A NIGHT OF TERROR

Esther's earliest memories were of brutal attacks against Jews. One upheaval followed another in the chaotic, anarchic years that followed the Russian Revolution. Change upon change. But her marriage to the older Jewish poet seemed to offer a promising new chapter.

Markish took her to Moscow. She bore him two sons. They lived among the most prominent writers of their time. Then World War II ended and the arrests began.

How had they managed to ignore it so long? How had they thought they could escape unscathed? Inevitably there was a knock at the door. Markish was taken. His papers were searched, his rooms sealed.

And Esther was left to wonder when she would see him, *if* she would see him again. . . .

THE
LONG RETURN

Esther Markish

With a foreword by David Roskies

BALLANTINE BOOKS · NEW YORK

English translation and foreword Copyright © 1978
by Random House, Inc.

The lines beginning "Got a bit of heart? . . ." appearing in the
Foreword are from the poem "1917," by Peretz Markish,
translated by Irving Howe, from *A Treasury of Yiddish Poetry,*
edited by Irving Howe and Eliezer Greenberg, copyright ©
1969 by Irving Howe and Eliezer Greenberg. Reprinted by
permission of Holt, Rinehart and Winston, Publishers.

All rights reserved under International and Pan-American
Copyright Conventions. Published in the United States by
Ballantine Books, a division of Random House, Inc., New
York, and simultaneously in Canada by Ballantine Books of
Canada, Ltd., Toronto, Canada. Originally published in France
as *Le long retour* by Editions Robert Laffont—Opera Mundi.
Copyright © 1974 by Opera Mundi. Translated from the
French by D. I. Goldstein

Library of Congress Catalog Card Number: 77-6137

ISBN 0-345-24803-1

This edition published by arrangement with Opera Mundi, Paris

The photographs in this volume are from the collection of
the author.

Manufactured in the United States of America.

First Edition: May 1978

CONTENTS

FOREWORD

ON THAT DRAB Saturday morning in Moscow, surrounded by a motley group of Jews, she stood out in her stylish pants suit and well-kept coiffure. She seemed to inhabit her own world in defiance of the Secret Police who kept a constant surveillance. Though we were strangers, and foreigners at that, she greeted us warmly in Yiddish and insisted upon our visiting her at home. But the essential fact of her uniqueness escaped us at this first encounter, on September 18, 1971—the very fact that Esther Markish, daughter of a former oil magnate and widow of a decorated and martyred poet, now stood among her people in an empty lot opposite the only synagogue in Moscow. This was testimony enough to the torturous and tragic path she had taken. Nor did we know then that this was to be the next-to-last lap of her "Long Return."

My wife and I paid two visits to the Markishes' apartment on Gorky Street, or to be precise, to that half of the apartment they had managed to regain on returning from exile (see chapter 19). During the second visit we had occasion to see their home transformed once more into a literary salon, for Esther had invited a group of leading Jewish dissidents to hear me lecture on a most subversive topic: contemporary Hebrew literature. We met some of the people who figure so prominently in the chronicle that follows: her son, David, and daughter-in-law, Irina, her older brother Shura, and the daughter of the "old man," Solomon Mikhoels.

Before my lecture began, I noticed David go over to

the telephone and, without lifting the receiver, turn the dial all the way around and lodge it in place with a pencil. He smiled at my amazement and explained with perfect nonchalance that this was a time-tested method of foiling the ubiquitous Secret Police, who use the telephone as a listening device even when it is on the hook.

Books lined the wall on one side of the room, and half of that bookcase, Esther explained, was occupied by the combined works of all the Markishes: Peretz Markish in Yiddish and Russian; Simon Markish's innumerable translations of Greek and Latin classics; Esther's many translations from the French, and, most recently, David's short stories and poems. There must have been a massive housecleaning in Soviet libraries and bookstores after the Markish family left for Israel!

It should be noted that any association with the Markish family was by this time an invitation to police harassment. A widow of a Yiddish writer who had been among the first victims of the purges pleaded with us not to visit the Markish home. And sure enough, on our way out of the Soviet Union, we were given special treatment by the customs officials, who confiscated all the materials Esther Markish had given us.

On returning to Boston, where we lived at the time, my wife and I organized a publicity and protest campaign for the Markish family. As things went from bad to worse—Esther suffered a stroke in April 1972, and David went into hiding three weeks later to avoid the draft—we began to despair of their ever being freed. From Esther's memoirs we know that this last year was indeed one of the most difficult of her life. Like the incredulous student described in the Preface, we too could not believe our eyes when, on November 6, 1972, the newspapers reported that Esther and David had arrived in Vienna the day before. Our reunion with them, fittingly enough, took place in Jerusalem.

The abundance of people, places and events described in this memoir should not obscure the presence of the two central figures whose stories are diametrically opposed. One is the rags-to-riches story of a small-town Jew, and the other tells of the move from aristocracy to *aliyah* (immigration to Israel). The two stories meet in the vortex of a revolution that overturned all lives.

Peretz Markish was born in the Pale of Settlement, the western part of the Russian Empire with the largest concentration of Jews (some five and a quarter million in 1897) of any place at any previous time in history. Markish grew up in a typical shtetl, or market town, the locus of Jewish life in Eastern Europe for over five hundred years. Here he received a traditional Jewish education, and even his youthful rebellion was expressed in terms of sanctioned Jewish activity. But, like so many of his generation, the Great War and the October Revolution disrupted the gradual course of his development and thrust him headlong into a new society in the making. In life as in poetry, Markish exemplified a radical break with past traditions.

> Got a bit of heart? Forget it!
> Want a little peace? Choke on a bone!
> Somewhere strum the balalaikas
> Bursting wildly on a stone.*

This was Markish's call to youthful abandon in 1917. For him the revolution meant freedom from the neoromantic, melancholy and controlled verse that had chacterized Yiddish poetry of the previous decade; it meant the physical freedom to travel and work wherever he chose, striking roots nowhere. The titles of his earliest collections of poetry best illustrate this mood: *Shveln* ("Threshólds"), *Pust un pas* ("Idle"), *Shtiferish* ("Mischievous"), *Nokhn telerl fun himl* ("After Pie in the Sky"), and *Stam* ("Just Like That"). By the time Markish left the Soviet Union and settled in Warsaw (1921), he had come to embody the achievement and promise of the Revolution

---

* Translated by Irving Howe. Of Markish's thirteen volumes of poetry and four volumes of prose and drama, only eight short poems have thus far been translated into English. They appear in *A Treasury of Yiddish Poetry*, ed. Irving Howe and Eliezer Greenberg (New York: Holt, Rinehart and Winston, 1969).

for all the young Polish Jews of leftist persuasion. "We saw in him the messenger of the new Jew from 'over there,' from the other side of the Red border," one of his youthful admirers recalls.*

From Warsaw to Paris to London and then to Berlin, followed by a short visit to Palestine and back to Warsaw. Finally, at the end of 1926, Markish returned to the Soviet Union, lured by the promise of a Yiddish cultural renaissance supported and funded by the government.

This crucial decision must be understood. Markish was among many prominent Yiddish writers who left the Soviet Union during the civil war only to return in the late twenties and early thirties (David Bergelson, Der Nister, David Hofstein, Leyb Kvitko, Moyshe Kulbak were some of the others). Though these writers were soon to discover that government support was contingent upon making their work conform to ever-tightening Party regulations, they were, in fact, treated as an elite class—they were housed in desirable apartments and their books enjoyed unprecedented press runs. Never before in history did Jewish writers and artists achieve such recognition—as Jews—from the powers that be. In the West, this would be analogous to Sarah Bernhardt, Max Reinhardt and Saul Bellow winning accolades and prizes for acting, directing and writing in Yiddish—not for enriching their respective host cultures. In the Soviet Union, during that brief, exhilarating honeymoon, Solomon Mikhoels' Yiddish State Theater in Moscow was honored as the pride of Soviet culture and Peretz Markish, a Yiddish poet of lowly origins, received the Order of Lenin. Finally, the ultimate mark of distinction was bestowed upon both Jewish men of genius: they were murdered on order from Stalin.

Esther's life runs in the opposite direction. She was born and raised far from the concentration and poverty of Jewish life in the Pale of Settlement. Her upper-class home in oil-rich Baku was a model of high Russian culture. As she herself admits, she knew not a word of Yiddish when Markish entered her life in

---

* Esther Rosenthal-Shnayderman, "Around the Markishiada" (Yiddish), *Di goldene keyt* (Tel-Aviv) 64 (1968): 219.

1929. By then, of course, she and her family had been stripped of their wealth and she had already been won over to the proletarian struggle. Yet, as her memoir illustrates so clearly, Communism, rather than establish the "classless society," gave rise to a new caste system more rigid than the one it had set out to replace.

By dint of her marriage and her own intellectual achievements, Esther entered the charmed circle of the Soviet intelligentsia. If famous names keep popping out of the pages, it is not because Esther likes to name-drop, but simply because most of her adult life in the Soviet Union was spent in the company of writers: they shared the same apartments, hung their laundry out together, were evacuated on the same train, and starved together. Esther's attitude to writers is typically Russian. Whereas we in the West have long delighted in the foibles and misdeeds of famous men and women of letters, Russians expect moral guidance from their writers. We are not nearly as shocked as Esther is by the misbehavings of those she considers "engineers of the human soul." On the other hand, because we almost expect a writer to misbehave, we are amazed at Markish's generosity, concern and courage. We need only compare Markish's record in the tragic years 1939–1952 with that of Colonel Itzik Feffer to see what price some intellectuals were willing to pay in return for power and privilege.

Esther maintained her sense of self despite the upheaval wrought in her life by Markish's arrest and by her subsequent exile to Kazakhstan. But from her account it would seem that her Jewishness did not become central to her self-identity until the last period of her exile, spent in the exotic city of Kzyl-Orda. There, thanks to the down-to-earth and rather comic figure of Ksil Pokhis, Esther found her place among the Jewish people—not the intellectuals this time, just the plain folk with their undaunted faith. From there the road of return led not to Moscow, but to Jerusalem.

The Long Return belongs to the ever-growing body of writing some have called the "literature of survival." This book invites comparison with Nadezhda Mandelstam's celebrated memoirs *Hope Against Hope* and *Hope Abandoned*. Both works focus upon the unforgettable presence and unsilenceable voice of the murdered poet. But Esther did not share in her husband's poetic experience to the same extent as did Mrs. Mandelstam. Furthermore, Esther missed out on Markish's stormy career in Warsaw, Paris, and Berlin, where he was acclaimed as one of the leading exponents of expressionism in Yiddish. All this would have to be the subject of another book.

There can be no doubt, however, that *The Long Return* is an essential work in its own right because of the living presence and passion of its author. The book is a lasting indictment against a regime that outdid its own past record of barbarity on the night of August 12, 1952, and a lasting reminder to us never to forget that date. Remember we must, for the executioners have gone unpunished, the survivors' wounds have gone unhealed, and the plague that brought it all about has gone unchecked.

David G. Roskies
New York City
Summer, 1977

PREFACE

MY REMINISCENCES and my life are part and parcel of the life of Peretz Markish and those reminiscences of his that remained unwritten. This is true of my whole life—before the night of January 27, 1949, when he was led away, and after—to this very moment when I am writing these lines here in my new home, in my ancestral country. And so it will be until I draw my last breath.

It is not important that Markish "created" me, that he molded my views and beliefs, that he drew me into Jewish culture and the Jewish world. That goes without saying and needs no explanation. But there are at least three facts that must be fully and clearly understood.

Markish loved his people. He loved them without any trace of pretense, hysteria, or affectation, like many great and sincere lovers of people of the past and present. His love did not contain one iota of scorn for other peoples (such as one finds, for example, in Dostoevski, particularly in his *Diary of a Writer,* with its almost shamanistic prophecy of "the new word" and its tirades against "Yids" and "Pollocks").

Markish loved his people as one loves a large and magnanimous family, rejoicing in its virtues and decrying its vices, but incapable of doing without it for even a day, because he owed everything he had to it—his understanding, his feelings, his humor, his honor, consciousness of his own dignity, and the ability to distinguish right from wrong. And just as you could not

1

possibly imagine forgiving the murderer who had wiped out your entire family, so, too, Markish could not forget the six million Jews who had been exterminated by German fascism, or ever forgive those who followed in the footsteps of their murderers. The bullet that was fired into the back of his head took not only his life, but the life of the culture that had been his whole reason for being. If Markish could rise up from the ashes scattered to the winds by his executioners a quarter of a century ago, he would forsake Russia forever, no matter how much grief and pain the separation would cause him. That is why I am in Israel—not instead of him, but together with him.

I have said that this separation would have caused him grief and pain. With every fiber in his body and with all the tenderness of his soul, Markish was attached to the Jewish culture of the Diaspora; he believed in its vitality as he believed in a long and glorious future for the Jews of Russia. He exalted the Soviet regime, not for personal gain or out of opportunism, but because it was his unshakable conviction that the regime had emancipated his people, had torn down the walls of the ghetto so that they, his people, could blossom anew and flourish in an atmosphere of freedom. Markish was wrong, and he paid for the error with his blood, which spattered the walls of the cellar where he was shot. If he could rise from the ashes, Markish today would be here in Israel, where a young offshoot of the ancient trunk of Israel sprouts green and grows strong. That is why I am here, and I am sure that he would be happy to know that I am: "You did the right thing, Firka, bravo!"

And finally this. In Katsetnik's novella *A Clock Overhead,* there is the following scene: At the threshold of the gas chamber, in one of Hitler's death camps, a Chasidic *tsadik* says to his disciple that in their martyrdom there is the unseen hand of God; a new Israel shall be born out of its ashes. And so it was with the death of Markish and his comrades. Their assassins imagined that it would spell the physical and spiritual annihilation of Russian Jewry. And yet, by the end of the sixties, the pogrom of 1949–1952 had become

2

one of the most powerful determinants of our painful decision to break forever with the past.

The name of Markish, his memory, is like a clarion call to Russian Jewry, mobilizing the Russian *aliyah*, as it is called in Israel. That is why I am in Israel—together with Markish.

Without knowing about the life and death of Markish, without comprehending it, it would be as difficult to understand this latter-day Exodus as it would be to understand Solzhenitsyn without knowing and pondering what he went through and experienced at the front, in prisons, in camps, in exile, and during the breathing space under Khrushchev. That is why I wanted to write this book and record all that I remember.

I am in Israel, and I am happy not only in the freedom I feel, but in the knowledge that I have done my duty. I am grateful to those who helped me to do so and without whose help our dream of freedom would never have been realized. My only regret is that I am unable to see them all and put my arms around them. They are numerous and come from every race and nationality, a genuine "International of good people," which the village sage Gedali, the hero of one of Isaac Babel's stories, dreamed about as he contemplated the cruelty of the Revolution.

Five of these people were there to meet us in Vienna: Barbara Oberman from England, Joel Sprayregen and his wife from the United States, Alex Buchenger from France, and Yitskhak Katz from Germany (West Germany, of course!).

I express my gratitude to Father Michel Riquet, the intelligent and charming French Catholic priest who visited us in Moscow. He came to us at a time of trouble and his wise words and active efforts restored our hope when all seemed lost. I wish to honor the memory of the French advocate André Blumel, a courageous man with a good heart, who manifested sincere sympathy for the "Israelis of Moscow" and did all that he could for them. My thanks go to Madame Winkler, who met me in Israel shortly after my arrival there. She urged me to write this book and helped me to publish it. I will always remember with a feeling of gratitude Greville Janner, British M.P., whose weekly Friday telephone calls from London to us in Moscow shored up our spirits.

And finally I wish especially to recall a startling encounter in Boston that shook me to the foundations of my soul. Before one of my lectures, a young man rushed up to me in the foyer of the theater and exclaimed: "Oh, Mrs. Markish, can it really be you? You really made it, after all?" And he put his arms around me and cried like a baby. I also cried. I never found out his name. Before the anonymous and pure-hearted love he incarnated in that fleeting moment, I kneel and touch my forehead to the ground.

Yes, we made it, but Markish did not. And to the memory of all those who did not make it, this book is dedicated.

1 / The Yekaterinoslav Pogrom

To THIS VERY DAY, Baku is divided into two parts: the Black City and, simply, the City. Today there are no boundaries between these two parts, and the Black City is as green as the "white" City. At the turn of the century, the Black City was the site of the oil industry, which was just then beginning to develop. Derricks and oil pumps jutted out of the ground like bare iron bushes and trees.

The house of my father, Yefim Lazebnikov, an oil magnate and owner of oil fields, was located in the Black City. It is there that I would have been born had not my mother, Vera Markovna, decided a few months before my birth to go to Yekaterinoslav to be with her parents, Marko and Olga Krichevsky.

There was nothing surprising about her decision.

Family ties in the Krichevsky family were unusually strong and warm. The wise and energetic Olga Lvovna was, until the end of her days, the uncontested authority for her children—five sons and one daughter, Vera, who was to be my mother. Everyone turned to Babushka Olya (as she was known) for advice; they came in times of trouble and in times of joy. Later, the same kind of relationship grew up between my mother and me, and, still later, between my children and me.

Babushka Olya worked with my grandfather Marko, who managed the houses and storehouses of the rich Yekaterinoslav banker Kofman. They occupied an apartment in one of his houses.

It was there that I was born, February 6, 1912.

A few months later, my mother returned with me to Baku.

We lived luxuriously; oil was profitable and my father knew the business well. He loved living on a grand scale, surrounded by beautiful things. He had received his technical training in France, where he met my mother, who was studying medicine there. Her family had taken her to the South of France to escape the Russian pogroms of 1905. My parents were married in France in 1907 and returned to Baku before my mother had finished her studies. A year later, my brother Alexander was born.

Many Jews in Baku looked disapprovingly on our family's way of life: it was too lavish. In 1914, my father was one of the first people in Baku to acquire an automobile. This prodigy of technology drew crowds of onlookers, especially when it got bogged down in the slimy, oil-soaked mud and had to be hauled out by a pair of horses.

"What folly! Yefim Lazebnikov should never have bought that machine," the Baku Jews said. "What nonsense for him to be buying an elegant apartment in the center of Baku when he could live so peacefully in the Black City. How foolish of Lazebnikov to spoil his wife the way he does, giving in to her every whim and fancy—why, her diamonds only attract more attention to her beauty. The Christians and the Moslems are beginning to take notice. . . ."

My mother was, in fact, very beautiful, and whenever anyone mentioned my father's name, the question inevitably followed: "Which Lazebnikov do you mean? The one with the pretty wife?"

But my father paid no attention to these remarks and lived as he saw fit. Our home in the Black City, and, later, our apartment on Stock Exchange Street, was always full of guests. Our cook, Kondratyevna, was famous throughout all Baku for her culinary talents.

My parents were not particularly religious, though my father did, of course, have a regular seat in the synagogue and gave generously to it. The only holiday we observed strictly with all of its traditions was Passover. My father read the Haggadah, and I searched for the hidden matzo. The stories of the Exodus from bondage in Egypt would linger in the childish imaginations of my brother and me for many days afterward.

My brother, Alexander—or Shura, as he was called in the family—became extremely religious. My family began keeping kosher again, to the delight of my paternal grandfather, Moishe, a cantor, who had come to visit us. Kondratyevna was initiated into the arts of the dietary laws and, albeit with grumblings, reconciled herself to the new state of affairs. Not really knowing too much about the whole thing, she regarded the division between milk and meat dishes as some sort of aristocratic caprice.

The Russian Revolution turned our way of life inside out. My father looked upon the Revolution as a *fait accompli* that had to be adjusted to if life were to continue. But the adjustment was no simple matter: his oil interests were confiscated.

My father joked bitterly, "When all is said and done, I was right, and not those Jews who criticized me. Everything they had was taken away, too, just as with us. But we, at least, lived like human beings."

In 1918, mother took Shura and me to Yekaterinoslav to visit with her parents, from whom she had been without news for a long time. My father remained behind in Baku.

6

The momentous events of 1917 in Russia—two revolutions and the Civil War that followed—had added to the trials and troubles of the Jews in Yekaterinoslav, a city on the Dnieper. The Jews had no illusions about the changes that were taking place; the experience of many centuries had taught them conclusively that any alteration in the social fabric leads to persecution of the Jews, to looting, pogroms and murder. Consequently, when the vodka-fired mobs poured into the streets of Yekaterinoslav, excited by the prospect of impunibly trampling on laws that only yesterday had been in force, the Jews set about preparing themselves for a pogrom. They began by dismantling and hauling away the wooden fences that separated the houses. This seemingly insignificant operation, dictated by past experience, had considerable practical importance: it is infinitely easier to flee from pogromists if the area is clear of barriers; scrambling over a picket fence with small children is difficult, if not impossible.

Our family, my mother, my nine-year-old brother, and myself—the baby—was staying in the yardkeeper's quarters of banker Kofman's house on Broad Street. Broad Street was predominantly Jewish, and the pogromists were heading straight for it. The air rang with the sound of shattering windowpanes, and the feathers of disemboweled eiderdowns floated all about. There was the smell of burning, too; somewhere they had set fire to something.

Gavrila, the yardkeeper, my grandfather's faithful and loyal servant, showed signs of nervousness. He listened anxiously to the piercing and increasingly audible cries of people shouting "Help!"

"They mean business today," Gavrila finally said. "I'll go see what's up." And he left.

The cries for help now rent the air just a few houses away.

"Gavrila won't betray us," my mother said, "but if they should burst in here . . . "

She was hoping that the hoodlums would pass us by. They were not, after all, looking into every house.

Gavrile returned, exclaiming, "Flee for your lives! They've already killed the Rabinoviches and . . . "

7

The Rabinoviches were our neighbors; they lived just a few doors away.

My mother stood up and took us firmly by the hand. "Let's go, children!"

We stepped out of the overheated yardkeeper's lodgings into the raw, black night. The autumn mud squished underfoot, and for a moment I imagined that it was mixed with the blood of old man Rabinovich, with his beard and jolly fat belly. . . . Or perhaps I am merely imagining it now, and that autumn night I was only trembling with fear.

We ran through strange backyards, pursued by that eerie, piercing wail for help. One of the houses seemed to have been abandoned by its owners. My mother dragged my brother and me through a wide-open door and rushed headlong into a room.

In one corner lay a body; it was half covered with a torn curtain, as if it had been wrapped in a shroud. A pogromist was bent over the body going through the dead man's pockets. Startled by the sound of our footsteps, he spun around. My mother's diamond ring caught his eye. He got up from the floor, grabbed hold of my mother's hand, and tried to wrest the ring from her finger.

"Take your hands away," my mother said calmly. "I'll give it to you myself."

At that moment, someone called out from the next room, "Hey, Pashka!"

Pashka turned around drunkenly and staggered out in answer to the summons.

As for us, we leaped through an open window and continued our frantic search for a corner, a niche, somewhere that would hide us for the night.

My memories of the Yekaterinoslav pogrom are, perhaps, the first thing in my life that I recall distinctly. My notion of time begins with that autumn night, with the recollection of viscous mud and blood. The first memory is like the first impression of an etching—it is the sharpest, the most distinct. The memory of that night illuminates practically every event in my life of any importance at all . . . and not with the light of the sun or the moon, but with the glow of fires set by assassins of old Jews.

Who was doing the killing? The Whites? The Greens? Makhno's band? Petlyura's*?

People were killing people.

Monsters were killing Jews.

It was a time when power changed hands in Yekaterinoslav every day. It even happened that different groups were in control simultaneously, the Monarchists in one quarter, the Anarchists in another. Such confusion might seem almost comic, but the shots that crackled throughout that night in this or that part of the city were not shots fired into the air, but at people.

The Anarchists withdrew, and the Reds arrived. Then the Whites ousted the Reds, and already cartloads of peasants were lumbering into the city, attracted by the prospect of looting.

All movements, all travel took place at night. The pogroms also took place at night, as did the silent dashing from house to house over grounds no longer marked by that symbol of private property, the fences. During the day, both the victors and the vanquished scattered, and so too we Jews, escaping from the jubilation of the victor and the wrath of the vanquished.

On one of those days, my father came from Baku, determined at all costs to get us on a train back home and deliver us from the horrors of a Yekaterinoslav gone mad. It wasn't as easy as all that, though. For days on end, my father scurried about the city trying to secure all sorts of laissez-passers. And then, one early autumn night, he was intercepted as he was engaged in this pursuit.

The night was as black as India ink. Paneless windows looked like black yawning holes against the background of a distant conflagration. A nearby street

* Simon Petlyura was part of the government of the independent Republic of the Ukraine founded in November 1917. He put no restraints on his soldiers' treatment of Jews, and the pogroms he fomented in 1918 caused him to be assassinated in Paris in 1926 by a Russian Jew, who was acquitted after a dramatic trial. Nestor Makhno was chief of a Ukrainian band of counterrevolutionaries. Unlike Petlyura, he restrained his men from killing Jews.—Trans.

9

resounded with the thump of hoofbeats and tramping feet. There was the sound of gunfire. No one knew for sure who was in control of the city.

Staying close to the walls of buildings, my father was making his way home. He was no more than a block away when the clatter of hooves behind him stopped him dead in his tracks. He froze. The next thing he knew, a horse bore down upon him, jolting him hard and almost knocking him over, and a blow from a whip struck his back.

The rider leaned forward from his saddle and peered into my father's face. His breath smelled of onion and stale vodka.

"Yid," he said, as if trying to confirm a supposition. "Get a move on, Yid."

Striking my father again with a light blow of the whip, he drove him on in front of his horse.

There was no place to flee to; escape was impossible. Slipping and stumbling in the claylike mud, my father kept moving ahead of the horse. At the end of the street, they turned left and passed through a gate and into a passageway that ended in a blind alley.

A tall, bright bonfire was ablaze in the alley. A dozen or so soldiers wearing motley dress—red riding breeches, green and blue field jackets, sheepskin coats, expensive women's coats, astrakhan *shapkas,* some with red piping—huddled close to the fire. There was also a machine gun mounted on a carriage. Close by, a group of some twenty Jews sat in a circle on the snow. My father recognized several of them as prominent, well-to-do members of the Jewish community. He nodded to an old, bearded Jew, the director of the Jewish gymnasium. Another, the owner of a dye works, did not acknowledge my father's greeting; his eyes were closed, his face a swollen mass of black and blue.

A guard was standing near the prisoners, smoking a cigarette.

"Well, what do you say, let's get it over with!" the horseman who had brought in my father called out to his comrades. "It will be daybreak soon. . . . On your feet!" he barked, moving toward the Jews sitting in the slush.

They got up slowly, like a herd of cattle.

"Take off your rags," the guard commanded impassively as he rounded up the prisoners with the butt of his rifle, to which a bayonet was fixed. "Your boots, too. And line up against the wall." A middle-aged Jew who was slow in undressing inspired a familiar taunt. "Abie"—the guard shouted the diminutive for Abraham menacingly—"that goes for you, too!"

The mounted horseman who still had my father in tow leaned down and ripped off his coat. My father removed his galoshes with the shoes inside and walked over to the wall, sinking up to his ankles in the mud and slush, which was yellow with horse urine.

"For what?" my father murmured, his lips hardly moving. And then he cried it out: "For what?"

One soldier, his jacket spread under him, was already positioned behind the machine gun.

Several Jews, their faces turned to the brick wall of the enclosure, were praying, swaying back and forth. One of them slipped in the mud; he was left lying there.

Suddenly, a burly horseman with long black hair came galloping in. From the way the soldiers snapped to attention and fawned before him, it was clear that he was their commander.

My father lunged toward him.

"Tell me why, commander," my father asked as he tugged at the horse's reins. *"Why* do they want to shoot us?"

"Why? Now, that's a good question, don't you think?" the commander, mimicking my father's voice, asked the soldiers.

"Why? They're Yids, you know, *batka* [chief]," the machine gunner replied. "Let's finish them off!"

"Let us go, sir . . . *batka,"* my father said, still tugging at the reins. "What are we guilty of? Just because we are . . . Jews?"

"Well, what do you say, boys, should we let them go?" the *batka* asked the soldiers. They kept silent, not daring to speak.

"Clear out of here, the whole bloody lot of you!" the *batka* yelled, wheeling his horse around. "Well, hop to it! Clear out!"

11

The Jews stepped away from the wall and flew out of the alley, leaving their clothes in a big black stack behind them.

My father ran off, too.

"Hey, Jew!" the *batka* called after him. "What's your rush?"

My father stopped dead. What could this mean?

"Put on your galoshes, Jew, otherwise you might catch cold!" the *batka* said, breaking into a broad smile.

My father ran to the gate and disappeared into the darkness of the street.

The man who saved my father's life was the Ukrainian counterrevolutionary *batka*, Makhno.

My father's escape from death was, undoubtedly, only a quirk of fate, a temporary reprieve. The threat of a senseless, absurd end hung over us like a suspended stone. My father racked his brains trying to discover a way out.

"Our best bet is to get to Kislovodsk," my father said. "From there to Baku is only a short distance."

"We'll all be killed on the way," my mother said. "Think of something really good!"

And my father did. "We'll hire a Russian general," he declared, "or, at worst, a colonel."

We didn't find a general, so we had to be satisfied with a colonel. Since the train to Kislovodsk passed through territory controlled by the White armies, we naturally got hold of a White colonel. My father explained his duties to him: the colonel would pass himself off as our grandfather—or father, if he preferred —and, decked out in his colonel's uniform, post himself at the entrance to our compartment whenever pogromists boarded the train. The colonel agreed, and my father gave him an advance.

We set out a few days later. The colonel came to pick us up in a carriage. The chest of his uniform was covered with medals; his mustache and goatee were trimmed to perfection. He was an intelligent man with a distinct awareness of his own dignity. He obviously felt it awkward for a man of his age and station in life to be earning money in such an outlandish fashion.

12

It was probably to hide his embarrassment that he chose to regard us as baggage. Whenever "controllers"—pogromists—came through the train, the colonel held the door of our compartment ajar, posted himself on the threshold, and nonchalantly blew smoke rings.

"I am traveling with my family," he would casually declare. Nobody in his right mind would ever have suspected that a colonel of the White Army was harboring Jews in his compartment.

At the Kislovodsk station, my father gave the colonel the second half of his fee, and we bade him goodbye.

"We'll stay at the very best hotel," my father announced. "It's safer that way."

As we entered the luxurious hotel room in the company of the manager and the floor staff, my father scanned the walls of the room and then, glowering at the service staff, he angrily struck his walking stick against the floor.

"You bunch of good-for-nothings!" he roared. "A Russian can't live decently any more! Where are the icons?"

The manager stammered his apologies, and the servants dashed off in pursuit of icons. The hotel was soon buzzing with rumors that a "rich and tyrannical Siberian merchant" had moved into room twelve.

And my father, further solidifying our position, demanded a samovar, rolls, black caviar, and vodka.

We returned to Baku shaken by what we had lived through, but now inured to the sight of blood and to mortal danger. For a great deal had changed in Baku during our absence. It was now under Bolshevik control—twenty-six commissars were in charge of the city.

One of the characteristics of the new regime was unannounced visits to private homes, so we were not surprised early one morning to hear a loud hammering on our apartment door. My mother opened it and let a group of soldiers with rifles into the vestibule.

"Clear out of the apartment!" one of them ordered. "Our commander will be moving in!"

13

"I have children," my mother said. "Where do you expect me to go with them? Out on the street?"

The soldiers consulted among themselves. "All right," they said. "But you belong to the bourgeoisie, so you'll have to suffer. You'll move into two rooms, and our commander will take over the other four."

That evening the commander, Alexei Dzhaparidze, arrived; he was one of the twenty-six commissars in charge of the city. Dzhaparidze was an idealist, naively believing that the Revolution would bring happiness and success in equal measure to everyone. The first and sacred duty of revolutionary idealists was to destroy people who were either opposed to or doubted the possibility of "universal happiness." The idealists did their awful duty because they believed in it. And later, still believing in it, they fell under the bullets of their friends and enemies—like the other twenty-five commissars, Dzhaparidze would be shot by the English and his wife and daughters sent away by Stalin to camps, where they languished until the dictator's death in 1953.

Alexei Dzhaparidze turned out to be a likable and even shy man. He felt uncomfortable about crowding us.

"You stay in the four rooms," he said. "I'll manage all right with two."

Soon after our return to Baku my father made up his mind to leave Russia. It would take a lot of time and money to get all the necessary papers, but there was no trouble about deciding on our destination. America held no attraction for my father, but Palestine did. One of my mother's brothers, Nathan, had been in Palestine since 1914, as part of the Jewish pioneer movement there. He lived in Petah Tikva, not far from the small seaside village of Tel Aviv. My father let him know of our plans and his hope of meeting him in Constantinople on the way to Palestine.

2 / From Baku to Moscow

IN THE SUMMER OF 1920, after disposing of our few remaining possessions and of my mother's jewelry, which had miraculously survived the Revolution, we moved to Tiflis, capital of the then independent Georgian Republic. My father busied himself arranging for the next leg of our journey, and I was put into school—junior preparatory grade of Princess Dolgorukova's gymnasium—where an incident occurred that remains etched in my memory.

One day the princess came into the classroom accompanied by the supervisor. Sniffing the air, she said, "My God, it reeks of garlic here! How many Jews do you have in the class?"

In the anti-Semitic mind of the aged princess, the smell of garlic was synonymous with "stinking" Jews. Actually, practically everyone in Tiflis used garlic—Armenians, Georgians, and Russians. When I returned home, I told my father what had happened. He answered me with a sad smile: "You see, my daughter, we are in an alien land. Perhaps someday soon we shall reach our own shores."

Early in 1921, our long-awaited papers came through, and we left for Batum, where we boarded a big Italian liner, the *Cornara,* bound for Constantinople. My father had booked a lovely, spacious cabin, and we settled in comfortably. It was aboard the *Cornara* that I celebrated my ninth birthday.

Constantinople was overflowing with Russian emigrants of every stripe. We finally found rooms in an

15

apartment belonging to a childless Jewish couple, Naum and Liza, the owners of a small hotel in the port area. My father notified Nathan of our arrival, and he promised to come to Constantinople and pick us up. In the meantime, my brother and I resumed our schooling. I became a boarding student in a French convent, returning home only on weekends; Shura was enrolled in the College of Saint Joseph.

Naum and particularly Liza were very kind to Shura and me, showering us with affection and presents. Liza left for the small port hotel every day around two o'clock, not returning until dawn. Naum went there only rarely; his energetic wife ran the whole business herself.

Uncle Nathan finally arrived from Palestine. He was a handsome young man, bronzed by the sun. The winsome Liza lost no time in manifesting her sensibility to the charms of the attractive *kibbutznik,* a fact that did not escape the notice of my perspicacious mother.

One fine day while we were strolling about the city with Nathan, we lost the apartment key, and so we set out for Liza's hotel to get a spare. Neither Nathan nor I had been to the hotel before, and it took us quite some time to find our way to the dirty side street in the port section. Scantily clad ladies were sitting on the stoops of the houses along this street: blonds, brunettes, old and young, Orientals and Europeans. A neat little red lantern was hanging over the entrance to Liza's "hotel."

The following day, after devising some plausible pretext, we moved out of Naum and Liza's apartment. My father had a good laugh; Mother was thoroughly shocked—for almost half a year we had been living under the same roof as the keepers of a bordello!

In many long talks with my father, Nathan told him about life in Palestine, describing it as difficult, one that only the strong in heart could adapt to. Nathan did not mince words: whoever will not or cannot do physical labor, whoever does not have capital to start up his own business, should forget about coming to Palestine. My father did not have capital and—gentleman and sybarite that he was—was not made for construction work or picking oranges.

At that time, émigré circles in Constantinople were buzzing with rumors about the NEP—the New Economic Policy—of the Bolsheviks, which gave some leeway to private ownership and, above all, to private enterprise. So my father, leaving us behind in Constantinople, set out on a reconnaissance mission to Odessa to see for himself what the possibilities might be.

What he found appealed to him. The Bolsheviks, who were short of specialists in every area, were making welcoming noises and promising practically all the world's earthly blessings. My father believed all that he heard and decided that Russia was the place to be. It was a decision that would cost him first his freedom and ultimately his life.

On his way back to Constantinople, he stopped in Baku and made all the necessary arrangements for opening his own paint factory. The immediate heavy orders for paint seemed to be a good omen for a profitable future in Baku.

In the fall of 1923 we returned to Russia.

The Baku businessmen, having lived through the hurricane of revolution and the Civil War, were optimistic: the NEP was in full flower. My father threw himself into his work, stepped up the production of paint, and brought my mother's brothers, intelligent and efficient young men, into the business. The only one not needing any help was Nathan; he was living in Petah Tikva, going around in bare feet and ragged trousers, living happily by the labor of his hands.

Once again we were living in Baku, inside the ancient fortress wall that surrounded the Old City, with its magnificent Tower of the Virgin looming up by the sea. (In the old days, according to legend, a young girl, grief-stricken over an unrequited love, had thrown herself from the tower into the water below.) In our elegant, comfortable apartment, we often thought of Uncle Nathan. Had we, after all, made a mistake by returning to Russia and not settling in Palestine? The paint business was apparently flourishing, yet my father seemed to feel his situation lacked security. Every once in a while he would say to Shura and me, "It's very doubtful I'll leave an inheritance, so get an education while you have the chance. Study languages, interest yourself in music. . . ."

From my early youth, I had studied ballet, and I continued the lessons now. (Later, when the pursuit of a "bourgeois" art became an obstacle to my joining the Young Communist Youth League—*komsomol*—I had to give them up.) I was received somewhat coldly at school. There were several reasons for that: my stylish "foreign" dress, a rather decent command of French, my passion for the ballet, and my "social origin"—for I was, in effect, the daughter of a NEP man.

The system of education in Soviet schools at the time was extremely curious. It was called the Dalton Plan Brigade Method. The class was divided into brigades, and each brigade studied only a particular part of the lesson, completely oblivious to what the next brigade was studying. The prerevolutionary method of teaching was now branded "reactionary," "counterrevolutionary," "regressive." I had a hard time with mathematics, but the humanities came easily to me, probably because I had the advantage of having private tutors: my father engaged a French woman to teach me the language, and another teacher for the history of literature.

In school we plugged away at an entirely new discipline, social science. One day during the lesson, the teacher pressed us to "work with our parents," wean them away from the practice of religion, which was, she proclaimed, "the opiate of the people. God does not and never did exist. It's all a fabrication of the enemies of the Revolution. If you fail to carry on illuminating atheistic work at home, you are supporting the enemies of the Revolution and the world bourgeoisie."

We eleven-year-old children thought over the words of the teacher. Many seemed inclined to believe her. Suddenly, one of the students got to her feet and said, "My grandmother observes all the Jewish holidays. She is very old. Why should I begin fighting with her? Can she possibly do any harm to Communism?"

18

"Tell your grandmother to cut out that *zhid* [kike] nonsense!" a boy yelled out.

The entire class was shaken. Anti-Semitism was practically unknown in the cosmopolitan city of Baku —at least I had never encountered it before. And then to come up against it in one's own class. . . .

We decided to try the boy before a people's court, and I was asked to serve as prosecutor—my schoolmates felt that I had a pretty glib tongue.

At the crucial point in my indictment, the "defendant" rose to his feet and said, "Tell me, why have you all ganged up against me? I was only joking. After all, I'm a Jew myself."

This was the last straw, and for a long time thereafter we had nothing more to do with him.

Several years later, when I was a student at Moscow University, I witnessed another overt manifestation of anti-Semitism. We were studying political economy, using the text of the French scholar Charles Gide, when one of the students yelled out in the lecture hall, "What a blockhead I am! What have I done with my Gide? I can't find him anywhere!"

A Russian student immediately chimed in, "You've lost your Gide. Why, you just have to look around you —here, in Moscow, you'll find a *zhid* standing at every street corner."

On that occasion, all I could do was to boil inside; the university authorities would never have tolerated bringing an anti-Semite before a people's court.

I have no clear recollection of the death of Lenin, in 1924, except for the long, plaintive whistling of locomotives and the perplexity of my father: what will happen now, what is in store for the NEP men?

Fate dealt with us rather brutally. At the beginning of 1925, my father was arrested. The first step toward official and final liquidation of the NEP by the Stalinists was the dismantling "on the quiet" of the most important private enterprises. My father was accused of having accepted a bribe of five rubles from a customer. The charge was absurd, but he was sentenced nevertheless to three years in prison, and his factory was confiscated and taken over by the State. Prison awaited the most important NEP men. It was preferable to be imprisoned earlier rather than later, and in that sense my father was lucky; in the beginning prison conditions were quite tolerable. (The prison in which I was incarcerated in 1953 was a far cry from my father's "rest home.")

The court had ordered my father to pay severance to his workers and compensation to various people who suffered from the closing of the factory. My mother sold everything we possessed and paid off all the debts in full. And then, at long last, we were permitted to visit him. We set off for Bailov, on the outskirts of Baku, where the prison was located. On our way there, I imagined the most lurid scenes: the prisoners in shackles, damp cells. . . .

The meeting took place in the prison yard, which was screened off by a low iron grill. My father looked rather well, although he was exasperated by his cell mates, who were criminals, and by the bedbugs. But the prison administration had taken notice of my father and planned to use him for office work. This would mean an improvement in his living conditions.

A short time later my father was transferred to the prison office. After that things went smoothly. One day the warden came by our apartment to inform us that my father wanted to renovate his cell at his own expense, and also exterminate the bedbugs and cockroaches. Mother immediately hired a crew of workers, who put my father's cell in shape. He was also authorized to have an iron bedstead and mattress brought from home. In those days the inmates of Bailov Prison had it good. . . .

My father served a year and a half and was released before his time was up because of "exemplary conduct." During his last six months, he frequently came home for dinner, with the warden as escort, of course. The warden sat at table with us, praised the cooking, and then withdrew for a couple of hours to leave my father alone with his family.

Following his release, my father got a job with Azneft' (Azerbaidzhan Oil). But not even a year had passed when the Chekists* burst into the apartment one night, turned it upside down, and arrested my father again. As it turned out, the grounds for his arrest were simply ludicrous: it was alleged that while working in the prison office he had deliberately squandered paper and ink supplies. My father was back home in twenty-four hours, but he was now firmly decided on leaving Baku forever. He naively supposed that in a huge city like Moscow, people would forget about his "bourgeois, NEP-man past" and leave him in peace.

It didn't take very long to pack, since my father had lost everything. My parents left for Moscow where Father joined the managerial staff of Glavneft' (Chief Oil Administration). I stayed behind in Baku to finish the school term.

My eighteen-year-old brother Shura had already left for Moscow not long before to "acquire proletarian credentials." Because my father had been a NEP man, no career was possible without them, and Shura was interested in journalism. So he began working in a factory in Moscow and did journalism on the side. Although such work in a factory was of no use to anyone, it qualified as "official re-education." Without a "proletarian present," Shura would simply not have been permitted to appear in print.

My mother was hoping Shura would enter the university and become an educated man "with diplomas." But Shura, some 1,800 miles away from Baku, had no intention of going to the university. His articles were already being published under the pen name "Alaze" (Alexander Lazebnikov). He had the makings of a fine journalist and a few years later, in fact, became associate editor of one of the sections of the newspaper *Komsomolskaya Pravda* ("Young Communist Truth"). His lot was to be the same of many prominent journalists, however: in 1937, he was arrested along with the entire editorial board of his newspaper, accused of espionage, and sent away to a concentration camp. He served twelve years and was

---

* The Cheka was a special commission set up in 1917 and charged with preventing counterrevolutionary activities.—Ed.

released and rehabilitated after Stalin's death. Our Shura was lucky—he survived.

For me the provincial life of Baku was unexciting. I have no doubt that there was some political and economic effervescence, but I was far removed from those spheres where the temperature rose above normal. Thus, for my school friends and me, the arrival in Baku of three famous Moscow poets—Joseph Pavlovich Utkin, Alexander Bezymensky and Alexander Zharov —was a major event in our lives. They were known as the *komsomol* ("young Communist") poets and enjoyed an enormous popularity at the time. In 1925, Utkin wrote "Poem about Motele, the Redhead," which he dedicated to Trotsky. It was unique in its use of both Russian and Yiddish, and it reflected the great hopes the impoverished Russian Jews had placed in the Bolshevik Revolution. He was a talented poet, infinitely more so than Zharov or Bezymensky, both of whom survived by betraying the rosy ideals of their youth—Zharov as the author of such propaganda poster captions as "We have outstripped America in milk yield," and Bezymensky by doing the best he could to exist on his past reputation. Bezymensky fully merited this epigram composed by his fellow poets:

> Hair on end,
> Teeth extend,
> An old rapscallion,
> With his *komsomol* medallion.

Utkin died in a plane crash in World War II, but he might have suffered a worse fate had he lived: either ending up in a camp or leading the degrading life of the "eternally youthful" poets Bezymensky and Zharov.

But these were not the concerns of 1927. Poets had come from Moscow, and the most pressing problem of the moment was how to get tickets to the poetry evening: they had already been sold, resold, distributed and redistributed. My two girl friends and I were sitting on a bench on the promenade along the waterfront, mulling over the futility of the situation. On an adjacent bench, a young man had settled down with a sketch-

22

book and pencil. I sensed that he was sketching my portrait and, momentarily inspired by an Eastern modesty, I got up from the bench and prepared to leave.

"Wait a minute," said one of my girl friends. "Why, that's Rotov!"

The artist Konstantin Rotov had come down from Moscow with the poets.

"Sit still, young lady," said Rotov, "and I'll give you a pass to the evening recital."

Having apprehended the imploring glances of my friends, I replied, "Fine. But we need three tickets. There are three of us, you see."

That evening, we sat on the steps in the aisle of the auditorium and listened to Utkin's account of his visit to Gorky on Capri.

A few days later, I left Baku forever, to join my parents in Moscow. I had very little money, so I traveled in a dormitory-car. Armed with the advice of wise relatives, I attached my valise to my berth with an iron chain: trains were full of pickpockets and crooks. While I was standing at the door of the car, I caught sight of Utkin walking along the platform, followed by the wide-eyed glances of his female admirers. A white jacket of foreign cut was thrown over his shoulders, red kid shoes shone like burning embers on his feet. To me, who dreamed of a leather jacket and who, unbeknown to my parents, wore a visored cap, the attire of the *komsomol* poet seemed like a sacrilege. And besides, he was traveling in a wagon-lit, which was all right for the well-to-do, but certainly not for a proletarian poet!

At one of the stops along the way, Rotov caught sight of me. He introduced me to Utkin and his two companions. I gave vent to my feelings, and Utkin declared, "If you write good poetry and earn good money, why not travel in style and dress well?"

That riposte clashed with the Soviet slogans that had become part of me, but it set me to thinking. All told, Utkin was right, but it was terribly hard for me to accept. The few years I had been in school had turned me into, if not a fanatic Communist, at least a rather narrow-minded individual. I was beginning to

23

see that Soviet life could, in no time at all, remove the rose-colored glasses and blinders that school had fitted me with.

After Baku, Moscow seemed to me like a huge, wild crazy quilt of a city. A new page in my life had turned and was now to be filled in, but I was a bit frightened about taking up my pen.

In the spring of 1928, the Sixth Congress of the Communist Youth International opened in Moscow, and I got a job there as a French interpreter. There was a lot to see and hear. The young German Communist delegation, headed by Kurt Fischer, were quick to express indignation over what they observed—especially the arbitrary distribution of wealth and the results of the Russian "cultural revolution." In their view, prerevolutionary culture had not been sufficiently pulverized. They regarded the aspirations of the people to normalize their everyday life, to live better, as a "manifestation of bourgeois tendencies." In their dogmatism, they were more left than the leftists, "plus catholiques que le Pape." The young French Communists, on the other hand, had a more emotional approach to the question. Everything they saw excited their boundless enthusiasm, and they looked askance at the German carpers. Not that they were opposed to breaking up the old culture, but if the Germans wanted to carry out the experiment in a more radical way, then let them do so in their own backyard, in Germany. Why demand it of these wonderful, hospitable Russians?

A few months after the Congress, and armed with excellent references from my work as interpreter, I entered the Department of Philology at Moscow University.

My father had rented an apartment in the outskirts of Moscow in an area known as Tsygansky Ugolok ("Gypsy Corner") in Petrovsky Park. The houses had been erected by "private builders"—small-time NEP men—in a large, heavily wooded section. The Soviets had used their services in an effort to alleviate the housing problem. The one-story wooden dwellings

24

provided housing for transients who poured into Moscow to try their luck. The State derived revenue from the taxes it levied on the private builders, who, for the most part, had lost their shirts in big deals or who had come to the city from rural areas with money they had put aside.

Our builder, Sergei Ivanov, had put together a house with four small apartments. The house had two porches facing the woods. In the summer, the trails were filled with cyclists and in the winter, skiers. Moscow lay to the east, beyond the quaint, gingerbread palace of Peter I, which had been turned into a flying school. The student pilots were among the tenants in Petrovsky Park, too, along with the gypsies, who had a large encampment in one of the clearings.

Sergei Ivanov occupied one of the units in his house. He was as heavy as lead and as indestructible as a drop of mercury. He had escaped being shot by the Food Requisition Detachments, survived the year of the Volga famine, and avoided the fate of the kulaks who were deported to Siberia. He had come through all of these volcanic eruptions physically unscathed, but had nothing save blind hatred for the Soviet regime. His life, like that of so many others, was now merely a matter of survival.

Sometimes he would drop in and chat with my father. He couldn't get over my parents' attitude toward our maid Sasha. The fact that she was treated just like a member of the family surprised and troubled him.

"Don't let her eat her fill, or keep her on too long with you!" Ivanov lectured my father. "If she has it too good, here's the kind of pigsty you'll end up with!" And he made a sweeping gesture meant to include not only his own house, Petrovsky Park, and Moscow, but the whole expanse of Russia to the shores of the Pacific Ocean.

Among our neighbors were a couple with one son. They were Russified Jews, and had come to Moscow from Kazan with the most noble intentions: to work for the welfare of the triumphant masses, to give their son an education, to live like human beings. Their fate was quite otherwise. The head of the family, an engineer, was arrested in 1937 on a trumped-up charge (the fact that he had concealed his nationality was also held against him); his son was killed during World War II. Although the woman was a pediatrician, she could not hope to find suitable employment, for she was the wife of a "traitor." Officially, therefore, she obtained a divorce from her "unworthy" husband (but while he was in prison and in Lubyanka, she clandestinely supplied him with money) and, by Soviet standards, she did very well, becoming the director of a kindergarten.

The house next to ours belonged to a Bukharan Jew. At the beginning of the NEP, he had come to the capital with a load of rugs and opened a rug store. After serving time in prison when the NEP was in full swing, he built a small house with rental units using money he had secretly laid away. By this time his outlook on life had taken on a decidedly Oriental flavor: he was a fatalist who believed in "swimming with the current," as the saying goes. Nine years later he would be washed away by that current; he was arrested a second time and perished God knows where. His family broke up and scattered over the towns and villages of boundless Russia.

The gypsies were the most picturesque element of the population of Petrovsky Park. They were authentic gypsies, with horses, wagons, tents, fortune-tellers, and flocks of dirty, bare-bellied children. Under one pretext or another—or none at all—they would invade the neighboring quarters, but they allowed no one to penetrate their campsite. The Soviet regime decided to make "settled citizens" of them, and for a time the gypsies did acquiesce to such an unnatural way of life. Their children danced wildly for kopeks on the dusty streets in front of the private houses; the women in gaily colored dresses told fortunes for a modest sum, predicting a bright future and solace to the soul. The men sat on the ground the whole day through, smoking tobacco and tinning copper pots. I imagined that life in the camp would go on only until all the copper pots had been lined with tin and then, one fine day, the gypsies would fold their tents, load the carts with their belongings, and move on to an unknown destination.

The gypsies looked upon me as one of their own, I think because I was slender, had an olive complexion, and often wore an embroidered Arab dress, which my Uncle Nathan had brought my mother from Palestine, and which she had passed on to me.

Whenever I passed near the camp, the gypsy women clustered around me and asked affectionately, "Are you a gypsy?" I would shake my head and run away, frightened of their reputation for thievery and cheating. But the gypsies would follow me with their eyes. They persisted in believing that I was one of their kind but for some reason was concealing my origin. Now I regret that I didn't get to know them better. They, at least, preserved their spiritual freedom under the Soviet regime.

The street we lived on—as well as the other streets in the neighborhood—did have a name, but I have forgotten it. All Moscow referred to our immediate area as Gypsy Corner—Tsygansky Ugolok. Even today, when the gypsies are no more and the houses of the private builders have been razed to make way for the multistoried apartment houses of the Writers' Cooperative, old-timers still call the area Tsygansky Ugolok.

In 1929, a new calamity shook the country when the regime introduced the passport system. A passport is evidence of full citizenship; it is the iron cable attaching you firmly to a place of residence and binding you to the omniscient Department of Personnel and police files. The booklet is issued only to people with an "unblemished past." Having a passport was bad enough; but not having one was much worse. At best a passport was like a cattle brand, but the absence of a brand signified lack of affiliation, "passportlessness," and could ultimately mean prison or terrible deprivation.

People who were unable to secure passports were tagged with the label, *lishentsy*—disenfranchised ones. First on the Soviet's list of *lishentsy* were the NEP men. There were two *lishentsy* in our house in

Tsygansky Ugolok: the landlord, Sergei Ivanov, and my father.

Very soon after Ivanov had been entered on the rolls of the disenfranchised, the State confiscated his house. On being notified of this action, he got roaring drunk and, eyes white with hate, seized an ax and proceeded to hack away at the building. When he had finally spent his wrath, he realized he was in danger for having violated what had become State property. Ivanov took the only decision possible: he fled that very night, vanishing into thin air.

3 / Peretz Markish

IN 1928, Moïsei Ravitch quit the Cheka (six years later he would be arrested for "spreading criminal Trotskyite ideas") and, on orders of the highest authority, assumed the eminent post of director of the National Literatures Section in the State Literary Publishing House in Moscow, one of the country's most prestigious publishers. His new situation gave him a certain rapport with many writers, and he kept himself fully informed of not only their literary problems, but their everyday troubles as well.

Even in Moscow, the Ukrainian Ravitch remained a Jew, instinctively seeking out other Jews so that he could have the pleasure of speaking Yiddish, singing old Jewish songs, and losing himself in childhood reminiscences of his native Cherkasskoye. One of the houses to which Ravitch-Cherkassky repaired to recapture his Jewish past was that of Joseph Avratiner, a brave Jew with sad eyes and a good soul. Joseph did not work in the Cheka; nor did he later graduate from the Institute of Red Professors, as did his frequent visitor. He was a simple wage earner who loved the plaintive melodies of the Diaspora and the bittersweet, radiant, explosive literature of his people—of the modern Yiddish writers, Sholem Aleichem, Mendele Mocher Sforim, and Isaac Leib Peretz, and of the poet Peretz Markish.

Joseph Avratiner was a friend of my parents, and I often dropped in to see him at his apartment. Many times Ravitch-Cherkassky would be there, locked in serious discussions about Jewish literature with the master of the house. I was sixteen then, and did not know a word of Yiddish; my head was still full of clanking Soviet slogans about universal happiness and the inevitability of world revolution.

"I've some interesting news for you," Ravitch-Cherkassky told me one day in the spring of 1929. "Peretz Markish is back from abroad. I suspect he's in Moscow already." And then, with a twinkle in his eye, he added, "The young ladies of Moscow better barricade themselves—Markish is as handsome as a god!"

"I suppose he wears a hat," I said defiantly. For Soviet youth at the end of the twenties, wearing a hat meant that you were a bourgeois, a NEP man. In 1928, even while the NEP was still in force, my father, a bourgeois oilman and "Red merchant," could not allow himself to be seen wearing a hat. And if he had donned one, I would probably have been the first to condemn him on the flimsy and superficial criteria of the *komsomol*.

"You're right, he probably does wear a hat," Ravitch-Cherkassky allowed. "And I've heard he wears a scarf thrown over his shoulder, too. He has traveled over half the world—he's even been to Palestine."

"Do you know of any Jew who doesn't want to go to Palestine?" Joseph Avratiner broke in. "I don't."

I forgot this conversation until a few days later, when I was in the Avratiners' neighborhood. I decided to drop in. A man of about thirty opened the door. He was breathtakingly beautiful; I couldn't take my eyes off him. The soft outline of his face was crowned by a shock of dark curly hair that fell casually on his fore-head. In the obscurity of the hallway, his deep-set eyes flashed like dark-blue gems. And he was well dressed, a rare thing in Russia in those days, when the country was going through yet another round of "momentary difficulties."

"Get acquainted," Avratiner called out as he appeared in the hallway. "Meet Peretz Markish! Don't just stand there, come on in. You haven't turned into a pillar of salt, have you?"

Markish and Avratiner spoke Yiddish to each other and, sitting at the table, I bitterly regretted not knowing a word of the language. Several times Markish glanced in my direction and, seeing the blank expression on my face, switched to Russian. But before you knew it he was gesticulating wildly and again speaking Yiddish, completely oblivious to my presence. I felt a bit offended, but also annoyed at myself and at my parents for failing to teach me my mother tongue. I decided to leave.

Markish saw me to the door and asked, "Do you have a telephone?"

"Find it yourself if you're interested," I snapped.

"But I didn't ask for your number," Markish chuckled. "I just asked if you had a telephone."

On my way home, I practically cried over my own stupidity. Why hadn't I given him my telephone number!

When I got home I told my father that I had met a Jewish writer—Peretz.

"Well, aren't you the lucky one!" He grinned. "Isaac Leib Peretz. Why, he died even before you were born."

"What do you mean died!" I said indignantly. "He just got back from abroad."

"Oh, you mean Peretz Markish!"

"Yes, yes, Peretz Markish, of course," I sputtered. "He even took down my phone number."

My father's face fell; he had evidently heard about Peretz Markish's adventures, many of which, incidentally, were simply the product of the wildest rumors.

Pretending I wasn't feeling very well, I spent all the

following day sitting by the telephone. There were lots of calls—from boys, girls, friends of my parents—but not the call I was waiting for. I was at my wit's end when finally . . . he called.

"May all the gods smile on you!" I heard Markish say.

"If one of the gods is you, I can't think of anything better," I responded.

"Avratiner has asked us to the country. Will you join me?"

"With pleasure," I said.

My family was terribly concerned—rumor had it that the divine Markish had a wife and child in every town! Women spoke about this with excitement, men with envy, but Markish only laughed when he heard such talk. "So long as people are envious of you, you're riding high," he would say. "When they start feeling sorry for you, you know you're finished." Later on, I heard Markish repeat this dictum often, whenever his numerous enemies accused him of being shamelessly handsome, shamelessly talented, shamelessly productive as a writer, shamelessly rich.

In one of our conversations not long after we first met, I told Markish that in 1918 our family had lived in Yekaterinoslav on Broad Street. He stared at me as if he were setting eyes on me for the first time in his life.

"In 1918 you lived on Broad Street, near the railroad station? You're absolutely sure now?"

"Absolutely. But what's so strange about that?"

Markish burst out laughing, so hard that tears came to his eyes. I looked at him almost panic-stricken; until that moment he had been quite calm.

"It's miraculous," Markish said, suddenly becoming very serious. "You may call it coincidence, but all the same it is miraculous. It all depends on how you look at it. . . . In 1918, Avratiner, Misha Svetlov, Misha Golodnyi, and I were part of the Broad Street detachment for Jewish self-defense in Yekaterinoslav. Well, how do you like that! If I had had any inkling you were living on Broad Street, I would never have thought of defending it," he joked.

31

Markish had occupied a key post in the detachment and enjoyed the esteem of his comrades: he had fought in World War I and had been wounded on the battle field. At one point a black-bordered press communiqué had announced that soldier Peretz Markish had met a hero's death to the glory of Russian arms! Markish's military prowess served him well in the fight against pogromists, whether the Whites, the Reds, or the Greens. And for all I know, I might not have come through the fires of the Russian Revolution had not Markish's detachment patrolled my street.

A year after we met, Markish asked me to marry him. I accepted joyfully.

"There's one thing, though, I must confess to you before we become man and wife," Markish said and paused a moment. "And then it will be up to you to decide."

"Fine," I answered, shivering at the thought that something could interfere with our happiness.

"I have never been married before," he said, "but I do have a small child, a daughter. When you're a little older, you'll understand how such things happen in life. But for now, I simply wanted you to know. Well, what's your verdict?"

"Okay," I said, "now I have something to tell you."

Markish was taken aback and exclaimed, "What is it? It can't be!"

"No, it's something else," I said. "When we met, I lied to you. I told you I was seventeen."

"Well, and so what?" he said impatiently.

"Just that I wasn't," I confessed. "I've just turned seventeen."

Markish roared with laughter. "You had me worried there for a moment—I figured you were only fourteen!"

The following day he came to meet my parents for the first time. Turning to my mother, he said, "Vera Markovna, would you by any chance have a small valise, the smaller the better?"

"What do you need one for—are you going some place?" my mother inquired.

"We are going off together,'" he answered, with a

nod in my direction. "I have decided to take your daughter away. As for the small valise, that's so it will be easier for her to carry."

"So you'll take a cab!" my mother remonstrated—she was terribly concerned about me!

That same evening, Markish and I left for Kharkov.

It was a hot, humid day when our train pulled into the Kharkov station. Since there was little hope of our finding a decent room in a hotel, Markish hailed a cab and gave the driver the address of his friend, the well-known Jewish militant, Henokh Kazakevich.

Henokh, a big, strapping, broad-shouldered man, was a newspaper editor and a prominent figure in OZET ("Society of Jewish Tillers of the Soil"). He was also one of the first to advocate the idea of establishing Birobidzhan as the Jewish Autonomous Province in Russia, an idea he defended vigorously, with all the passion characteristic of him. Henokh was in the process of moving there with his family—his wife and younger son Ema. Ema was attending a Jewish technical school (there were such schools in the Ukraine in those days) and hoping to become an engineer. But fate would decide otherwise, for Ema became a prominent Soviet writer.

Henokh was an old Party member, an idealist and a dreamer. And he was a good Jew who wanted happiness for his people. Half an hour after our arrival, Markish and Henokh were having a heated discussion about something in Yiddish, while I sat in a corner of the room not understanding a word. A bystander might have thought that Markish and Henokh were mad as hell at each other, but it was nothing more than the clash of two hot temperaments.

Markish told me later what it was all about. Henokh had laid out his ideas about Birobidzhan, and Markish had disputed each in turn, contending that the settling of Jews in Birobidzhan was artificial, that this godforsaken Far Eastern territory could never become a real homeland for the Jews for which they would work and suffer privation, and that this dangerous and costly experiment would end up in a fiasco. Nothing could succeed unless the hand worked in harmony with the

33

spirit, and could there be any doubt that the wilderness of Birobidzhan was alien to the Jewish spirit? The only other Jewish writer sharing Markish's pessimism about Birobidzhan was Der Nister, which in Yiddish means "the concealed one" and was the pseudonym of Pinkles Kahanovich, who died in a prison hospital in 1950.

It turned out that Markish was right. In 1934, he and a group of Jewish writers visited Birobidzhan to see the "Jewish Republic" for themselves. Living there in one community were Jews from all over the world who naturally differed widely in character and customs. They could probably have blended with each other had they been united by a feeling of allegiance to a homeland, but Birobidzhan was not a homeland for them, not the land of the Jews that Israel later became. And Markish (who around that time had written, "Rocks of glory of a bygone day/ Intoxicate me . . .") foresaw that.

He came back disheartened and disillusioned. And, as time proved, the situation turned out to be even more terrifying than could have been anticipated in 1934. The majority of those Jews who had come from abroad to build a new Jewish homeland were sent to camps, where they perished in 1937. Birobidzhan, which is now in decay and remains the Jewish Autonomous Province in name only, still hangs like the sword of Damocles over the head of Soviet Jewry, since it is an ideal place for "fractious" Jews who are fighting for the right to emigrate from the USSR to Israel.

As for Henokh Kazakevich, fate was kind to him: he died his own death before he could be thrown into prison and tortured, as he certainly would have been had he lived to the time of the purges in 1937.

From Kharkov we went on to Kiev. We were met at the station by the keen and talented Jewish literary critic Nokhem Oyslender, whom Markish called Nyuka. Markish thought highly of him and respected his opinions and judgment. They had plenty to talk about; Markish was just then putting the final touches on a new book of poetry, *Farklepte tsiferblatn,* about which he had written to Nyuka.

Nyuka's wife, Mira Khenkina, a dull and rather mediocre poet, hung on every word Markish spoke, doing her utmost to get him to put his seal of approval on her poetry so as to advance her literary career. But Markish was unwilling to do so, in spite of his fondness for Nyuka; that refusal later cost Markish Nyuka's friendship. No doubt Mira continually harassed her husband with endless complaints that "his" Markish did not appreciate her talent. Later, during those terrible days in 1949, the integrity of the Oyslenders deserted them altogether: following Markish's arrest, Nyuka and Mira publicly declared their shame at having associated for so long with the criminal and traitor, Peretz Markish.

After Markish's rehabilitation and Mira Khenkina's death, Nyuka, learning that I was in Moscow, asked if he could see me on a matter of the utmost importance. We met, but hardly spoke a word. Then, avoiding my eyes, he handed me a packet. "These are Markish's letters to me which I saved," he said. "Take them. They are extremely valuable and interesting."

No doubt Nyuka was ashamed. I was grateful to him and appreciated the risk he must have taken by not destroying the letters during the years when they could have been used as criminal evidence against him.

But, to return to Kiev in 1930 . . . When the news got around that Markish was in town, a number of people—writers, poets, painters—came to see him for help and advice or simply to chat. He seemed to radiate a certain magnetism for people who had anything to do with Jewish culture. His personality was so forceful that often a first-time visitor would leave the house as either a loyal friend and disciple or an enemy.

It was dry and dusty in Kiev that summer, and friends suggested that we get away to Vorzel, a vacation spot. Markish agreed, without giving any thought to the practical side of the question. As usual, he had his briefcase containing paper and manuscripts with him, and his friends joked, "This time Markish has brought not only his briefcase, but a young wife too!"

We reached Vorzel toward evening and, after straying through shaded byways, we finally found the small house where we had reserved a large room with balcony—both of which were completely bare, providing nothing even to sleep on. But the absence of a bed wasn't what bothered Markish.

"Can you imagine—a room without a table?" he remarked with some irritation. "What am I going to work on?"

We called in the landlady to discuss the matter. Throwing up her hands in despair, she said, "What's this now, vacationers without their own furniture? If only you had let me know sooner, I would have found something. Now it's too late. It's already dark out."

The landlady gave me a kerosene lamp—electricity was as yet unknown in Vorzel. I finally found a can of kerosene in the dark passageway, but then I was confronted with the problem of figuring out where to pour it. I removed the glass shade from the lamp and twiddled with the wick. But where in the world did you put the kerosene? I was aware of a hard lump in my throat and was on the verge of tears; I felt helpless and alone. This was not quite the way I had pictured my honeymoon with the famous poet Peretz Markish. Finally, when I couldn't stand it any longer, I rushed over to him.

Markish grinned. "Come now, you don't know where to put the kerosene?" "After all, you do come from Baku, and you have plenty of kerosene there. Well, give me the lamp."

In a short time our room was illuminated by its steady glow, and life no longer seemed so gloomy.

The landlady dragged down a wooden bed frame from the attic and gave us a ball of twine. Then from somewhere she produced an empty sack before bidding us good night.

Until midnight, Markish and I were busy stringing the bed frame like a hammock; then we stuffed the sack with hay. The result was a fine bed.

The next morning we were able to borrow a shaky table from some neighbors; Markish set it out on the balcony and sat down to work. I was left to myself and the household chores.

At that time, I didn't have the vaguest idea about housekeeping. That didn't bother Markish a bit; he was busy working. He would swallow whatever

36

food I managed to slap together (it would be an exaggeration to describe it as a meal), go out to stretch his legs, and then sit down to work again. Now and then—at his work table, over dinner, or pacing back and forth in the room—he would mutter something unintelligible in Yiddish, and as I sat listening to him, I again bitterly regretted that I had never learned the language. I made up my mind to do something about it.

Two weeks later a telegram arrived announcing that Markish's father was coming to Vorzel to see his son and to make my acquaintance.

4 / David the Pious

BEFORE PRESENTING ME to his father, Markish decided to tell me about his family's life in the shtetl of Polonnoye, where he himself saw the light of day in 1895.

He came from a poor family: his mother, Khaya, sold herring; his father, David, possessed a bibical kind of beauty and was also a wise and learned man, none of which earned him a livelihood. Khaya's father, Shimon-Ber, was a tailor and relatively well off. David was taken into the family because of his erudition and was not expected to work. Day after day, David sat studying the Talmud, leaving the resourceful Khaya with the responsibility of providing for their seven children. She eked out a meager living from her herring; she would buy a whole fish, cut it up in small pieces, season each morsel with onions and sunflower oil, and sell them. The family would probably have had to go out begging if not for the support of Shimon-Ber. The help he gave, however, was not sufficient to keep all the children clothed and shod. When, at the age of three, Markish was sent off to *heder*, he could not get there on his own: it was winter, and little Peretz had neither a coat nor shoes. But David insisted, so Peretz's older brother, Meir, who was seven and had a pair of shoes, wrapped his baby brother in a blanket and carried him on his back to the *heder*, where he also studied.

Fate lavished all its gifts on just one of David and Khaya's seven children—Peretz. His five sisters and one brother grew up to be reasonably bright, reasonably successful, reasonably good-looking people. But little Peretz became Peretz Markish.

The reputation for beauty and intelligence of David's younger son spread to the neighboring shtetls, and Jews made their way to David's house to have a look at the gifted child. When Peretz was about seven, he developed a remarkable voice and began to sing in the synagogue. But as time went on he began to feel pent up in his father's ramshackle house with its small opaque windows, and stifled in the shtetl, with its hunched-over Jews weaving fantasies of a better life and its omnipresent white goats wandering through the twisting streets. At the age of ten, he ran away from home to the hamlet of Romanov, where he sang in the synagogue and led a free but half-starving existence until he moved on to Berditchev.

One day, a prestigious "big city" cantor from Kiev was stopping in town. The rabbi of Berditchev, who held out high hopes for Peretz, persuaded the cantor to audition the young singer. Peretz was given a few kopeks for food to fortify himself before the decisive test. For practically the first time in his life he treated himself to some fat meatballs with oil-fried potatoes, gobbled them down—and lost his voice from gorging himself with such unaccustomed fare.

Thus Markish's musical career ended. He was born to speak to God in other ways. Fifteen years later, in his poem "The Forty-Year-Old," he wrote:

> Even if my throat be in fever,
> Through the vapors and the pain,
> This word of mine goes out to You . . .

Following Peretz's misadventure with the rabbi of Berditchev, Markish's oldest sister, Leah, came to take him back home. The virus of freedom, however, had infected him permanently. Two years later, he dared do something that his contemporaries in Polonnoye would have been afraid even to think about, but which excited their admiration and envy: he, a Jewish boy from the shtetl, walked around in broad daylight in rubber boots and a cap! David closed his eyes to the brazen behavior of his "wayward" younger son, while Khaya said wistfully, "Ah, if only he would become an accountant. He has the brains for it!" Shortly thereafter he was fixed up with a job in the Polonnoye Savings and Loan Society.

It was just about that time—he must have been around fifteen—that he began to write poetry. His poems, which he wrote in Russian, were in a religious-mystical vein and suffused with his feelings, his desires and his impressions about the world opening wide before him. He wrote reams, impulsively, wherever he was, at any time whatever, and using any paper he could lay his hands on. He scribbled one of his early poems on a bank check. When the customer received the check, he was unable to cash it and he complained to Markish's superior, who, after a moment's bewilderment, suspected some skullduggery—a forgery had been committed or a robbery was brewing. Finally, the trail led back to Markish. The "culprit" received a severe reprimand and was threatened with dismissal should there be a repetition. David took it all fatalistically; Khaya wept over her Peretz and his involvement in a situation that no good Jewish boy should get himself into.

But this was nothing compared with the scandal that broke out a few months later. One fine day a troupe of itinerant Jewish actors straggled into Polonnoye—a rare event. You can be sure that it was not good fortune that brought them to such a godforsaken hole as Polonnoye; nor was it the prospect of an especially warm welcome or of making some money. In fact, on the evening of their arrival, Peretz Markish was the only person who went to the local inn to greet the actors.

The inn, which was packed full with snoring customers, was not the ideal place for discussions about art. So the young Markish took the keys to the Savings and Loan Society building out of his pocket and led the troupe there.

In no time at all, the building was ablaze with light —you would have thought it was the day of Tsar Nicholas's coronation. A flood of laughter and song filled the darkened street. Thick smoke poured out of the window of the director's office, where they had set up a samovar and were boiling water for tea.

The night watchman came running—but then must have had second thoughts about going in to investigate. Instead, he rushed to the director's home and informed him that bandits had broken into his office and were ransacking it. It was not long before the Jews of Polonnoye, "answering the call to arms," had surrounded the brightly lit building. Bursting inside armed with spears and axes, the first thing they saw was Markish standing on a table and reciting his poetry to the actors, who were seated on the floor around the puffing samovar.

The next day, Peretz Markish was fired by the Savings and Loan Society. Nothing could save him: not the tears of Khaya, the sighs of David, or the "palm-greasing" of his grandfather, tailor Shimon-Ber.

Peretz Markish would be neither a cantor nor a banker; it was not in the cards.

His father, David, a wise man who was accustomed to the blows of fate, merely threw up his hands and resigned himself to the situation: little Peretz, who had shown such promise, would not make his way in the world, would never be an accountant.

And now David was coming to visit us in Vorzel.

Markish left in the morning for Kiev to meet his father. The old man was coming by boat from Dnepropetrovsk (formerly Yekaterinoslav), where Markish's entire family had settled before the Revolution. As I awaited his arrival, I was nervous and at loose ends. Markish had told me that his father didn't know a word of Russian and that, in general, there

40

was no need for me to speak to him if I didn't feel like it.

"But at least tell me what I can say to welcome him—a word or two of Yiddish," I implored.

"Well, all right. If you wish, you can say *vos, ver, vemen*. That will please him."

I took down the words and committed them to memory.

Late that evening, Markish arrived with his father. The old man was strikingly handsome: he had a stately bearing, a flowing white beard, and pale-blue eyes. He was wearing a long, black satin caftan and a visored cap. The cart that brought our guest was laden with a number of wicker baskets, bales and sacks of books.

"Vos, ver, vemen!" I blurted as I ran to welcome him.

He shuddered, and stared at me in complete consternation. "Don't you know Russian, my daughter?" he asked in Russian with a heavy Jewish-Ukrainian accent.

I looked toward Markish in an effort to find out what all this could mean. But Markish showed no reaction. It was only then that I noticed in the darkness that Markish's hand was bandaged with a blood-soaked handkerchief.

"What's wrong, Markusha?"

"Let's get a doctor!" Markish said impatiently. "It's those things," he said, glowering and pointing to his father's baggage. "At the station I got my finger caught in the door of his compartment. I think I've torn out my fingernail."

We got the doctor out of bed. He removed the upturned nail and bandaged the finger. Once the operation was over Markish brightened.

"What does it mean, *vos, ver, vemen?*" I asked him on the way back home. "Your father didn't appreciate it one bit."

"It means, 'what, who, to whom,'" Markish replied. "Remember, you insisted on my telling you a few Yiddish words."

When we got back, we found his father on the balcony, seated at the table and reading the Torah by the light of the kerosene lamp. Markish said something to him in Yiddish, but the old man shook his head. Then Markish used all his persuasion to try to convince him of something, gesticulating and pacing back and forth in the room. The old man didn't say very much, but it was clear that he wouldn't give an inch.

"He's no old man, he's some sort of demon," Markish finally said in Russian. "He refuses to sleep in our room."

"Why?" I asked.

"You'll find it hard to understand. According to Jewish law, he is not allowed to sleep in the same room with a married couple."

"But it's terribly cool out on the balcony. He'll catch cold," I pleaded.

David himself solved the problem by determinedly dragging the folding cot we had prepared for him out of our room and into the corridor.

The next morning, as usual, Markish sat down to work, and the old man came over to me to have a chat and get to know me better.

"Do you have parents, daughter? Papa, mama?" he inquired.

"Yes, in Moscow. I have a brother, too."

"Your parents, are they Communists?" the old man asked, fixing me with his eyes.

"No, they're not."

"Good!" he said, obviously relieved, but suddenly he looked worried again. "Oh, and your brother, is he a Communist?"

"No, he's not either," I informed him.

"Good!" he repeated, now thoroughly reassured. "Tell me, what did your parents give you for a dowry?"

I hadn't received any dowry, so I countered his question with a question of my own: "And what did you give your son?"

The old man beckoned me toward the window.

"Look!" he said, indicating, with a broad sweep of his hand, the sky, the river and the woods beyond. "I give all of that to you besides my son Peretz!"

The question of kosher food bothered Markish's father more than anything else. He didn't have to ask —he could see that we hardly kept kosher, and so he made a suggestion.

"Why should you bother about the cooking, daughter? I'm a very good cook! It will be delicious and as it should be, and, besides, it will save you some money. Why don't you go out for a walk, daughter, and in the meantime I'll prepare a borscht the likes of which even your mother never made for you."

I didn't go for a walk but stayed and watched how the old man prepared the soup. He sliced the tomatoes, pared the beets—everything looked so tasty. Now and then Markish poked his head into the kitchen and suggested, "Watch closely, Firka, see how he does it! Remember, it's not just any old borscht, it's kosher borscht!"

When we sat down to the table, the old man removed the cover from the gurgling pot, which emitted a piquant, fragrant aroma, and filled his son's plate first.

"Tell me how you like it, Peretz," he said with triumphant serenity. He did not doubt either his culinary talents or that his son would fully appreciate the merits of his cooking.

Markish had barely touched the spoon to his lips when he jumped up from the table and yelped, *"Sam! Sam!"*

The old man looked frightened, and I had no idea what was going on. Nor did I know then that *sam* was Yiddish for "poison."

In no time at all, the mystery was dispelled. Instead of seasoning the borscht with vinegar, the old man had used essence of vinegar by mistake. Following that incident, Markish resolutely barred his father from the kitchen. The old man was crestfallen.

So I set out for town and the Jewish cookery there. My father-in-law, contritely shaking his head, went along with me. After satisfying himself that the cookery was strictly kosher, he regained his composure. We bought a dairy meal, as he desired, and returned home with food in containers.

The next day I went out to get the dinners myself. The meat soup was poured into the same container

43

that had been used the previous day for the milk dishes. After sniffing the soup, the old man put the container down on the table with a bang.

"Why did you use the same container for *milkhik* [dairy] and *fleyshik* [meat]?" he inquired sadly. "Do you want to get me into trouble with God, my daughter?"

After that, the old man went out to take his meals in the cookery.

Friday evening also created problems. One Sabbath eve Markish and I got home rather late. The landlady met us at the door with the news: "Your dad won't go to bed. He refuses to extinguish the lamp."

Markish laughed. Not without a certain feeling of pride, he explained to me that on Friday, after the first star appears in the heavens, an orthodox Jew is not permitted to work, and putting out a light is among the things regarded as work.

"I'll go and put it out myself, then," I volunteered. Markish grinned. "You just go and try!"

"Papa, let me put out the light," I said as I walked over toward him and took a deep breath to blow out the flame.

"Don't do it! Don't do it!" he cried, waving me away with his hands. "You're a Jewess! We need a *shabes-goy* [a non-Jew]."

Our landlady did not fit that role either, the old man lost no time in explaining to me. We had no choice but to trouble our neighbors and enlist their aid.

The next morning we were discussing Sabbath rules and David told us of an incident that took place on the boat. One of the baskets he had placed in the baggage room contained his siddur, or prayer book. Not surprisingly, none of the ship's crew was willing to rummage around in the baggage room for the old man's basket, so he resorted to a stratagem. Among the passengers, he had spotted an enterprising, Jewish-looking young man, and he went up to him. "Pardon me, young man," he said, "but you are Jewish, aren't you?"

"Yes, I am," he answered.

"Well, I've noticed that you have access to the

ship's captain," the old man continued, looking pensively at his interlocutor.

"That's right," he confirmed. "I'm a journalist."

"Let me tell you what's on my mind, then. There's a basket of mine in the baggage room and it contains some medicine I am supposed to take twice a day. But nobody wants to go and get my basket for me. Be good enough, young man, to speak to the captain about it, and you will be doing a virtuous deed!"

The young man did as he was asked, and Markish's father retrieved his basket with the siddur.

"And I didn't deceive that young man," he declared as he concluded his story. "The siddur is the medicine of the soul, and I must take it twice a day, morning and evening."

That same day, my brother Shura turned up quite unexpectedly in Vorzel. He had come to see how his baby sister was getting on with that "harebrained ladykiller" Peretz Markish.

The first person Shura bumped into at the door to our house was Markish's father.

"Oy!" exclaimed David as his eyes fell upon Shura. And that was all he said.

As it turned out, Shura was the young man who had helped the old man retrieve his siddur.

While in Vorzel, Markish finished his first play *Nit gedayget* ("Do Not Grieve"), which dealt with life in one of the first Jewish communal settlements "on the land," near Dzhankoi in the Crimea. Jews on the land was a theme that stirred Markish's imagination and commanded his attention for a rather long time. In fact, his play was the further development of the theme he had already treated in a poem of the same name.

Putting the final touches on his play, Markish became preoccupied and withdrawn. This was particularly noticeable in the mornings. He would rise early and awaken me, but he seemed lost in another world. While I went about preparing a quick breakfast, he would wander around the neighborhood by himself. If I asked him anything, he would answer curtly or simply ignore the question altogether and go outside.

No matter what I said, it would irritate and anger him. Before sitting down to work in the morning, he hated to talk to anybody.

So our breakfasts passed in silence, except for an occasional staccato exclamation. That disturbed and upset me. I interpreted in my own, feminine way Markish's stubborn morning taciturnity. It was only much later that he explained to me what it had all meant.

During the night, Markish dreamed about the sequel to what he had been working on during the day. No sooner would he close his eyes than subconscious images started to emerge. When morning came, they would linger on for but a fleeting moment—until he had got down to work. In that brief interval—between the time he awoke and the time he sat down to write—Markish continued to live with these images, no longer in a dream now, but in a state of consciousness. This was more challenging than in the dream state, for it meant retaining these images and prolonging their vitality until they had been fixed on paper. Anything that could possibly distract Markish during this crucial, half-hour interlude had to be dismissed.

By lunchtime his work for the day was finished. He would whistle some tune, more often than not "Come Back to Sorrento," and from the way he whistled I could tell whether or not he was satisfied. After lunch, he would take a nap for a half-hour or so. He woke up refreshed but reluctant to talk about his work. The entire afternoon until nightfall was set aside for relaxation.

After he had finished his play and sent it off to Moscow—to Mikhoels at the Korsh Theater—I imagined that he would take it easy for a few days, but the next morning he was his usual taciturn self and, after breakfast, he sat down at his table to work on some poems. He regarded a morning not spent in work as a morning killed by his own hand. I recall a few such workless mornings, and on those days, until Markish turned in at night he was gloomy, glum and withdrawn.

After his afternoon nap, Markish was unrecognizable. We took walks together, went swimming or visited friends. Isaac Markovich Nusinov, one of the most brilliant Jewish literary critics, and his family spent that summer in Vorzel. Despite his youth—he was only a few years older than Markish—Nusinov was already a professor at Moscow University and head of the literature faculty at Bubnov Pedagogical Institute, where he gave a course, in Yiddish, on the history of Western literature for future teachers in Jewish schools and technical institutes. A number of his pupils subsequently became writers—the poet Shloimo Roitman, for example, now living in Israel, and the critic Gersh Remennik. The faculty was, naturally, shut down in 1937, the year that inaugurated the official attack on Jewish culture in the USSR.

With his fine-features, moist Eastern eyes and small beard, Nusinov bore a striking resemblance to pictures of Jesus Christ. One of his artist friends had even given him a caricature showing him crowned with a wreath woven of thorns and roses. It was captioned with a line from Blok's poem "The Twelve": "Crowned with wreath of roses white/Out in front steps Jesus Christ."

Markish spent long evenings at Nusinov's house in discussions that lasted into the late hours of the night. They conversed mostly in Yiddish but sometimes in Russian. I recall their reaction to Mayakovsky's suicide. Neither accepted the official version, according to which the poet had shot himself over an unsuccessful love affair. They discerned something more profound and troubling in his death.

I took the liberty of interjecting myself into their conversation, citing some of Mayakovsky's own lines:

"Passerby! Is thisTchaikovsky Street?"
"No!
"It's been Mayakovsky's for a thousand years!
"He shot himself at the door of his beloved here."

"Oh, no!" Markish countered. "It's not important that he wrote about his death. What is important lies elsewhere: a real poet rarely dies peacefully in his

47

own bed. Yes, Firka, you made a poor choice of a husband!"

Those words made a deep impression on me.

During the first days of July, the reply came from Moscow that Markish's play, *Nit gedayget,* had been accepted by the Korsh Theater, and Markish was summoned to Moscow to give it a reading. He was delighted: the theater had a first-rate troupe of actors —the veteran actress Blumenthal-Tamarina, the brilliant Mezhinsky. Leaving me in his father's care, Markish left for Moscow. This was our first separation, and although not a long one, it was very hard for me to take.

The old man followed Markish's instructions with a lofty sense of responsibility. He considered it his duty to go to the market every day and also to have a number of talks with me. He told me about Jewish history and religion. And he also intimated to me in a gentle way that he regarded his son Meir, who had gone into accounting, as the most successful of all his children. He didn't take Markish's occupation very seriously, although he refrained from openly criticizing it. He didn't understand his son's poems, and maybe he didn't even read them. But Meir's work—that was a proper occupation for a young Jewish man! Meir was the unshakable pride of his father; Peretz was an enigma, and a somewhat frightening one, at that.

About ten days later, Markish returned from Moscow, exuberant, overexcited, and with the ever-present briefcase in his hand.

"Avratiner gave me a present for Sonya," Markish said, taking a package out of his briefcase (Avratiner's family, in whose house I had met Markish, was spending the summer in Vorzel). "Take it over to her! But I haven't brought a thing for you."

"I don't need anything, Markusha!" I said, and I meant it sincerely. "You're here, and that's what counts."

To my great surprise, the "iron" Markish was moved deeply. He turned away from me, but not before I noticed that his eyes were moist with tears.

"I was just kidding, Firka," he confessed, as he

handed me a small box. It contained coral earrings, the first earrings I had ever had.

There was a gift waiting for Markish too: I was expecting a child.

When I told him, he said excitedly: "I am ordering a boy. Watch your step, I won't accept a girl!"

I didn't know if Markish was joking or meant it seriously, and I was terribly worried until the baby came. It was a boy, as Markish had wished.

In the middle of August, my mother arrived in Vorzel; we were going to return to Moscow together because I had to get back to the university. Markish liked Vorzel and planned to stay on there to get some work done.

My beautiful and statuesque mother made the acquaintance of the patriarch David, clad in his flowing black caftan, on our balcony in Vorzel. To Markish's great astonishment, the old man extended his hand to my mother, although religious law forbade him to take the hand of a married woman. When we were sitting at the table, though, David paled perceptibly and stubbornly avoided looking at my mother. That troubled me, and I drew Markish's attention to his behavior.

"I'll fix everything," Markish whispered as he led my mother away from the table into our room.

"You are wearing a short-sleeved dress," Markish remarked to my mother, "and quite properly so, Vera Markovna, for you have beautiful arms. But just look at my poor father—he's not himself; he is not allowed to behold a woman's uncovered arms, even arms like yours. . . . Throw a shawl over your shoulders."

My mother put on a shawl, and the old man regained his composure.

The time came for me to leave, but Markish was reluctant to let me go. "What's the point of your studying?" he asked. "I didn't finish the university myself, and so what, I'm getting along all right. Stay here with me! If worse comes to worse, you can resume your studies next year."

But I wanted to go and held my ground.

"Forget about the university," Markish persisted.

49

"I want you to give me six children, and you need time for that. Why study, when you know very well you won't have time to do your homework?"

"And what about the equality of men and women?" I protested with all the ardor of youth. "I am in favor of total emancipation! A woman must be able to fend for herself in life."

"Ah," Markish grumbled, brushing me aside. "Your duty is to build life, my duty is to make a living. If you want to call that emancipation, then do so to your heart's content!"

Nevertheless, Markish didn't seriously interfere with my studies. On the contrary, he took pride in my modest achievements, and he never failed to praise them in front of his writer friends, as though he himself were amazed. My achievements were a source of pleasant distraction for him.

At the end of August, my mother and I left for Moscow. I settled down once again in my fifteen-foot-square room in Tsygansky Ugolok. When Markish arrived, I just about managed to squeeze in a small table. In those days, the celebrated Markish had neither house nor home—not that it mattered to him in the least under whose roof he spent the night. He was absolutely sincere when he wrote:

> "Instant" they call me . . .
> With free outstretched arms,
> The world I greedily embrace,
> And gaze in mute exultation
> Afar and aloft into the vast before me!

5 / My Father's "Gold"

THE INGENIOUS SCHEME the Soviets had devised in the form of the *lishentsy* gradually acquired a much broader application than it had had at the outset. The "sins" of the parents were now visited `on the children. The Soviets' first organized public campaign was a dirty and sickening spectacle: the press began publishing declarations of children repudiating their parents, of wives repudiating their husbands. The repudiators beat their breasts, gushed tears of "pure-hearted" repentance—it was only by an absurd quirk of fate that they had ties of blood with the bourgeoisie, with the NEP men, with the enemies of socialism. . . . Those few who failed to make public declarations were threatened with severe retribution: they bore the stigma of being "relatives of the disenfranchised"; they were refused work and admission into schools, and were subjected to persecution and harassment.

We were aware of what went on, but only rarely did the situation penetrate our lives. Markish was moved by national, not class interests. What interested him in postrevolutionary society was Jewish life, not the life of society as a whole. The destruction of millions of Russian peasants did not touch us directly, and we shut our eyes to it. No matter how painful it is for me to make this admission, I cannot refrain from saying today that it was a tragic failing on the part of Markish, a failing which he shared with almost all of the Soviet intelligentsia. We did not see the misfortune of others, or, if we did, we tried to find a justification in stereotyped rationalizations—"historical

51

necessity," "class struggle," and so on. Only years later, in the midst of our own tragedy, did we realize the sheer horror in its entirety—not only the torment of the Jews and of the intelligentsia, but the torment of the whole country, of all society, of all the peoples that are part of it. After Markish's arrest, our maid, who had lived with us for more than fifteen years and had become virtually a member of the family, said to me, "Now, you're weeping, but why did you think nothing of it when they dispossessed my father as a kulak, when they destroyed him with no reason, when they ruined my family?"

Her words bore no trace of malice or even resentment; they were simply a cry of grief over the human blindness and egotism that we, like others, were guilty of.

The Revolution promised not only the destruction of the old culture, but the creation of a new one. Naturally nothing practical could ever come of it, so the regime concentrated on developing "new, socialist relationships" between people. These relationships often assumed curious and occasionally monstrous forms. We, in our blindness, did not see this . . . until our eyes were opened.

In those times it was considered shameful to take your husband's name after marriage and, for that matter, the very institution of marriage was considered shameful: how can you still tolerate those "bourgeois survivals"? The idea of wearing a wedding ring or formalizing a marriage was simply outlandish. Freedom! No limit! No holds barred! The authorities were satisfied: playing at freedom, their subjects, in the heat of the game, took the clank of chains for joyful music.

It is curious to note what has become of those antibourgeois practices. The tradition of wedding rings has been restored—it is considered unseemly for a newlywed not to wear a wedding band—and the bride puts on a veil for her wedding ceremony. "Free love" belongs to the distant past; rarely has a young girl lost her virginity by the time she visits the *ZAGS* (Registry Office) to get married.

The cultural revolution is over, and time has erased the traces of destruction. In 1931, though, experiments in that revolution were still going on. In that year, for some inexplicable reason the Faculty of Philology of Moscow University was shut down. "Philology is an obsolete science ill-adapted to the spirit of the times" was the official motive. It was preceded, nevertheless, by a "social purge of the student body," which had lots of unpleasant consequences. As the daughter of a former NEP man, I was obliged to go to work in a button factory so as "to work off my social origin through proletarian labor." I combined work in the factory with my studies in the university and for that reason I was not "purged." After our faculty was disbanded, students were given the choice of continuing their studies either in the Herzen Institute of Social Sciences in Leningrad or in the Bubnov Pedagogical Institute in Moscow. There was also a third alternative, which I preferred to the first two: study in the Moscow Foreign Language Institute. I continued my studies there in the French-language department. The classes were taught, on the whole, in impeccable French. A number of teachers were workers in the Comintern—foreign Communists who had come to Russia to "build a new life." In 1937 those who didn't manage to get back home in time fell victim to repression and finished their lives in camps and prisons.

In the spring of 1931, when my child was expected, I left for Baku to stay with relatives and have my baby there. It was difficult getting into a clinic in Moscow; besides, I was frightened and Babushka Olya wanted me to come. Markish was jubilant over the birth of a son; he named him Simon. As far as I was concerned, my baby was, of course, the most beautiful, the most intelligent . . . the most everything. And, amazingly enough, he actually began talking when he was nine months old.

The production of Markish's play *Nit gedayget*—now called *The Land*—on the stage of the Korsh Theater coincided with the birth of Simon. This was Markish's first stab at playwriting, and he was pleased by its success, and decided to continue writing plays.

Shortly after the birth of the baby, we took on a nursemaid who was to share the life and fortunes of our family. She was a Russian peasant girl from the region beyond the Volga, and her name was Lena Khokhlova. She looked after the child, did the cooking and helped with the housework, but this does not begin to describe the position she occupied in our household: she became a member of the family.

From Lena we learned something about the lot of the peasants in postrevolutionary Russia. Her father, a hardworking muzhik, owned a cow and four sheep. He didn't have a horse, however, and was therefore known as "a horseless one," which, by rural standards, means a poor man. Nevertheless, quite soon after the Revolution he had been hauled off to prison as a "prosperous" peasant. It was a flagrant mistake, and the peasants appealed to the town authorities, the Cheka, who ruled that Khokhlov was a toiler and ordered the poor man's release. Issued a discharge certificate, Lena and her mother set off for the prison to obtain the father's release. When the guard unbolted the cell door and called out, "Khokhlov, Mitri, step out!" Dmitri Khokhlov fell dead with a heart attack. He had imagined, no doubt, that the "liberators of the downtrodden" had come to take him to be shot. Lena's husband and children had died from hunger or cholera or something else, and Lena had come from her village to the city to earn her living as a domestic. She was short and slightly humpbacked, a condition she would invariably explain as "the contraction of my waist due to overexertion."

Markish loved to listen to Lena's stories about peasant life, stories told in the rich, vivid speech of the people. My children—first Simon and later David —grew up on these remarkable stories. And I cannot help thinking that if they developed into writers, it was thanks not only to their father's genes but to Lena's stories as well.

Markish and I moved into my father and mother's room in the apartment in Tsygansky Ugolok. As usual, Markish worked a great deal, and it distressed me that he wasn't paying enough attention to our child. Markish did love Simon's precocious wit, his *khokhme,* and he swelled with pride whenever his son came up with something funny in front of visitors. But I wanted Markish to be in constant admiration of our joint creation. In my parents' home and in our family circle, I was accustomed to children being the center of life, the object of adulation. But Markish lost patience whenever I alluded to this, and went off to work. I think he wanted to avoid offending me with a cutting rebuff, which, by the way, he was quite capable of.

"A father and son can be bound by spiritual ties," he said to me once. "Right now"—Markish nodded in the direction of his son—"he is simply a piece of flesh, mine and yours. Can I, let's say, get excited over my finger, not because it is a perfect instrument, but precisely because it is *my* finger? Don't ask me for the impossible. My relation with my son will come later."

On one occasion when we had guests, one of them brought Simon a big box of candy. The boy grabbed the box and, gurgling in pleasurable anticipation, carried it over to a corner and opened it. Markish suddenly became very serious and gazed at his son in silence for a moment.

"Simon!" he shouted. "Come over here to me at once!"

The child obeyed, looking nervously and questioningly at his father.

"Why aren't you offering the candy to anyone? Don't just stand there, do as I tell you," Markish ordered.

Simon made the rounds of the guests, offering the candy. From the way Markish looked, I knew that this was not the end of his lesson in behavior. When the child had done his duty, he looked diffidently at his father and was just about to attack the candies.

"Hey, son, not so fast! You were not thoughtful enough to share your candy with our guests, and for that you'll have to be punished. So go to the window and throw out whatever is left in the box!"

Our guests were uncomfortable, and I was on the verge of tears, but we kept silent. The child walked sadly to the window and, barely able to reach the windowsill, he obeyed his father's orders. Then he silently left the room, tears rolling down his cheeks.

"Children must be taught," Markish declared, sensing our displeasure. "Especially if they are as smart as my son, Simon. That lesson will come in handy someday. He won't stop loving his father for that and he'll remember that lesson forever. He'll even tell his own children about it."

Markish found time for his son only when his head was free of work. If the child happened to come up to him while he was preoccupied with his own thoughts, he summoned me—"Firka!"—and the look in his eyes seemed to say, "Rescue me, I've no time for him now, nor for you, for that matter, or anyone else." Markish's character was, it seems to me, vividly reflected in his attitude toward his child: the character of a poet and creator.

And so everything was fine and splendid with us. The world seemed to me like an immense green playing field. Markish advanced along his chosen path confidently and imperiously. Fame pursued him, although he did not seek it.

The outline for Markish's play *The Fifth Horizon* had been accepted by the Vakhtangov Theater and he planned to go to the Donbass mining region in order to gather material for it. Shortly before he left, a letter came from his brother Meir, the hope and pride of his old father, David. During the NEP, Meir had engaged in big business in Yekaterinoslav, where Markish's parents lived, but now he made his home in Makeyevka, a town in the Donbass. He worked quietly and unobtrusively there as a simple accountant.

After reading the letter, Markish became depressed. Now he had a second reason, probably the more important, to visit the Donbass. He didn't tell me what was in Meir's letter, merely noting that his brother, who knew a great deal about mining affairs, could be of considerable help to him in his investigation.

Before his departure Markish had to finish up the work he was doing with the Russian translators of his first collection of poems, *Rubezh* ("The Boundary"), which he was then getting ready for publication. Russian poets and translators would come to our place in

Tsygansky Ugolok: strapping David Brodsky, small and impetuous Pavel Antokolsky, perpetually sad and dreamy Tarlovsky. No sooner would a translator enter the room and I leave it than the air would be filled with shouts, in Russian and Yiddish, singing, stamping, and general clamor: Markish was working with the translator—that is, he was tearing the translation to pieces, demonstrating that words were only the receptacle for feelings and that poetry could not be translated by trying to match up words with the original. It was the poet's feelings, not his words, that must be conveyed in another language. In an effort to explain the feelings expressed in his verse, Markish would often demonstrate with dramatic gestures. On one occasion, alarmed by a strange thud, I peered through the crack in the door. Markish was prone on the floor, arms spread wide, literally embracing it: the verses in question represented the author embracing the whole world, the entire universe.

After *Rubezh* appeared, many critics noted with astonishment that the translation of "The Last One" ("Poslednii"), one of the poems in the collection, differed radically from the original, not only in the words but in the imagery. The fact was, however, that Markish, in the course of his work with Pavel Antokolsky, had reworked his own original imagery, suggested new comparisons and metaphors, and insisted that Antokolsky incorporate them in his translation. And Antokolsky, fired by the passion of Markish, did just that.

By the time Markish left for the Donbass, I had guessed that Meir, as a former NEP man, had fled to Makeyevka and was still in danger. In the Russia of the thirties, it was quite a common occurrence for a NEP man to go into hiding, although sooner or later he was usually apprehended and thrown into prison for having participated in the New Economic Policy of the Bolsheviks. Up to that time, Meir had been lucky.

Toward evening a few days after Markish's departure, there was a knock at the door. "Is Lazebnikov in?" a man inquired.

"He's not back from work yet."

"Excuse me," the stranger said and left.

We didn't attach any importance to this visit; in fact, we had forgotten about it by the time my father came home. But no sooner had he sat down at the table than there was another knock at the door. My father got up and went to the hallway to see who was there.

A minute, two minutes passed, and there was no sign of my father. My mother and I went out into the street and saw an automobile driving away from our house. This time my father had been arrested without a warrant and without his family's being informed.

For days we sat at home, in tears and in despair, until finally the mailman came with a letter, with no return address, that said: "Whoever finds this note, please forward it to the following address. . . . " On the other side of the paper, my father had written: "I am being transported in a prison train. Why I was taken, I have no idea. I think we are traveling in the direction of Yekaterinoslav. I am going to toss this note out of the window at the nearest station—with God's help, someone will pick it up."

Knowing now that my father was alive, my mother began at once to take action. She sought out former Yekaterinoslav NEP men or, to be more precise, their families: all the men, without exception, had been arrested and shipped off to Yekaterinoslav. Their wives told my mother something she wasn't aware of: *zolotukha,* or "gold fever," had set in. Every city undertook to arrest as many former NEP men and simply rich people as possible so as to curry praise and favor. To this end, they even resurrected house registers and other documents to ferret out former residents who had moved to other cities. Cheka agents were then dispatched to these cities to nab their victims on the quiet—as they had done with my father—so as to prevent their having time to "appropriate" another place of residence. My father had never had any business dealings in Yekaterinoslav, but he was married to a woman from there, a fact on record at the Civil Registry Office. So the decision was taken to arrest him and transfer him to Yekaterinoslav in order to "swell the numbers and fulfill the plan." An epidemic of *zolotukha* spread through the land of the Soviets!

What exactly was this *zolotukha* that raged throughout the Soviet Union?

The State needed money, and lots of it, and it decided that the most effective way of getting it was simply to take it away from its citizens. That meant rearresting all those NEP men who had neither died a natural death nor been murdered, and "shaking them down" until they had surrendered all the gold, money or other valuables that they might have stashed away. Rather than imposing taxes on them or persuading them to subscribe to loans, they just plain took their money. They would seize a NEP man by the scruff of his neck, shake him, beat him up, threaten him with death, take his money, and then, when he was no longer of any use, let him go. It wasn't a difficult task; no more difficult than robbing a passer-by of his wallet on an open field in the night.

I got in touch with Markish, whose first reaction was to want to return to Moscow immediately to rescue my father. But after thinking it over, we decided that the best thing to do was for me to go to Yekaterinoslav myself.

Laden with provisions I had purchased with Markish's coupons in the special distribution center (after the dismantling of the NEP, the country experienced a scarcity of food and manufactured products), I boarded the train for Yekaterinoslav. I had decided to go directly from the station to Markish's parents.

Markish's father, David, was despondent. Khaya, his mother, kept on repeating, "They'll end up putting everybody in prison, everybody." David was frightened for Meir, the pride of the family; they had already come looking for him. Because of that, David agreed to accompany me only to the beginning of the street where the prison was located: he did not want to attract unnecessary attention to himself and, in turn, to Meir.

The square in front of the prison was swarming with humanity; you might have thought some big celebration was taking place or a fair or black market center in full swing. People were milling around, eating food they had brought with them, talking to one another. Seeing I was a new arrival, they began firing questions at me:

"Who's been arrested, your father?"

"Where's he from?"

"What's his name?"

"How long has he been holding out?"

I didn't quite understand the last question. They clarified it for me: How many days has the prisoner, under torture, resisted signing a confession? One sturdy old NEP man had been holding out for seventy-six days.

Knowing for certain that my father had nothing left of his former fortune and, consequently, that he had no reason to hold out, I made my way to the prison administration.

"I'm the daughter of Lazebnikov," I said as I presented myself through a narrow window. "Is my father here?"

"Why, we have been waiting anxiously for you!" a young blond, with clear, pale-blue eyes said to me cordially, even tenderly. "Come along."

And opening the door, he led me along the corridor of the prison and into one of the interrogation offices.

Here, his tender cordiality vanished into thin air.

"Where are the imperials? Where are the diamonds? Where are the gold bars?" he roared like a wild beast. "Have you brought them? Hand them over! Hand them over now and you can have your father!"

His bellowing wasn't spontaneous; it was obvious that he shouted these words over and over again every day.

"Imperials? What are you talking about?" I yelled, unable to contain myself. "What do you want from us?"

"Imperials—that's money, money, money!" the blond stormed. "The country needs money! Where are they? Hand them over! How did you know your father was here? Who do you live with? Answer, and be quick about it!"

"I'm the wife of Peretz Markish," I said. "I am living at his father's."

The blond paused for a moment and then returned to the charge: "See here, you're bourgeois, the whole

60

bunch of you! Where's Meir Markish? Come clean, where's Meir?"

"I don't know," I answered.

"And where's your father's gold?"

"He doesn't have any gold," I said.

"Doesn't have any gold?" he cried. "Ha, ha, ha! And you expect me to believe you! Stay here, then, and try to remember where the gold is, where Meir Markish is. You won't leave this place until you do— do I make myself clear?"

With these words, the man dashed out, locking the door behind him.

It wasn't until evening that the key turned and the blond burst into the room, this time accompanied by a stranger—a tall, emaciated, twitching Jew with a sickly, yellow complexion. Darting nervously about the office, he resembled a folding ruler that an unknown hand had let fly into the room.

"Your father has confessed everything!" the Jew announced as he walked about. "He said he had sacks of gold as big as this!" He made a gesture suggesting something almost the size of a full-grown man. "Where are the imperials? Have you brought the imperials?"

"Ah, so!" I cried out, nearly in hysterics. "If my father has been hiding his gold from the family, bring him here! The only thing we have is a piano, my mother's ring, and a gold watch. . . ."

My mother also had a string of rose-colored pearls, but I didn't mention it—I was very fond of it.

"And the string of rose-colored pearls!" the gaunt Jew roared. "Why have you concealed that from us? The necklace has thirty pearls!"

"I didn't think it was genuine," I ventured. "If you need it, then take it. Take the watch, and the ring. That's all we possess. Take them and let my father go."

I gathered that my father had told them about the pearls, the watch, the ring, the piano. But that was all he could have revealed.

"Keep the pearl necklace for yourself!" the tall Jew decided. "You're a tasty morsel; it will look good on you."

61

"How dare you talk to me like that!" I exploded. "My husband is a poet, a famous man!"

"A poet?" he repeated, somewhat surprised. "What's his name?"

"Peretz Markish."

He paused for a moment, then, still pacing to and fro in the office, he said, "I know Markish from Berditchev. I used to write poetry myself. Where does he live now?"

"He lives where you took my father from."

The Jew and the blond withdrew and again the door was locked. I sat in the room until it was almost dark. In the evening, the Jew appeared again, alone.

"Well, have you decided to surrender the money?" he asked, this time using the polite form of address.

"I don't have any money," I insisted. "The best thing you can do is to take this parcel to my father, and also this pillow."

He told me to hand over the parcel. "But as for the pillow, he can get along without it. This isn't a health resort here. Leave the food and get out of here!"

Despite the advanced hour, the same dense crowds still filled the square. As soon as I came out, I was assailed with questions:

"Where did they take you?"

"What took you so long?"

"Whom did you speak to?"

As a matter of fact, I was anxious to find out who it was that had spoken to me. I had hardly begun to describe the tall Jew when from all sides the answer came: "Why, that's Varnovitsky, the head of the *zolotukha* campaign!"

That evening when I reached Markish by telephone I asked him if he remembered Varnovitsky.

"I don't recall the name," Markish said. "I'm on my way and I'll take a look at him and be able to tell you better."

Markish arrived forty-eight hours later, twenty-four hours after they released my father, who was emaciated, black-and-blue all over, and suffering from sharp heart pains. He told us about the beatings, and about the sleepless nights in the ward, when the inmates were ordered to hold "meetings" and recant under the light of a blinding electric light. Then an agent provocateur would be sent up to the podium to proclaim:

"Lenin said that in the land of the workers gold would be used for the construction of public toilets! Let us, then, surrender all our gold! Let us repent and give back our gold!"

And the prisoners listened to all this raving madness and were not permitted to close their eyes until dawn; even during the day, they were forbidden to lie on their bunks.

With a trace of a smile, my father recalled how one of his cell mates, the Jew Gusatinsky, had not been able to stand the beatings, the humiliations, the torture, and had made a declaration:

"After the last session, citizen investigator, I made up my mind to turn in my gold. I have lots of gold and want it to be used for the construction of a public toilet in the center of Kiev opposite my house. And I would like a plaque to be affixed to it with the inscription that it was built with my gold. My children and I, and my grandchildren, all of us will go and use this toilet with great pleasure!"

"We'll build it, we'll build it!" the investigator promised. "You are a highly conscientious citizen. . . . And the gold, where is it?"

"I hid it. I buried it in my apartment in the center of Kiev."

"We will go straight to Kiev tonight, then," the investigator said. "You shall be a shining example to others, Citizen Gusatinsky!"

Gusatinsky blushed. "Come now. I merely find the idea very appealing, it's so unusual: a toilet made of gold bearing the name of NEP man Gusatinsky."

Gusatinsky was given a splendid dinner, and he slept blissfully in the office of the investigator until evening came. He then left for the station with the investigator, and they boarded a first-class train. While sitting in the dining car, Gusatinsky amused himself discussing with the investigator the advantages of socialism; he enjoyed the relaxation after his long nightmare in prison.

The next day they arrived at Gusatinsky's house and were met at the door by Gusatinsky's wife. She was speechless with joy.

"I have decided to give everything back!" Gusatinsky announced to his wife while still at the door. "We'll give it all back: the gold, the diamonds, the pearls, the platinum tiara, the silver-fox stole. The whole lot!"

"What in the world are you talking about?" she asked, throwing her hands up in the air. "What stole?"

"Come on, you know!" Gusatinsky persisted. "I stashed all those valuables away in our bedroom, under the floor."

A workman was called in to tear up the floor in the spot indicated by Gusatinsky. There was nothing there.

"I must have got it mixed up a bit," Gusatinsky said. "Let's rip up the floor in the dining room."

The workman attacked the floor, and nothing turned up there either.

By evening, they had torn up the entire apartment without any results.

"Now, citizen investigator, you know as well as I do that I have nothing," Gusatinsky declared. "And now you can shoot me, hang me, cut me to pieces. . . . I feel a bit rested and I enjoyed a good night's sleep."

Gusatinsky was returned to the Dnepropetrovsk prison but released a short time later. He was arrested a second time in 1938 and perished in one of the camps.

6 / The House for Writers

OUR FAMILY OF THREE was a little cramped for space in the one tiny room in Tsygansky Ugolok, so we decided to move. The Writer's Union had just built a House for Writers in Nashchokinsky Lane—since renamed Furmanov Street—and Markish was able to buy an apartment there.

The House for Writers was a three-story structure erected over two adjoining two-story houses. It was a pleasant, quiet neighborhood. One end of the lane gave onto the Arbat, the other onto Gargarin Lane. The idea of a private apartment plus the desirability of the location gave rise to considerable maneuvering among the writers; proletarian writers had had their fill of living in communal apartments or occupying corners in a room. It was no simple matter to come by living space in Moscow.

The apartments on Nashchokinsky Lane were sold according to a person's merit, situation, connections, and God knows what other criteria. Among our neighbors were Boris Pasternak, the poet Osip Mandelstam, Mikhail Bulgakov and Vsevolod Ivanov, dramatists, Ilya Ilf and Yevgeni Katayev (as Ilf and Petrov, collaborators on two successful comic novels), aspiring writer Yevgeni Gabrilovich, and the already well known writer and critic Victor Shklovsky. A few Yiddish writers moved in: the poet Samuel Halkin and Isaac Nusinov, our neighbor from Vorzel. There was also an American tenant: Henry Shapiro, distinguished foreign correspondent and, later, head of the Moscow bureau of United Press International.

Markish left the arranging of the apartment up to me and got down to work the day after we moved in. He wasn't the least bit interested in who our neighbors on the floor were. The very idea of a House for Writers left him cold; all he cared about was that there were walls, a floor, and a ceiling. Naturally, then, there was no likelihood of the Markishes having a housewarming!

Soon after our arrival, Vsevolod Ivanov invited us to visit his apartment to be part of a gathering of participants in the recent plenary session of the board of the Writers' Union honoring the memory of the Ukrainian poet Taras Shevchenko. Markish had attended the session and had told me what a fine and intelligent man Ivanov was. He had also been very impressed with Ivanov's beautiful wife, Tamara, a former actress in Meyerhold's theater and a woman of liberal views who knew her own mind and possessed a great deal of self-respect.

Ivanov's invitation had been written in an old-fashioned style; I was referred to as Markish's "spouse," a word whose use in those days said something about a person's status. His literary situation at the time was ambivalent. To his misfortune, his early Siberian stories had pleased Stalin, perhaps because they were a true reflection of Siberia during the revolution—cruel and bloody. In any case, Stalin had taken a keen interest in the writing of the young Siberian and in his literary development. On one occasion he ordered the editors of a big Moscow magazine to send him the proofs of a novella by Ivanov. Stalin liked it and proposed writing a foreword for it. Someone in Stalin's entourage, foreseeing a precipitate advancement in Ivanov's career, telephoned the writer and informed him of Stalin's proposal. But Ivanov took the news coldly, declaring that he saw no need for a foreword by a political figure and would prefer a writer or critic to make such a contribution. His novella did not appear in the magazine, and until the end of his life, 1963—he outlived Stalin by ten years—Ivanov carried the stigma of insubordination and "fractiousness" as far as the politico-literary authorities were concerned. A number of his novels never saw the light of day. Throughout his life he maintained his independence and integrity. Acutely aware of where and in what times he was living, he steered clear of polemic and public declarations.

Gathered around the tastefully arranged table that evening at the Ivanovs' were two of the Serapion brothers—Benjamin Kaverin and Konstantin Fedin—the brilliant and perceptive literary scholar Boris Eikhenbaum (who in the postwar anti-Semitic campaign was to be listed among the "rootless cosmopolitans"—Jews), and his loyal and favorite student Irakli Andronnikov, who was still a young man and a marvelous storyteller. Amid the friendly laughter of the assembled guests, he interpreted scene after scene from the literary and theatrical life of Moscow. I'll never forget his story about a famous actor of the Moscow Art Theater.

Returning home one night after having got thoroughly drunk at a party given by the hospitable Alexei Tolstoy, the actor fell out of the hackney cab and rolled into the gutter, where he promptly fell sound asleep. He was discovered by passers-by, who shook him out of his torpor to protect him from being robbed. In answer to their questions, he simply mumbled, "I am on my way to Tolstoy's." So they put him into another cab and sent him off there. It was around daybreak when he showed up, much to Alexei Tolstoy's consternation.

Andronnikov told the anecdote brilliantly, impersonating the voices of Tolstoy, the drunken actor, the considerate passers-by, the listless cab driver, and the miserable thieves who had beset the drunken man.

Markish listened amusedly enough, but he was bored. He regretted sacrificing the time he had set aside for rest and relaxation simply to go to some large party, which he did not enjoy. But a small group of friends—two, three or four at the most—was something else.

Our neighbor Boris Pasternak dropped in on Markish quite often. He would sit himself down in Markish's study and just watch him as he spoke. Markish's conversation was inseparably linked with movement and gesticulation, and Pasternak understood that better than anyone. He sat and watched, eyes wide open, a shock of hair falling low on his forehead. And when he spoke, it was sparingly, always waiting for Markish's reaction and reply. Pasternak was exactly like his poetry—multifaceted and burning with an inner flame. Problems of everyday life did not preoccupy him in the least. His work as a translator had not yet become his "poetical service," and money came in only irregularly. The Pasternaks were having a hard time of it.

One winter day Markish and I were coming back from somewhere on the streetcar. It was fiercely cold, so cold that if you touched any metallic part of the streetcar it stripped the skin from your finger. At the front, bent over and ruffled up like a bird, sat a figure in a rubber raincoat. He was sitting absolutely motionless, lost in thought.

"Why, that's Pasternak," Markish said, and, leaving me where I was, he went over to him and began speaking very low. When he came back to me, he said, "Give me all the money you have with you."

At the same time he took from his own pocket whatever money he had, put it with mine and went back to Pasternak. After handing him the money, he continued talking to him until it was time for him to get off. Ours was the stop after, which was closer to our entrance.

Markish said nothing until we got home, and then only one sentence: "The great poet Pasternak has no bread to eat." Throughout supper that evening he was completely silent.

Markish held Osip Mandelstam, another neighbor of ours, in high esteem as a poet, but they were not friends. Undoubtedly they respected each other, but it went no further than that.

One morning—it was the thirteenth of May, 1934—there was a knock at our door. It was early and I was still in bed. Markish answered it himself and a moment later he came back to the bedroom. He looked pale and his movements were brusque.

"They've taken Mandelstam away," he said. "Get up and go down to see Nadezhda Yakovlevna. Take her some money—I imagine she will be needing it now."

The first question that came to mind at a time like that was "But why?" Naturally, neither Markish nor I could find an answer, and that made it even worse.

After doing his day's work, Markish, too, went to see Nadezhda Yakovlevna. As Anna Akhmatova has noted in her *Reminiscences,* Markish was the only male writer who called on the wife of Osip Mandelstam on the first day of his arrest.

Fate was to deal a heavy blow to our neighbor two floors below, the Hungarian writer Máté Zalka. The charming and gracious Máté was a political emigré. His wife, Vera, and I were very good friends. In 1936, a crestfallen Vera told me that Máté was leaving on a mission that would take him far away for a long time. I could see that she was reluctant to say any more about it, so I didn't question her.

A short time later, the newspapers began writing

about the heroic battlefield exploits of a certain General Lukács, Commander of the Twelfth International Brigade in the Spanish Civil War. And then came the communiqué announcing that General Lukács had been killed in action. Few people at that time knew that the legendary Lukács and Máté-Zalka were one and the same individual. Or at any rate, I didn't know, so I did not understand the tears shed by Vera as she read the obituary. After Zalka's death, the Soviet Government gave Vera a substantial súm of money but refused to reveal the identity of General Lukács. They strictly forbade Vera to say anything about it either.

Markish was rather oblivious to the things going on in the house. The only person he saw with any regularity was Isaac Nusinov, who enjoyed coming to our apartment. He had only recently got married for a second time—to a young student of his, and his home life wasn't very peaceful. I think he found it pleasant to be with us, where everything was subject to the routine, wishes, and habits of the master of the house. Lena Khokhlova doted on Markish, and the children —by then we had taken Markish's daughter, seven-year-old Lyalya, under our roof—spoke quietly and didn't dare to play noisily. The household existed for Markish—it was simply a law, and it required no explanation.

When Nusinov came by, the two would repair to the study. Markish liked to have Nusinov's opinion and occasionally would read aloud to him his fresh verses, listening patiently to what his guest had to say. He listened, of course, but that was as far as it went: he knew the value of poetry, his own and that of others. Nusinov, an old, fanatic Communist of pre-revolutionary vintage, always tried to approach Markish's writing from a Marxist point of view. Markish would roar with his infectious laughter until tears came to his eyes. Poetry and political economy, the spirit and the word: Markish could see no connection between them, and Nusinov would get angry at him for his political myopia, for his complete ignorance of the "laws" of Marxism-Leninism.

"Do you know what you and Marx have in common?" Nusinov asked. "Only the fact that you and he are on the same page of the encyclopedia."

But, knowing that Markish was incorrigible, Nusinov's anger would quickly subside. His love for Markish's poetry took precedence over his love for Marx, at least during the hours he spent in our home.

Unfortunately, Nusinov was in a certain sense correct in calling Markish politically myopic. The Soviet notion of "political grounding" becomes in practice quite the opposite—that is, total political blindness, Orwellian double-think, the capacity to believe absolutely in today's *Pravda* editorial, notwithstanding what it proclaimed yesterday and will proclaim tomorrow. Markish was politically grounded to the extent that was necessary, but he was incapable of thinking through a political situation to the end and drawing the conclusions. But, then, perhaps he did not want to. If he had thought through and drawn conclusions from a situation like the signing of the Nazi-Soviet Pact of 1939, for instance, he would either have had to commit suicide or, at the least, stop writing—which for Markish would have been no real choice anyway because to stop writing would have been the same thing as death.

I recall one particular conversation in the home of some friends, a very frank and, for those days, mortally dangerous conversation about Stalin and the terror. Markish could stand it no longer. He ripped the collar off his shirt and cried out, "Enough! I can't take it any more!" And he got up and left. Out in the street he said to me, "If I stop believing, I won't be able to write another line."

If I dwell at such length on the residents of the House for Writers, it is because the house was like a microcosm of the entire great fraternity of writers who lived throughout Russia at the time. And one result of such a concentration was that a man like Vsevolod Ivanov was compelled to live in close proximity with a man like Konstantin Finn.

Konstantin Finn—who had opportunely changed his Jewish name of Khalfin to the ethnically unintelligible

70

name of Finn—was married to an attractive young woman with whom I struck up a friendship. Finn liked to drink, and on those occasions when he did so would wax eloquent over his unusual talent—in all seriousness he would call himself "the great Russian comedy-writer"—and also try to persuade everybody around him that his national origin was a pure accident—he was completely ignorant of Yiddish, had a Russian soul, and so on. Once, when I was visiting his wife, an old Jew rang the doorbell; he was shabbily dressed and looked forlorn. As it turned out, the old man was Finn's father. He had come to his rich and respected (by the authorities) son to ask him for a little money. Konstantin Finn did not allow his father even to cross the threshold; he showered him with abuse and insults in the perfect Yiddish his father had taught him as a child. The old man suffered the vituperations of his son in silence and then departed, shaking his hoary head in sadness and bewilderment.

"You should be ashamed!" I said, unable to contain myself. "After all, the old man *is* your father!"

"Old men should be crushed like bedbugs," he said, with malice in his voice. This was the "engineer of human souls," the renowned and respected Soviet writer Konstantin Finn.

He had a most successful career cooking up his talentless plays in the oven of current events to please the authorities. When he was sixty years old, he joined the Communist Party—to facilitate his traveling abroad. My friend—his wife—had left him long ago for someone else. Feeling he had been robbed, Finn used to shout out for the whole house to hear, "I am a great Russian comedy-writer and you are a stinking kike!"

Occasionally, Markish received a visit from the talented poet and satirist Alexander Arkhangelsky, an intelligent man and trenchant critic. He would come, as he was wont to say, "to air out his brains and trip on the clouds," and Markish ignited him with the fire of his own temperament. He was fond of children and became pals with our bright, five-year-old Simka. The child would sit with him for hours on end reading satirical magazines of the twenties. Simka was crazy about him. Arkhangelsky lived in the apartment directly above ours, and whenever he wanted Simka to come up, he tapped his cane on the floor according to a prearranged signal.

This friendship between Simka and Arkhangelsky almost led to a major literary scandal. Toward the end of the thirties, Stalin for some reason ordered the restoration of a few bourgeois traditions abolished during the Russian "cultural revolution"—to wit, a few traditional holidays. Among them was the winter celebration of the *yolka* ("fir tree"), except that it was shifted from Christmas to New Year's! A few years earlier, anyone who dared to have a Christmas tree with all the trimmings in his home at New Year's would have been taking a great risk: he would have been accused of kowtowing to old bourgeois customs, lacking political vigilance, bigotry, et cetera. But now, thanks to the "all-gracious magnanimity from on high," New Year's trees were ablaze with candles in many Moscow houses. Even in the Hall of Columns at the House of the Trade Unions, candles had to be lit on the State New Year's tree intended for the children of high officials so as to give a bold example to private households.

Markish took a dim view of this scheme of the "Father of Peoples." "In my father's home, I didn't see Christmas trees or other trees and bushes. It's not a Jewish custom. But if you want to amuse the children, please, go ahead and get one."

The children were delighted, and even I liked the idea of welcoming in the new year by decorating a fragrant fir tree.

Our Simka was invited to a children's New Year's party in the home of Victor Gusev, a Russian poet who enjoyed great popularity at the time. He had a glorious tree hung with marvelous toys that he had picked up somewhere secondhand—it was still quite impossible to find nice toys in the stores. Some twenty children of writers gather around Gusev's tree under the avid eyes of their parents, who waited to see their offspring come up with some especially funny jokes, songs, or poems. Markish, naturally, stayed home, but I accompanied Simka to the party.

From "Grandfather Frost," Simka received a "Bi-

Ba-Bo," a pair of hand puppets—in this case a muzhik husband and wife—with which he immediately proceeded to put on a little play. Climbing up on a high stool that had been placed behind a screen, Simka presented a skit involving the muzhik couple arguing. The dialogue was punctuated with popular, often earthy expressions, but it was clever and funny. The child was not, of course, improvising; he had taken his text from one of the satirical reviews of the twenties that he had read at Sasha Arkhangelsky's and learned by heart. The wives of the writers were flabbergasted, and they practically dragged Simka bodily from behind the screen. While the Soviet *beau monde* vociferously expressed its displeasure, the children were as happy as they could be over Simka's escapade. Still, we had no choice but to leave.

When he heard about what had happened Sasha Arkhangelsky split his sides laughing—as did Markish, who hated the philistines' sanctimoniousness. Simka became the hero of the day, but, all the same, he took his banishment from society hard. "Don't you ever take me visiting again!" he said to me. "Whenever I am in a crowd of people, I go crazy."

The most cordial relations developed between Markish and the Yiddish poet Samuel Halkin, who had taken an apartment in the adjoining block. Halkin was younger than Markish, and he possessed a languorous, serene beauty and sad, dreamy eyes. His poetry did not have the detonating, explosive, incandescent quality of Markish's; on the contrary, it was soft, meditative, filigreed. He read his poems in a muted voice, his eyes half closed as he swayed gently back and forth, whereas Markish pelted his words like so many sharp stones. No doubt it was their artistic dissimilarity that attracted these two poets to each other, a rather rare occurrence in the literary world of Moscow, but they did have in common a keen interest in the affairs of the Jewish Section of the Writers' Union, although Halkin took no active part in them. Whenever he and Markish got together, they discussed "Jewish matters" as well as poetry. Markish headed the Jewish Section and was secretary of its Inspection

Committee, a post to which he had been elected at the First Writers' Congress in 1934.

The Congress was a most impressive event, unquestionably a milestone in the cultural life of the country. It was presided over by Maxim Gorky, and active roles were played by such writers as Aleksandr Fadeyev and Aleksandr Serafimovich. Among the foreign guests were André Malraux, well known for his pro-Soviet sympathies, and the Spanish poet Rafael Alberti, who converted to Communism in 1931. One of the principal reports—on foreign literature—was delivered by the brilliant orator Karl Radek. Few people could have imagined in 1934 that Radek would soon be arrested and executed, just as was another rapporteur at the Congress, who read a paper on poetry, Nikolai Bukharin. (In 1949, on the night Markish was arrested, the text of Radek's address at the Writers' Congress was found during the perquisition and confiscated on the grounds that it was a "subversive document by an enemy of the people.")

Even closer to Markish than Halkin was the Jewish writer and playwright Ezekiel Dodrushin. They had been friends ever since the early twenties, during Markish's Kiev period. Shortly after Markish and I met, he introduced me to Dodrushin—"Khatsya," as he was called—at a May Day picnic. The outing, or *mayovka,* had been organized by the students and teachers of the Moscow Jewish Theatrical Studio, where Dodrushin taught the history of the Jewish theater.

The studio was run by Solomon Mikhoels, the eminent Yiddish actor and director. For me, a university student, the actors' milieu was something new and fascinating. I was charmed—and, I admit, somewhat shocked—by the free and easy atmosphere that characterized this world. I didn't have a clue as to how to conduct myself amid these attractive, uninhibited aspiring young actors and actresses. They all seemed to be quite special, fashioned, as it were, out of a different dough. Besides, I was jealous of these beautiful young girls, who made no secret of their admiration for my handsome future husband. And Markish, of course, responded good-humoredly to

74

their flirtatiousness. They were forever talking Yiddish together and, to my extreme regret, I didn't understand a word. I was aware that Dodrushin had noticed my discomfiture and the tears in my eyes. When I told Markish why I was feeling so distressed, he delivered a lecture asserting each individual is above all an object of observation for a poet, that a poet belongs to the world, that I was ignorant of the actors' milieu and therefore goodness knows what had got into me—why, an actor's demonstrativeness was nothing more than part of his stock-in-trade. . . .

At seventeen, I was no match for an argument, and all I could do in response to Markish's explanations was swallow my tears. But not long after, I got my chance to teach him a good lesson.

We had gone to a performance at Mikhoels's Moscow Yiddish Theater. Literally everyone in the theater adored Markish, from the leading actors to the make-up men and stagehands. His loud, intense voice seemed to resound in every corner of the theater simultaneously, offering encouragement to the actors or relating some wise and amusing folk parable—parables were his forte. I had been lingering in the wings and then, quite unexpectedly, I ran into the charming Benjamin Zuskin at the door of his dressing room. Zuskin was playing one of his most brilliant roles that day, Sendler in *Voyage of Benjamin the Third*. He greeted me with a warm embrace and a kiss, as was customary in the theater. Suddenly, Markish appeared from out of nowhere. He looked at me disapprovingly and led me into the auditorium just as the curtain was going up. During the intermission, we went to the foyer and he gave me a real dressing down: how could I have permitted Zuskin to kiss me! Markish spotted Dodrushin and promptly called him over as arbiter. Khatsya couldn't conceal his amusement as he listened to our squabbling.

"But Markusha," I said, seeking to vindicate myself, "you told me yourself that this was the way things were done in the theater, in your entourage. And Zuskin is an actor. And I want to behave in a manner appropriate to the circumstances!"

Markish could find nothing to say as his eyes traveled back and forth between me and Dodrushin, who, by this time, had burst out laughing.

"Well, what can you say to her?" he asked. "After all, you taught her how to conduct herself among theater people and, as you can see, she's an excellent pupil!"

7 / The Year of the Deluge

THE YEAR 1937 crept in on us like a beast of prey on soft padded feet.

That year can be compared to the year of the deluge, the plague, the eclipse of the sun. It was a year of death, arrests, and soul-shattering events.

First, Markish's mother, Khaya, died—serenely, naturally, like an overripe fruit that drops off the branch. Markish went to Dnepropetrovsk (formerly Yekaterinoslav) to bury her. He came back to Moscow wan and melancholic. His mother had not been for him an understanding friend and counselor; she had simply been a mother. The love he had for her was the traditional love of a son for his mother, but his grief was more than the customary grief; it was the grief of the artist, of a creative spirit.

Then my father, Yefim, fell gravely sick and took to his bed. He suffered from severely painful attacks of angina pectoris, the result of his incarceration in Dnepropetrovsk during the *zolotukha*. He realized full well that this had been the source of his illness, but he was a kind and gentle man and bore no hatred or resentment toward his oppressors.

My father lay in bed quietly fading away. Toward the end of the summer of 1937, he was transported to a hospital. Doctors held out little hope for recovery. One morning the telephone rang and we were told my father had died. My mother let out a scream.

"Grandpa is dead!" said little Simon. "I don't want to go on living any longer either!"

Among those who came to the cemetery were Markish's friends, the Jewish writers who thought well of my father and wished to pay their respects to a victim of the Russian Revolution.

Soon after my father's death, Markish's own father, David, died. Markish decided to go to the funeral in spite of the fact that he was ill, but before he could leave he was notified from Dnepropetrovsk that his father had already been buried. As Jewish law prescribes, the deceased must be returned to the earth as soon as possible.

It was just about that time that Markish's daughter Golda—or, as we called her, Lyalya—came to live with us. Her mother's husband had been arrested only a short time before, accused of Ukrainian nationalism and of attempting to overthrow the regime. He was an interesting and cultivated man and the translator of Pushkin into Ukrainian. Lyalya's mother, knowing that she, too, would be arrested, determined to save her child. Markish and I traveled to Kiev to pick up Lyalya and bring her back to Moscow. Her mother saw us off at the station with tears in her eyes, although never imagining it would be ten years before she would see her daughter again. Shortly after our departure, they came for her. She was sentenced to prison for harboring anti-Soviet sentiments.

My brother Shura's career in journalism was shaping up very nicely, or so it seemed: by 1937 he was deputy head of the news department of *Komsomolskava Pravda*. But then Alexander Bubekin, the editor-in-chief of the newspaper and a *komsomol* official, was arrested as an enemy of the people and traitor to the socialist fatherland. He was accused of other crimes as well: espionage on behalf of a foreign power and planning an attempt on Stalin's life. Shortly after the arrest, Mikhailov, the new editor-in-chief—who, following Stalin's death in 1953, occupied the post of first secretary of the Central Committee of the *komsomol* and later became minister of culture —called a meeting of Jewish staff members to suggest that they take Russian names. Rosenzweig would become Borisov, for example, and Shura would take Yefimov in place of Lazebnikov. The Jews were indignant and refused. Shura went one step further: he wrote a letter to a powerful man in the Kremlin, Wyacheslav Molotov. With unusual speed, someone called Shura from Molotov's office and thanked him for the "signal." Nevertheless, *Komsomolskaya Pravda,* which was about to publish a poem of Markish's, suggested that he sign it with the name "Pyotr Markov." Markish, needless to say, hit the ceiling.

It so happened that Shura was on duty in the city room the night before Markish's poem was to be published, and it was then that he learned where the order to substitute "Pyotr Markov" for Markish's name came from: the editor-in-chief, Mikhailov. That same night Shura wrote a second letter to Molotov; it was never acknowledged. However, the two letters were put in my brother's file and used against him later.

It was not long before other arrests were made among the newspaper's staff. When Shura's boss was taken, his friend, the pilot Valeri Chkalov, a hero in the Soviet Union, made direct overtures to Stalin on his behalf and vouched for Babushkin "with his own head." The "Kremlin mountaineer"—as Mandelstam described Stalin in a poem that led to his arrest and extermination in a concentration camp—responded with a favorite maxim of his: "You have only one head; it may still come in handy."

It was just about that time that I began working in the foreign department of *Komsomolskaya Pravda,* but my job lasted only a few days: my supervisor was arrested, and I was dismissed on the spot. Shura was also fired for having been associated with a convicted "enemy of the people." He had no trouble, however, in finding a job on the newspaper *Sovetsky Flot* ("Soviet Fleet"), which sent him out to the Soviet Far East. At first we received many warm letters from him, but suddenly they stopped. When I inquired about him at his editorial office, I was told, "Your brother is not even worthy of inquiry being made about him. In due course, you'll know everything."

The next thing we knew was that a perquisition had been made in the apartment in Tsygansky Ugolok and seals placed on Shura's room. Thus we learned he had been arrested.

My beloved maternal grandmother, Babushka Olya, had come up from Baku and was living with us. When she heard about Shura's arrest, she took to her bed. Panic and gloom invaded our home. I was not feeling myself and Markish insisted that my mother and I get away to the spa at Kislovodsk. After all, there was absolutely nothing we could do to help Shura. We had hardly even unpacked our bags there when a telegram came from Markish: "Babushka Olya has died." We hurried back for the funeral—we certainly had had our share of funerals in the past few months! Markish was crestfallen. He had been attached to Babushka Olya and had a deep appreciation of her subtle insight into the human heart. A patient and wise woman, she had had a far better understanding of the impulsive, volatile Markish than did my "decorous-bourgeois" parents.

In October we were notified that Shura had been condemned to eight years in camp with the right to correspond. We took warm clothing and a knapsack to him in Butyrki; from there he was shipped to the North. He had been convicted of spreading counter-revolutionary propaganda and participating in an underground organization.

Using all his connections, Markish succeeded in getting an appointment with Deputy General Prosecutor Rozovsky, a Jew who occasionally went to the Yiddish Theater. When Rozovsky looked through Shura's files, he threw up his hands: there was nothing he could do for my brother. Under torture Shura had confessed to belonging to an underground organization. Many people at the time put their signature to fake confessions—anything to bring an end to the torture. They ordered my brother to inform on his accomplices, and my brother, not without a touch of irony, had written, "Our organization was so clandestine, not one of the members knew any of the others." That confession satisfied his interrogators. Later on, during the war, when political prisoners were not being released, Shura received a second sentence: ten years for attempting to build an airplane—within the confines of the camp —in order to fly off and join Hitler!

As for Rozovsky, not long after his meeting with Markish, he was arrested and shot.

All around us people were being sent off to prisons and camps, some never to return. Jewish personalities, in particular, were being persecuted and suppressed. Moyshe Litvakov, editor-in-chief of the leading Yiddish newspaper *Der Emes,* was arrested. He was a dogmatic, fanatical Communist and active member of the notorious *Yevsektsiva* (the Jewish section of the Party's Central Committee). As might be expected, Litvakov regarded Markish as a nonideological poet, alien to Marxism and sympathetic only to Jewish nationalist aspirations, and accused him of writing exclusively about Jews and nothing about "workers and peasants." He had even protested the authorizing of Markish's return to Russia from abroad.

Major Jewish writers, like Moyshe Kulbak and Izi Kharik, were taken; Kharik was executed before the year was out, and Kulbak died in a slave labor camp in 1940. It seemed as if Markish's hour must be at hand, yet he was not touched during that awful time. It is difficult to say why. One story has it that Stalin, in a conversation with Aleksandr Fadeyev, mentioned that Markish was a remarkable poet. That opinion was apparently not lost on the powerful Fadeyev, who then held an important position in the secretariat of the Union of Soviet Writers. In any case, Markish, for a while at least, escaped the fate of many of his colleagues.

Markish knew what was going on in the country around him. Like everybody else, he knew. But, also like everybody else, he did not know that "ten years imprisonment without the right to correspond" was tantamount to being shot, that prisoners were being tortured in the basements of prisons, that millions of innocent people were languishing in concentration camps. He continued to believe in the justice of the ideas and actions of the "builders of a new life." It is painful for me to remember that now. But it is the truth, and I have no intention of concealing it.

At the height of the "Great Purge" Markish and I went off to Tbilisi to attend a session of the Writer's Union. As part of a national commemoration of the seven hundred fiftieth anniversary of the birth of the Georgian poet Shota Rustaveli, the Union had been directed to hold its jubilee session in Georgia. Markish and a few other board members were allowed to bring their wives along. The literary spectacle promised to be dazzling, and I was overjoyed at the prospect of the trip.

Markish and I did not make the trip together, because I had decided to go to Baku first to visit my dear Uncle Naum. He had been arrested and confined in the horrible prison in Sumgait but, thanks to the timely and vigorous intervention of my relatives, his case had been re-examined. He was discharged from prison and returned to Baku as an invalid. (In 1941, he was cut down by a German bullet during the defense of Sevastopol.)

Knowing that the once surfeited Baku was now on the verge of famine, I brought food and other delights from Moscow. They were primarily intended for my Uncle Naum, but just at the moment when he was freed from prison, the economic fallout of the Great Purge affected another uncle of mine, Isaac. He was charged with a "crime in the performance of his duties" —there was no further elaboration. The result was that the Moscow food parcel intended for Uncle Naum went instead to Uncle Isaac.

During that period it was not only the politicals who were apprehended, but industrial managers as well. Thus all five of my uncles—my mother's brothers—passed through prison. Babushka Olya had devoted herself to "saving" them—just as my mother would ultimately spend a full eighteen years "saving" her only son, Shura—by going to see them in the camp, bringing the food parcels that kept them from starving to death.

81

After having done my share of weeping in the once peaceful and happy Baku, I took the train to the Georgian capital to join Markish. Ilya Ehrenburg and his wife, Lyuba, also on their way to Ibilisi, were traveling in the next compartment. We had known each other for a long time—through Markish, of course. Ordering tea, which was traditionally served on trains, I joined the Ehrenburgs in their compartment. The hour was late and the soft light from the table lamp danced in the brick-colored tea as Ehrenburg spoke.

"You know, I made Markish's acquaintance in 1920, in Kiev. At that time, a whole group of young Jewish poets was working there; Markish was head and shoulders above them—he was forceful, handsome and fantastically gifted. A few years later, I ran into him in Paris, at La Rotonde I think . . . yes, yes, at La Rotonde! I don't believe you were with him in Paris then, were you?"

"I was only ten years old at the time," I said.

"Yes, but of course—how silly of me! He used to sit in La Rotonde with a Jewish prose writer from Poland, Oyzer Varshavski. I don't recall exactly how it happened, but Varshavski suddenly began telling a Hasidic tale. Markish probably knew it, but he listened attentively. I had never heard the story before. It went like this: One Yom Kippur, the Jews of a certain little shtetl were gathered in the synagogue atoning for their sins. They had prayed the whole day and, by their calculations, God should have already forgiven them. But evidently they were guilty of such grievous sins that God was not prepared to absolve them, and the evening star failed to appear in the heavens. The Jews could not leave the synagogue until the evening star came out. A murmur went up through the congregation as the people became fearful of the vengeance of God. The Jews started accusing one another of venality, of deceit, of bearing false witness. But still the evening star did not appear. . . . A poor, old tailor and his small son were at the entrance to the synagogue. The boy was restless; he had already made atonement for all his sins, and he was still too young to be worried by the sins of others. And lo and behold, he took a penny flute from his pocket and began to play. The Jews

82

threw themselves on the tailor— Because of a good-for-nothing like your son, God's wrath will come down upon us! But the rabbi restrained his flock, for he had perceived God smiling down on the child . . . and then the evening star emerged!

"I remember how this story shook me to the bottom of my soul. Markish gave me a sidelong glance, and I saw that his eyes were radiant with tears. 'Why, there you have the history of art,' he said with a sigh. 'Only today it isn't a penny flute that's needed, but the trumpet of a Mayakovsky!' "

The trip to Tbilisi passed quickly, thanks to Ehrenburg, and the city greeted us with its abundance, its intoxication, its Caucasian hospitality. Compared with Baku and its catastrophic food shortage, the Georgian capital was a paradise. Lavish banquets followed one after another, each presided over by the secretary of the Writers' Union, Abolgasem Lakhuti, a friend of Stalin's. Lakhuti had come to the USSR as a political emigré from Persia. It was common knowledge that the wall of his Moscow apartment was adorned with a large photograph of the master of the Kremlin inscribed, "To my friend Gasem Lakhuti from Josef Stalin." That photograph was Lakhuti's certificate of safe conduct.

The Persian poet was fond of writing letters to Stalin, full of flattery and praise in the true Persian tradition. But he got burned with one of them—much later, to be sure, after World War II—when he compared Stalin to a gardener cultivating a beautiful bed of flowers. The scent of every flower, in the words of the author, was known to the gardener. Only one marvelous blossom had escaped the attention of the cultivator of the garden: Mikhoels's Yiddish Theater. Lakhuti urged Stalin to visit the theater and give it its due. Such a recommendation was not one to gladden the heart of the anti-Semite in the Kremlin, and he ordered Lakhuti to refrain from writing to him in the future.

In 1937, however, Lakhuti's glory was in full flower. It was Lakhuti who was charged with the organization of the literary gathering in Gori, the town where Stalin was born. The meetingplace was at the foot of a broad, marble stairway leading up to the pavilion that housed and protected the modest little home of Stalin's parents. Could anything be more symbolic than the foot of a stairway?

There was no talk of literature at that meeting.

Pointing to the sun over our heads, Lakhuti said something like this:

"Oh, thou stupid sun! No longer need thee shine down upon us! We have our own sun—Stalin!"

The assembly was silent for a moment, as if struck by lightning. Then, wild applause broke out. People were afraid not to applaud lest they pay for their omission with prison.

Markish was standing at my side, his face ashen. He avoided the faces of others and lowered his eyes to the ground. The muscles in his jaw pulsated convulsively under his skin while people all around clapped, their eyes also fixed on the ground.

On December 31, 1937, a gala banquet was held to wind up the festivities honoring Rustaveli. At the entrance to the restaurant was Misha Svetlov, holding a big log in his arms. In answer to my look of perplexity, he separated the log in two, revealing a bouquet of charming spring violets in the hollow—where he got them, God only knows!

"Today I am going to give these flowers to the most gorgeous girl in the world," he declared.

He gave them to Radam Amiredjibi, of the Georgian royal family—she was, in fact, a devastatingly beautiful girl—who was soon to become his wife. Their marriage was not a particularly successful one, although it lasted quite a long time before falling apart.

"A Georgian princess was too much of a luxury for a poor little Jew," Svetlov would say later.

At eleven o'clock on New Year's eve, a group of writers—Svetlov, Golodnyi, Markish, and the Spaniard Plá y Beltran—started out for Batumi. In the morning we reached Sukhumi, the capital of Abkhazia, where Delba, the Party chief of Abkhazia, met us at the station and invited Markish to stay overnight. It seems that he had read a great deal of his work and dreamed of making his acquaintance.

That evening, we dined at Delba's house and, on the wall above his desk in the study, I noticed he had pinned a newspaper clipping with Markish's poem "Spain."

Delba didn't keep his high position in the Party hierarchy for very long; he fell into disgrace and went into scientific work.

In Batumi the first order of the day was a gigantic meeting in the opera house. One high official delivered a speech in Georgian that lasted for two hours. Practically every sentence contained the word Stalin, and each time the name was mentioned, people rose to their feet to applaud. I was sitting in the presidium, so as to translate Pla y Beltran's speech into Russian, and I noticed that Markish and Svetlov, on the podium, were playing ticktacktoe through it all, a most serious expression on their faces!

We were to leave Batumi by boat. The orchestra had played their final selection and the speeches of farewell had been delivered, but the boat did not leave. When the passengers began to complain, the captain responded by locking himself in his cabin. The port authorities offered no explanation, as the boat remained at dock, with the steam billowing out of the funnels, for more than an hour.

Finally, an automobile sped up to the dock and screeched to a stop. People jumped out of the car and rushed on board dragging crates with special labels—they were loaded with souvenir certificates that had been ordered for the visiting writers. The printers had not been able to get them ready in time.

We finally set sail, with the certificates, crates of brandy and fruit, and the songs of people who had come to see us off.

And I was carrying something else, too—what was to become, nine months later, our second child.

8 / Solomon Mikhoels

ON SEPTEMBER 23, 1938, we were entertaining a gathering of Jewish writers from Odessa in our home. The young Odessans, among them Notke Luria, looked upon Markish as an oracle, for he had become a living classic of Yiddish-Jewish literature.

The evening was in full swing when I suddenly felt the onset of labor. Not wishing to disturb Markish, who was engrossed in conversation, I managed to get to the telephone and call for an ambulance. It came quickly, and of course Markish then realized what was going on. He became terribly nervous, and I don't think it was because a second child was on the way. He looked at me forlornly, as if he felt at fault because I was suffering and he was helpless to do anything for me, to somehow share in it.

Our second child—a son—was born the next day. All of our friends and relatives naturally took an active part in the business of choosing a name, and there were suggestions galore, running the gamut from Abram to Ivan. Markish put an end to it by deciding to name his son David, in memory of his father.

Everything had turned out well, but for a long time afterward I could not forget that look of compassion and helplessness in Markish's eyes. Another person's physical suffering always oppressed him. He seemed to feel a debt toward the sufferer, and the sight of blood disturbed him deeply. He refused to intellectualize physical pain, as, for instance, the breakdown of activity within the organism, or to regard blood as simply a combination of red and white corpuscles.

Such a rationalist approach was foreign to his spiritual makeup.

Because he had received no formal education—in questionnaires, he always filled in the blank after "education" with "at home"—he looked on the scientist primarily with the eyes of a poet. I particularly remember Markish's reactions to the laboratory of the eminent scientist Pyotr Kapitsa, whom he visited in 1934. Kapitsa had just returned from England with his unique vacuum laboratory. It is doubtful that Markish understood the scientist's explanations, but what impressed him deeply was Kapitsa's vast knowledge, his fantastic instruments, his experiments. Markish saw in Kapitsa his exact opposite. Everything Markish looked upon in the world, everything his eyes apprehended, flowed back into his soul. Kapitsa's eyes seemed to grow out of his brain, and the information they gathered in the surrounding world was immediately registered in his brain and analyzed by it. For several days after his meeting with Kapitsa, Markish was enthralled by the figure of the scientist and by his knowledge in a field inaccessible to the poet. Anybody else who had found Kapitsa's area of research so impressive would probably have read some popularized study about it. Not Markish. To have learned something new about vacuum theory would not have added one iota to his understanding of Kapitsa the man.

Once, in the fall of 1939, Markish asked our very good friend Yakov Bruskin, a professor of medicine, for permission to assist at a surgical operation. Markish planned to use his observations in writing about the war that had just broken out in the West. Bruskin, of course, agreed.

Yakov Bruskin was more than a surgeon; he was a great scientist. His works on the methods of treating cancer were widely known. He gave consultations as a surgeon, as a therapist, as a phthisiologist. His circle of friends included a number of remarkable people. He had treated Yesenin and Mayakovsky, and was head of the Institute of Cancerology.

Bruskin invited Markish to assist at a complicated abdominal operation. Markish came home afterward pale, exhausted and taciturn. But later he spoke a great deal about the hands of the surgeon and of the enormous knowledge that guided their movements. Bruskin had held in his powerful, stubby-fingered hands the thin thread of human life. It verged on the supernatural; Bruskin was like a magician, a wizard.

Markish idolized knowledge like a pagan. Thanks to a phenomenal memory, he knew a great deal. Whatever he read, whatever he observed, he retained easily and effortlessly. But, outside of the fields of literature and language, he did not possess any systematic knowledge.

In 1934, I had registered as a doctoral candidate in linguistics at the Institute of Philosophy, Literature and History (IFLI). Markish was pleased and impressed with the fact that I was studying and learning, but when he'd had a look at my syllabi, he flew into a rage. He described linguistics as "gravedigging," contending that language was the product of the development of the human spirit and that to subject it to analysis and poke around in its living organism was blasphemy and utter nonsense. He thoroughly rejected the idea of linguistics as a science.

I continued my study of Romano-German linguistics at IFLI, where one of my fellow students was Alexander Shelepin, who became known in the mid-sixties as the "Iron Shurik" of the Soviet Party leadership. The IFLI had undoubtedly provided him with a better education than had been received by anybody else in the untutored high Party and governmental spheres of the Soviet Union. At one time, Iron Shurik had headed *Komsomol* (later, he was chairman of the KGB—the Committee of State Security, or Secret Police). Comparatively young (fifty-seven) and energetic, Shelepin did well at picking up points in the Russian political game. However, his efforts to take over the Ministry of Defense after the death of Malinovsky came to nought; Iron Shurik had been rising too fast. Grechko was named minister of defense; and Shelepin head of the Soviet Trade Unions. In the opinion of some specialists on the Soviet Union, this arrangement is not decisive: Shurik's hour is still to come. The feeling in some Moscow intellectual circles is that if Shelepin rose high in the Party hierarchy, it would mean still greater regimentation. The opposite opinion is that Shelepin "has gone further to the left" since he has been in disfavor, and that his accession to power might result in some liberalization of the regime.*

Another student in IFLI was Tatyana Litvinova, the daughter of Maxim Litvinov, people's commissar for foreign affairs, who played an active role in the founding of the country of Communism, but died in disgrace and oblivion.

His fall from grace began in 1939, when his policy of consistent antifascism and his favoring rapprochement with England and France suffered a defeat, and Stalin concluded his pact with Hitler. In the ensuing years his falling star momentarily rose again, only to vanish forever from the political horizon once the war was over: there was no longer any room for Jews in the Soviet diplomatic corps.

His daughter Tatyana was notable for her broad and liberal views. His grandson Pavel took part in the "Demonstration of the Seven" on Red Square on August 24, 1968, a futile, but strikingly bold protest against the Soviet occupation of Czechoslovakia. Litvinov's granddaughter, Tatyana's daughter, married a well-known champion of human rights, the physicist Valeri Chalidze. They now live outside the "land of triumphant socialism."

I met Maxim Litvinov through my work on *Vechernyaya Moskva* ("Evening Moscow"), familiarly known as *Vechorka*. The meeting itself was not of particular interest, but I record it here because it points up the simplicity of working relations that characterized the prewar period, a simplicity that was replaced by espionage-itis and the monstrous bureaucratization of the military-police machine, with its pathological fear of contacts between the "masses" and the "leadership."

Vechorka was planning to publish a round-up of

* On April 16, 1975, upon his return to the USSR after a disastrous trip to Great Britain at the invitation of the British Trade Unions Congress, Shelepin was dropped from the Politburo; toward the end of May, he was ousted from his post as head of the Soviet Trade Unions.—Trans.

materials on the notorious Stavisky Affair. The newspaper did not have the right to print it without the prior authorization and imprimatur of the Press Section of the Commissariat for Foreign Affairs, so, after making a selection of materials and getting the green light from Rokotov, my chief in the foreign news department, I set off for the Commissariat. The permit to publish depended on two men: the head of the Press Section, Konstantin Umansky, and his deputy Podolsky. But when I went to see them with my sheaf of materials on Stavisky, they refused to assume responsibility for issuing a permit.

"Go see Litvinov! He will, no doubt, issue you a permit," Umansky declared.

I couldn't believe it: I should go to see the commissar out of the blue, just like that?

"Go straight down the corridor. It's the last door on the left," Umansky added.

I knocked at the door timidly, and a voice said "Come in, please!" in a thick Jewish accent.

Sitting behind the desk was a rotund, middle-aged man wearing a pince-nez. "What can I do for you?" he asked.

I was terribly nervous, but I explained to him as best I could what I wanted. Litvinov hastily examined the materials and okayed them.

There wasn't a soul in Litvinov's office: no secretary or typist, no aides or bodyguards. For a Soviet citizen in the second half of the twentieth century, this would be beyond belief.

Our apartment on Furmanov Street was like a Jewish island in a Russian ocean. Our interests, our conversations, the whole atmosphere was Jewish. Markish —and, under his influence, I, too—naturally sought out the society of our own people. I do not mean that he was narrow-mindedly nationalistic and consequently limited his contacts with *goyim*. It was merely that associating with Jews was a sure remedy against assimilation, an infallible, age-old remedy, with which he had been inoculated since the day he was born. Jews were always, for Markish, "his own," whether they were good or bad. Although he did have a few intimate friends, the relationship was never unconditional, one he could not live without. He was in harmony or dissension only with himself; his entourage merely took part in that harmony or dissension.

We did not observe the Sabbath in our home, nor did we keep kosher, and Markish had no qualms about adding sour cream to a meat borscht. But he zealously guarded in a little red kidskin bag his father's mezuzah and the phylacteries that had been left to him—the attributes of the Jewish faith and the Jewish national consciousness. Markish the poet stood in admiration of the heroic past of his people and in dismay over its present: its dispersion throughout the world, its loss of statehood, the physical and moral impoverishment of the downtrodden members of the Diaspora.

In his poem "The Last One," Markish exclaims to God:

Do you remember the tribe of your chosen shepherds?

And he calls for an explosion capable of strengthening and renewing his people:

> A mangy dog in the valley of the ghetto
> Gnaws a miserable bone and cracks his chops.
> I need a wrathful knife, not that hyena,
> Not that rotten trash stuffed in sacks.

A "winged beggar," the descendant of the proud shepherds of Canaan, found for himself a new vocation in life, a new place under the skies of the Diaspora:

> Pieced and worn his century-old velvet,
> Like notes fallen due, his eyes are unfeeling.
> Thus, the seed of the patriarchs is spent,
> The raging winds of the Sinai quelled.

But there is one force, one stubborn dream uniting the people:

> Oh, miserable rabble of squalid bazaars!
> But burnt into your brows—"Jerusalem."

It would be erroneous to see anything Zionist in these verses. Markish is concerned here with a great spiritual heritage that has been squandered by its heirs, who are no longer worthy of it. The poet exhorts them to come to their senses and recognize their shame. Markish was not a Zionist, but the Hitlerite and Stalinist persecutions compelled him, when his end drew near—arrest, prison, execution—to realize his error, to understand that for a Jew who wants to remain a Jew there is no other way except to return "to the shores of his ancestral home." I recall how proud and elated Markish was over the birth of the state of Israel; how he went to the gates of the newly opened embassy to observe a Russian policeman guarding Jewish diplomats. (Need it be said that it would never have occurred to anyone at that time to enter the embassy? But should anyone have entertained such an outlandish idea, the policeman on duty would have inspired him with a healthier notion.) A few months later, in a conversation with Nusinov, Markish said, "I, too, would like to die there."

In this sense, Markish's death takes on an even more tragic dimension, for it was preceded by the shattering of the faith and ideals of a whole lifetime. But his love for his people, his allegiance to his people remained intact. And Markish's work drew its strength from this source.

Among the people Markish surrounded himself with, people in whom he found a common language and with whom he shared kindred interests, Solomon Mikhailovich Mikhoels occupied a special place. In 1929, not long after we met, Markish introduced me to the great Yiddish actor and brilliant director. Markish had taken me to the Moscow Yiddish Theater for the first time in my life. We saw *The 200,000* with Mikhoels in the role of Shimele Soroker. During the intermission, Markish took me backstage. I was a bit nervous at the thought of actually meeting Mikhoels, a man whose name was known to the vast majority of Russian Jewry and to many Russians as well.

I was struck first by Mikhoels's appearance: he was

very ugly, at least as this word is customarily understood: large head set on a short neck, irregular, protruding chin, drooping underlip. His short, stocky, thick-set torso indicated enormous physical strength. His glowing, melancholy, mischievous brown eyes seemed to possess a life of their own, independent of the rest of his face. Mikhoels looked at me teasingly when he saw my frightened embarrassment. But the very first words he pronounced, though quite possibly devoid of any significance, made me forget at once his extraordinary external aspect. Solomon Mikhailovich had something prepossessing about him, a knack for putting you at ease by what he said and the way he said it, by the capacity he had for poking fun at himself.

Several years later, in 1934, I found myself traveling to Sukhumi on the same boat as Mikhoels. He was depressed, despondent; he had recently lost his second wife, the actress Zhenya Levitas. Then, too, Mikhoels was in the process of preparing a production of *King Lear* and was getting himself "into the skin" of the tragic hero he was to portray.

In Sukhumi, the passengers took advantage of the opportunity to visit the famous monkey preserve there. Mikhoels went along, too, although without any particular enthusiasm. We were passing by the monkey museum, taking a quick look at the boring tables, diagrams and sketches, when all of a sudden Mikhoels, who had been silent until then, stopped me and took me by the hand.

"What do you mean, passing by my portrait like that," he muttered. I slowed my steps and glanced up. On the wall opposite, there was an immense oil painting of a chimpanzee. Not knowing quite what to say, I maintained an embarrassed silence.

"But that's me to a tee!" Mikhoels exclaimed with feigned enthusiasm. "Don't you agree?"

There was nothing I could do except smile graciously, because Mikhoels was not just joking.

"What an artist!" Mikhoels continued enthusiastically. "What a portraitist! He has captured my features to perfection!"

After that, he seemed considerably cheered up.

Markish and I had, of course, attended Zhenya's funeral and been terribly shaken by the extent of Mikhoels's grief. During the cremation ceremony Mikhoels, with a gesture only he would be capable of, drew up the convulsively clutching fingers of his right hand to his tightly clenched lips. Somehow, it was more horrible than a wail would have been, or the sight of the tears of a weeping man. The scene remained engraved in my memory as the ultimate expression of the pain and suffering of the human soul.

Some time later, at the premiere of Mikhoel's *King Lear,* there on the stage was the same poignant expression of grief that had so affected Markish and me at Zhenya's funeral—only this time it was not his wife's body lying before Mikhoels, but the body of Cordelia lying before her father, Lear. I looked at Markish. He nodded sadly; he too had recognized the scene. I could see his consternation over this transposition and the trouble it caused in his soul. Poets and actors—even great actors—are probably fashioned out of different material. . . . Be that as it may, Mikhoels's portrayal of Lear created a sensation. The critics hailed him as the "best Lear of the century." And this was due in no small measure to the Cordelia death scene.

The relationship that existed between these two giants of Russian Jewry is characterized by an incident that took place at the beginning of 1939. At *Pravda's* request, Markish had written an antifascist article for the paper and sent it off to the editors. The morning of the day before it was to appear, the telephone rang. As it was the time of day when Markish was always at work and would not take calls, I took the receiver off the hook and immediately heard the excited voice of Mikhoels.

"Where's Markish?"

Learning that it was the "old man," Markish took the call.

Ten minutes later, he came out of his study. "I'm off to the theater," he said. "The old man wants to see me. . . . In an hour and a half, he has to deliver a speech at a meeting and he needs my help."

An hour and a half later, Markish telephoned.

"Turn on the radio; the old man's going to speak now."

I turned it on. To my astonishment, Mikhoels was reading Markish's *Pravda* article. He hadn't yet finished when the phone rang again. Not surprisingly, *Pravda* was calling.

"Where's Markish? What has he done? Why, Mikhoels has been reading Markish's article at the meeting, and it's already been printed in the paper! The very same article!"

The article was, indeed, a remarkable one, and it was carried in the world press under Mikhoels's signature.

Later, when I told Markish about the phone call from *Pravda,* he took it in stride. "That's a lot of nonsense," he said smiling mischievously. "You heard yourself what a marvelous job the old man did!"

That evening Mikhoels was playing *Lear.* We never missed a performance if we were in Moscow, but this time we went more to see Mikhoels backstage.

Mikhoels was still on stage when we got to his dressing room—we could hear Lear's soliloquy over the theater's loudspeaker system. Finally, the door opened and he rushed toward us, pointing to a stack of telegrams on the table.

"Just take a look! They're all congratulations on my speech today! It's so awkward. I don't know what to do."

Markish was beaming; he was genuinely happy about having helped him out.

Relations between Markish and Mikhoels were not, however, always so cordial. There was much in the character of the "old man" that rubbed Markish the wrong way. They had vehement arguments and would all but throw chairs at each other. They both had hot tempers and each one of them felt, of course, that only he was in the right. Markish was not a particularly tolerant man, and since he would be the last to make any concessions, their quarrels would go on a long time.

One of Markish's most serious run-ins with Mikhoels occurred during the war, in Tashkent, where the Yiddish Theater had been evacuated. Mikhoels was so occupied with public affairs that rehearsals often took place in his absence. The theater was then rehearsing Markish's play *An Eye for an Eye*. Without the "old man's" firm hand, the actors grew increasingly undisciplined and rehearsals were slipshod affairs; if the actors fumbled Markish's text, they simply improvised. I had written Markish about the situation. He was then serving in the Black Sea fleet, but during one of his missions, Markish succeeded in altering his itinerary and showed up unexpectedly in Tashkent for the dress rehearsal of *An Eye for an Eye,* one day before the premiere.

Markish came away depressed.

"I had a run-in with the old man," he said. "I am responsible for what I write and I won't have anybody tinkering with my text!"

I learned afterward that Markish had raked Mikhoels over the coals and refused to hear any explanations. The next day he boycotted the premiere and left for the front without even saying good-bye to Mikhoels. Their quarrel was to last for a long time. Anastasya Pototskaya (whom Mikhoels married after the death of Zhenya Levitas) and I tried as best we could to patch things up, but without success. It was not until the end of the war that our husbands put aside their differences.

9 / Shura's Odyssey

MARKISH RECEIVED official recognition in 1939, when, for the first time, several writers were the recipients of awards. He was the sole Jewish author writing in Yiddish to receive the highest award, the Order of Lenin. Only a handful of Russian and Soviet writers of other nationalities were so honored, among them Samuel Marshak (who was a Jew but wrote his poems and children's books exclusively in Russian), Kornei Chukovsky, literary portraitist, translator and author of books for and about children, and Alexei Tolstoy, who is best known for his trilogy *Road to Calvary* and was one of the first Soviet science-fiction writers. The Order of Lenin had the stamp of Russian "national policy": it was not given on the basis of literary merit alone; also taken into careful account was the recipient's nationality. Two other Jewish, Yiddish-language writers received lesser awards—Leib Kvitko, poet and novelist executed in 1952, and Itzik Feffer, many of whose poems were about the Bolshevik Revolution. He, too, was executed during the Stalinist purges after the war.

Moscow was buzzing with rumors that Markish had been selected for the award long before it was actually made, but he would only smile when he heard them. He was quite offhand about it all—on the night before the list of laureates was to be announced, the telephone didn't stop ringing. Friends and adversaries alike were making haste to congratulate Markish, just in case; he finally asked that the phone be disconnected.

When Simon asked his father which award he'd received, Markish replied, "The badge of honor. Now that's not too bad, is it?" But Simon was disappointed with the answer. To tell the truth, so was I—I was more ambitious than Markish.

Later in the evening, Joseph Avratiner, our old friend and the person who had introduced me to Markish, popped in.

"Congratulations on your Order of Lenin!" he shouted from the doorway.

Markish merely smiled as he strode over to greet his guest.

But was Markish in fact happy about the award with which the Soviet regime honored him—in the wake of those terrifying years when that very same regime had put to death or interned dozens, if not hundreds, of people who were close to him? I am convinced that he was. His faith in "our radiant future" and in Stalin personally had not been destroyed, or even shaken.

97

Political blindness? Obviously. The irrepressible, irrational joy of someone who had miraculously come through a cataclysm? Yes, there was probably that, too. But there was something else: At the beginning of 1939, the Soviet Union still appeared to be the most resolute and consistent enemy of Nazism; Molotov's trip to Berlin and Ribbentrop's journey to Moscow were still six months away.

I believe that Stalin's deal with Hitler caused the first breach in Markish's armor of faith. Now, many years later, it is easy to condemn, particularly for those who looked on our life from the sidelines or who know about it from hearsay. But there is no worse injustice than supercilious and self-satisfied condemnation. I trust that no one of integrity will raise his hand to cast a stone at the ghost of Markish for political myopia and for believing as he believed.

But if Markish was genuinely pleased to receive the medal with the profile of Lenin, he had a quite different reaction to his entry into the ranks of the Party of Lenin and Stalin; that for him was a severe trial.

Early in 1940, Aleksandr Fadeyev summoned Markish to the offices of the Writers' Union. His message was clear: "The Party has demonstrated its faith in you. It has shown you great consideration, and it is now your duty to reciprocate this kindness."

The methods employed to swell the ranks of the National Socialist Party in Germany have been described by numerous historians. Intimidation and coercion were tactics used to fill the gaps created by those who lacked enthusiasm or were not natural opportunists. The same is undoubtedly true of the All-Union Communist Party tactics beginning in the second half of the 1930s. To refuse the proffered "honor" was to invite the direst consequences. People tried all sorts of subterfuge to find a way out, but I know of only one argument that could be used with impunity: religious convictions incompatible with the statutes of the Party. And it was an argument Markish could not use. Instead, he stressed his lack of discipline and his inadequate political grounding, but Fadeyev was inflexible. As a rule, Markish was discreet, almost secretive. But the minute he got home, he talked unrestrainedly about his conversation with Fadeyev—how he was being pressured to take this momentous decision and that he could not say no, because of his fear for his family's future. I was powerless to offer any advice, and he didn't expect any of me. I think the only thing that made it easier for him was that he didn't actually become a member of the Party until the war was on and the Nazis were shooting Communists and Jews indiscriminately and throwing them into the same pits.

After the birth of our second son, David, we were cramped for space in our apartment on Furmanov Street—there was Markish and I, his daughter Lyalya, our two sons, a nursemaid, and a house servant. The time had come to think about moving.

In Russia, to find an apartment like the one we needed is more than anything else a matter of good fortune, which in this instance turned up in the guise of a friend of Markish's, the Jewish literary critic Meir Vinner. He happened to drop in one day and told us that some friends of his were interested in exchanging their large apartment on Gorky Street, in the center of the city, for a smaller one. The friends were a German couple named Rohr: Mr. Rohr was a professor and historian, and his wife was the accredited correspondent of the *Völkischer Beobachter,* Nazi Germany's leading newspaper! They had decided to break with Hitler and had asked for political asylum in the USSR. Their request was granted and they had been given Soviet citizenship, but they were now compelled to give up their elegant apartment, which had been made available to them by the Diplomatic Department for Assistance to Foreign Nationals. Provided that we could obtain the support of someone high up in the Ministry of Foreign Affairs, the apartment would be ours.

I didn't like to bother Markish with such things, so I went to take a look at the apartment on Gorky Street myself, and I fell in love with it at first sight. Four large bright rooms! The furniture provided by the ministry was of antique mahogany and had been confiscated from palaces and landed estates. Everything was perfect, except that we still didn't have the right connection, someone who could give us access to Dekanozov, the deputy minister of foreign affairs in charge of administration. But once again, Fortune smiled on us. Another deputy minister of foreign affairs, Solomon Lozovsky, a Jew, happened to be in the Yiddish Theater one day when I was there, and he agreed to set up an appointment for me with Dekanozov. In no time, the arrangements were made; the Rohrs moved into our apartment, and we into theirs.

The Rohrs did not live very long on Furmanov Street. They were soon arrested and both of them died in camps. This was the way Soviet Russia expressed its gratitude to antifascists who had put their trust in them.

Among the furniture in the Gorky Street apartment was an elegant secretary dating from the time of Paul I, a veritable work of art from the Palace of the Tsars. It was the property of the Ministry of Foreign Affairs, and for a time, we rented it. Later the ministry offered to sell it to us. Markish had no objection—the price was quite reasonable—and the imperial, flaming-red mahogany secretary became our private property.

But there is more to the history of that piece of furniture. After Markish's arrest and after we were sent into exile, the secretary was confiscated, along with the rest of our belongings, and delivered to the special store for seized property. In 1955, following my return to Moscow from exile, I dropped into the library of the Writers' Union, and what should I see but our secretary! They tried to convince me that I was mistaken, that it had been in the library's possession for many years; but I opened one of its doors and pointed out a small hole in the inside back panel where David had dug out a knot in the wood. The documents were consulted and it was discovered that the secretary had been acquired in 1953. It was returned to us, the sole material evidence of our former life.

Fifteen years later, after we had filed our papers requesting authorization to emigrate from the USSR to Israel, the secretary once again changed ownership. We were forbidden to take it out of Russia, since artistic treasures are not permitted to leave the country. So, being without work or money, we decided to sell it. We, "traitors to the Soviet motherland" who were dreaming of going to Israel, were informed, in the greatest secrecy, that a certain highly placed personage was interested in acquiring the secretary. This personage came by the house one day and examined the secretary from top to bottom. He pretended he didn't know who we were; nor did we give any sign that we knew who he was. The State Historical Museum had appraised the piece at a rather high price, but our potential buyer haggled bitterly over it, arguing how poor he was. Finally, we had no choice but to let the secretary go at half its real price. The buyer was Deputy Minister of Foreign Affairs Semyonov. You can imagine how anxious he must have been to acquire the secretary if he was ready to risk contaminating himself by exposure to the Markishes, a family that had fallen into disgrace. . . .

At the time of the move into our new apartment, Markish was not in Moscow. He had gone off to Bialystok, Poland, which had been "liberated" by the Soviets, to attend a meeting of a group of Jewish writers and personalities active in the Jewish arts who had fled Hitler. Markish wanted to help them get resettled and re-established in their careers, but since he knew, or, rather, suspected what the real state of affairs was in Soviet nationality policy, he did not paint an especially rosy picture for the refugees. The authorities had resigned themselves to the presence of Jewish culture in the USSR, but had no intention whatever of encouraging its further development by representatives of the Polish Jewish intelligentsia. In the eyes of the Soviet regime, the refugees from Poland were not only Jews; they were also aliens, because they had not undergone Soviet psychological preparation. Thus it was doubly dangerous to allow them to be incorporated into the ideological front.

"At the present time, shoemakers are needed more than writers," Markish told the Bialystok meeting. The ironic truth of the remark is reflected in his poem "The Forty-Year-Old":

You need a shoemaker—your heel is broken,
And he's writing a book, puffing from his labors.

A few of his listeners failed to discern the point, and they made a firm mental note of it. Later on, distorting the true meaning of his words, they were to allege that Markish had disparaged the Polish writers by suggesting that they turn in their pens for the tools of the craftsman.

Some of the writers were able to get to Moscow with Markish's help: Rachel Korn, a Yiddish writer and poet who later emigrated to Canada, the novelist Chaim Grade, and Efraim Kaganovsky. Among others who made it were the dramatist and poet Israel Ashendorf, who in 1953 emigrated to Argentina, and Alter Kacyzne. All were refugees, with no place to live, so various families took them in. Alter Kacyzne came to stay with us. Fate was only briefly kind to him. He left Moscow and joined his family in Lvov but in 1941, the Germans came into that city. Alter was killed by Ukrainian anti-Semites.

In trying to help the Polish refugees, Markish exerted considerable effort on behalf of the Jewish Miniature Theater from Poland, which was directed by a famous Yiddish comedy team, Dzhigan and Shumacher. Among the troupe's members was a remarkable dancer, Rakhel Lyubelskaya. Her parents had been killed, victims of German occupation, but somehow she had managed to survive and get to Moscow. At this time, which was still the "honeymoon" period in the Stalin-Hitler relationship, Markish wrote his famous poem "The Dancer from the Ghetto," in which his people are incarnated as a homeless dancer.

Whither beckon you, whither drive you,
The icy wind and sorrow of the night?
The blizzard swirls, in the fields the blizzard
    swirls,
The portals and the gates locked tight.

Soviet censorship forbade any mention of Fascist atrocities, but Markish wrote:

In days of yore, here, amid the ominous growling
  of the winds,
Above the frozen multitude was uttered
The solemn promise—"Thou shalt not kill!"
Now killing is the command become.

But the angry thunder shall not the truth drown
  out,
Nor thought to darkness and to fear succumb.
Not he on whom the axe does fall shall perish,
But he who lets fall the axe on the block.

Unknowingly, Peretz was prophesying his own fate.
The poem was not published then, of course; it was
forbidden to abuse the Germans. Nor was it published
once the war had begun, for there were concerns more
pressing than Yiddish literature. And after the war,
it would have been viewed as glorifying Jewish nationalism. So it gathered dust in a drawer. Eventually it
did emerge in Russian translation. And then Markish
was arrested. He did not live to see one of his best
poems published in his native language.
  Markish did all that he could to help the Jewish
writers from Poland—the theater of Ida Kaminskaya,
the Miniature Theater of Dzhigan and Shumacher—
helping them survive as any Jew helps his fellow Jews
who have met with disaster.
  Certainly, the Russian authorities were not the least
bit concerned by the plight of Jews driven to the four
corners of the earth. When Markish was in Minsk,
on his way to Bialystok, he was summoned by
Ponomarenko, who was first secretary of the Byelorussian Party Central Committee (he subsequently became one of Stalin's inner circle). Their whole
conversation was distressing, but two of Ponomarenko's observations were particularly unsettling: the fate
of Polish Jews in Russia was a question dependent on
top-level politics, and, indeed, the future of Russian
Jewry itself was wrapped in a cloud of uncertainty.

Markish was anxious to visit my brother Shura, who
was confined in Arkhangelsk, in the north of Russia.

I was opposed to the idea—I was afraid Markish would get into trouble and himself wind up in the camp—so just my mother and I went to see Shura. Our journey was preceded by a humorous and rather symbolic episode.

In the course of securing authorization for the visit, I managed to obtain an appointment with GULag Deputy Chief Granovsky (GULag is an acronym of Russian words meaning "main concentration-camp administration"). Markish came with me to Granovsky's office, which was near the notorious Lubyanka prison, but was not permitted to enter; the pass had been issued to me in my maiden name.

I entered Granovsky's office. He jumped up from his desk and exclaimed, "Surely there's some mistake! You're not Lazebnikova, you're the wife of Peretz Markish!"

It turned out that a year before, Granovsky had been vacationing in Kislovodsk at the same time I was there, and someone had pointed me out to him as Markish's wife.

After this quite extraordinary reception, I explained I had come to request permission to visit my brother. To my great satisfaction, he gave me a permit that would be valid for seventy-two hours.

"But," Granovsky warned me, "bear in mind that there are not only political prisoners there! There are also real bandits—so be very careful!"

I then asked him for permission to take my mother along. Without batting an eye, he added my mother's name to the permit.

His parting words were: "When you get back, be sure to telephone me to let me know how things went. One thing, though, don't write down my number. Make a mental note of it."

Markish was to see us off at the North Station and bring a large knapsack filled with provisions for Shura. He had dressed as he always did: loose-fitting coat, hat drawn down over his eyes, a scarf thrown over his shoulder. Such a shady-looking character attracted the attention of a policeman, and Markish was summarily hauled off to the police station. They checked his documents and let him go with the explanation that they were on the lookout for a certain criminal and had mistaken Markish for him. Just as the train was about to pull out, Markish came running to us with the knapsack, and we took our seats.

The trip was not a restful one: a patrol of soldiers kept waking up the passengers to verify documents. Whether they were looking for anyone in particular, I cannot say; perhaps it was just routine. At long last, the train pulled into the halfway station, from which we had to make our way on foot. The taiga was all around us, and the air was buzzing with the monotonous drone of mosquitoes. We sank up to our ankles in the swampy earth as we plodded toward the camp.

On our arrival, the camp adminstration immediately rescinded the orders of Granovsky, and we were authorized a visit of only two hours in the camp guardhouse. Even so, Shura managed to tell us a number of extraordinary things.

He had been arrested in Vladivostok and his transfer to Moscow had taken a couple of months, because he had been held up at various transit prisons along the way awaiting transport. As he familiarized himself with the methods employed by his jailers, Shura became increasingly convinced that there had been a Fascist coup-d'etat in Moscow. His cries of "Long live Stalin!" from behind the bars of his cell drew the mockery of his jailers. Eventually he wound up in Lubyanka and was brought before an interrogator. Shura was accused of every crime under the sun and threatened with a sentence of "ten years without the right to correspond" —in other words, death by shooting (the Soviet legal code had no provision for capital punishment at the time, so people condemned to death received "ten years without the right to correspond"). On the last day of his interrogation, the examiner beckoned Shura to the barred window of his office in Lubyanka.

"Well, take a good look at Moscow—you'll never see it again!" he said.

Shura peered down on the square below, which, from so high up, looked like the bottom of a well. He could see the statue of Vorovsky and the crowds of scurrying people, unaware—or not wanting to be aware—of what was going on behind the walls of Lubyanka.

At that moment, the telephone on the interrogator's desk rang. He lifted the receiver.

"Svetlanochka, it's you. Well, it's about time! . . . Your husband has left on vacation? What a stroke of luck! So, today, then? At what time? . . . In a quarter of an hour? I'll be over in a jiffy! . . . Be an angel? That's not at all in my line. . . . For you? Well, okay, we'll see what can be done. . . ."

Replacing the receiver, the interrogator turned to Shura. His eyes glowed with genuine human happiness.

"Well, let me tell you, Lazebnikov," the interrogator said, "you can consider yourself born under a lucky star. It just happens a girl has asked me for a favor I can't refuse. So I'm putting you down for eight years instead of ten without the right to correspond."

And so, with his kidneys broken by the interrogator, some teeth knocked out, and his head laced with scars, Shura went off to a concentration camp for eight years.

The two hours with Shura passed like a flash. The following day my mother and I returned to the guardhouse in hopes of having another meeting with Shura, thanks to the complicity of a fine fellow named Sasha Sematsky, the head of the sector in the camp known as Black Stream. Sematsky was married to a Jewish woman by the name of Fanya, and because of her he did all he could for the Jewish political prisoners.

To our chagrin, in the guardhouse we ran into a certain Britsky, the second in command of the entire camp. He was a real brute and assassin. When he discovered why we were there—no mention was made of Sematsky, of course—he ordered us to clear out, or else he would set the dogs on us. A half-hour later, we were still loitering around the guardhouse area hoping for a miracle. It was then that Britsky made good his promise.

A pack of well-fed police dogs were set loose upon us. My mother and I took to our heels, stumbling, falling, driven by fear and desperation. Luckily, near the guardhouse there was a small wooden hut inhabited by some local people. They had seen us fleeing for our lives and, leaping out of the house, they grabbed us and pulled us inside. They were a kind couple; the wife's name was Lyubushka. They had saved our lives and now they gave us shelter. That same night, there was a gentle tap at the door. It was a prisoner sent by Sematsky to deliver a note from Shura: We were to meet him the next day at the work site—they were building a railroad—and bring food and vodka for the crew. The note-bearer would serve as guide.

We decided that this time I would go alone. At dawn, Lyubushka set me and the prisoner on our path —we had about six miles to cover. She had lent me her peasant dress so that I would not attract undue attention, but since she didn't have an extra pair of shoes, I went off in my high-heeled pumps.

Two and a half hours later, we reached a plate-layer's cabin, and before long Shura arrived. After emptying the food basket, he neatly refilled it with dozens of letters his fellow prisoners had given him; on my return to Moscow, I was to mail them. As you might imagine, correspondence with the outside world was strictly limited and censored.

Not even a quarter of an hour had passed when the telephone rang; someone had squealed to the camp administration that a woman wearing high-heeled shoes had been seen in the vicinity. Shura was given to understand that an *oper*—an operative of the Ministry of Internal Affairs—had been dispatched with a dog. I couldn't linger a minute longer: to be caught in possession of the letters would mean certain arrest.

Feeling as if lead weights had been attached to my feet and trying not to look back, I made my way along the railroad ties in the direction of the station. I had no other choice: if I had strayed from the tracks I would have sunk in the marsh. At length, I heard the footsteps of someone running after me, shouting "Firusha!" and I understood at once that the person could only have been sent by my brother, since this was Shura's name for me.

Shura's messenger told me that the danger was past; the *oper* had lost the trail and was heading in the opposite direction. I could return to the plate-layer's cabin.

On the way back, the messenger told me the extraordinary story of why he had been sent to the camp. In the kolkhoz, or collective farm, where he had been working prior to his arrest, the wife of the kolkhoz chairman had a tremendous weakness for the opposite sex; any man could enjoy her favors simply for the asking. My messenger had been among the beneficiaries of her largesse, but, having a mischievous streak in him, he didn't leave things at that. He decided to have a good laugh at the expense of the chairman, whom he hated. So while he was in bed with the chairman's wife, he stamped her buttocks with the kolkhoz seal, which he had pilfered from her husband's desk. It was not long before the chairman discovered his wife's new acquisition. Using the most devious means, he carried out a quick investigation and got to the bottom of the affair. He then wrote a letter of denunciation to the district authorities, informing them that a sacrilege had been committed against the state seal in his kolkhoz. The hapless lover was sentenced to ten years in the camps—but with the right to correspond.

On my return from Shura's camp, I telephoned Granovsky and told him the whole story: how we had been set upon by dogs, how they had countermanded his order authorizing a visit of seventy-two hours. The story about the dogs didn't seem to upset him unduly, but he didn't appreciate at all the fact that his order had been violated. At any rate, Britsky was soon recalled from his post and sent God knows where.

Many years later, I called Granovsky for the second time—it was after Markish had been arrested. A dry voice informed me that the individual was no longer employed there. I learned afterward that Granovsky had been arrested. For all I know, he has perished.

10 / The Evacuation Train

ON THE MORNING OF June 22, 1941, Markish and I were getting ready to leave for Ilinskoye, a small community near Moscow, to look at a dacha Markish was planning to buy. He had hemmed and hawed a long time before finally making up his mind. He personally felt no need for a dacha, or a car, either, for that matter. All he required was a desk and a typewriter. But Markish's brother Meir had a severe heart condition and the doctors had recommended he spend more time in the fresh air. This was what had finally persuaded him.

Markish was, by Soviet standards, very well off, but he simply had no pretensions to the "good life," and even abhorred its advantages: a house in the country, fine furniture and porcelain—everything that money could buy at that time in Russia. He was remarkably unassuming and modest in the way he lived. For example, he never changed the eating habits of his childhood in the shtetl: for breakfast every morning he had herring with boiled potatoes. He never stinted on money or asked me to account for household expenses, and it was usually days before he noticed if I had bought something new for the house. Even a week might pass before he would suddenly ask:

"Say, isn't that a new couch?"

"That's right, I recently bought it."

"But why? We did have something there before, didn't we?"

Occasionally an object pleased him, but it wasn't in his nature to develop attachments to things. He

109

gave generously of his money to strangers, like house servants, or elevator men. On New Year's Day, we always baked some special pastries for the service personnel in our Gorky Street house. Workmen frequently came by to get a bit of help or merely ask for advice. He was never aloof, always accessible—in contrast to the majority of the privileged occupants of the house.

Well, around noon of June 22, 1941, as we were leaving for the country to purchase the dacha, the telephone rang. When I picked up the receiver, all I heard was my mother's voice saying "War!"

I cannot say it was unexpected, although we had hoped, though without counting on it too much, that the "wise policy of Stalin" would preserve the Soviet Union from a confrontation with Germany. And yet the actual announcement came as a monstrous surprise, like a clap of thunder in a clear sky.

Five minutes later, Markish was off to the Writers' Union, which was a mobilization point. As for me, I set out to collect Simon and Lyalya at the Pioneer Camp on the outskirts of Moscow, where the children of writers vacationed in the summer.

A few hours later Markish returned home looking grim.

"In an hour, I'm going off to join the People's Volunteer Corps," he said.

I was practically without any news of him until July 6, when the children and I were scheduled to evacuate with the Pioneer Camp to the village of Bersut on the Kama River. I was disconsolate at the thought that I wouldn't have a chance to say goodbye to Markish before we left, and by the time I arrived at the courtyard of the Literary Fund, where buses were waiting to take us to the station, I was in tears. The yard was filled with writers and their families. It was chaos—agitated adults, screaming children, everyone pushing and shoving. Nobody knew if we would all get to Bersut, how long we would be away, if we would ever return . . .

And then, I spied Markish elbowing his way through the crowds. Against the background of the tired and sullen crowd, he stood out like a messenger

110

from another world. People recognized him, followed him with their eyes, and murmured, "Why, that's Markish."

He had obtained a few hours' leave to come to see us off. He was wearing his soft suede jacket—uniforms were still in short supply—and I thought he looked thinner.

From June to September I lived with the children in Bersut. From there we moved on to Chistopol, which had become a transit center for writers prior to their evacuation to remote areas in Siberia and Central Asia.

Bersut had the charged atmosphere of a reformatory. Lyashko, a so-called proletarian, worker-and-peasant writer, was put in charge of the writers' families. He was a boorish petty tyrant who took his new job very seriously, seeing his role as that of an ideological and educational mentor. Calling together the wives, he delivered a long and tedious lecture stating that we were now "like everybody else," and under no circumstances were we to use makeup or wear jewelry of any kind. With each day that passed, Lyashko became increasingly surly and churlish, more like the commandant of a camp than anything else. As a matter of fact, he forbade my mother to enter the nursery area where my children had been placed, and this despite the fact that I worked there as the night nurse. I made up my mind to extricate myself from the annoying "tutelage" of the proletarian penman and move to Chistopol, also on the Kama River.

I made several trips to Chistopol to look for lodgings, but my efforts were in vain. I went from house to house, knocking on doors, rapping on windows, inquiring, "Would you by any chance have a room for rent?" And the reply was invariably "We don't rent rooms to Jews!"

The inhabitants of Chistopol must all have been either anti-Semitic or simply scared that if the Germans came, they would punish anyone who had "helped" the Jews. But at the time I was in no mood to try to discover the whys and wherefores; I just walked about the streets crying my head off.

One day, as I was doing just that, a middle-aged man and his wife stopped me. They were sitting in front of a shop next to an old house. Sobbing, I told them my troubles.

"Please come and live with us," the man offered, pointing to the house. "It's not a palatial mansion, but there's room enough. Right, Shura?" he said, turning to his wife.

So we moved into a room behind the kitchen in the house of a wonderful Russian couple, the Vavilovs— Uncle Vasya and Aunt Shura. We lived there until we were evacuated to Tashkent several months later, sharing with them their food and their troubles. After we left, Boris Pasternak and his family moved in, on our recommendation. Later on, Pasternak corresponded with the Vavilovs, and his letters became their pride and joy.

Our friendship with the Vavilovs continued after the war. Whenever Uncle Vasya came to Moscow on business—he worked in a watch factory—he never failed to look up the Pasternaks and us.

Compared with Bersut, Chistopol looked like a real city: a few paved streets, two-story houses, a brick building that had been the gymnasium at one time, a main square lined with old trading stalls, a large harbor. Food was already scarce by then and people zealously guarded the sugar, oils, and soap they had put by.

Every day, we writers' wives used to go to the Chistopol market, though it didn't have much to offer, in hopes of getting a bit of food—either for money or in exchange for some clothing. One morning a peasant came to the market with a large barrel of honey. We were all milling about the bazaar in search of something to eat when we caught sight of him. Could there be any greater treat for the children than honey? A long queue immediately formed, and we all agreed among ourselves that each customer would limit himself to 150 grams; otherwise there wouldn't be enough to go around. We were happy as could be as we stood in line waiting for the vendor to set up his scales and open the barrel.

Just then, who should walk into the marketplace but

Leonid Leonov, the prominent Russian writer and official of the Writers' Union.

"What's he selling?" Leonov asked, as he neared the queue. "How much is it?"

When he found out, he went up to the vendor and started whispering something in his ear. The vendor thereupon put away his scales, loaded the barrel back on his cart, and followed Leonov out of the market.

So our children went without honey. Leonov, who had offered the vendor a higher price, bought the whole barrel for himself. Naturally, he remained impervious to our reproaches and appeals to his conscience as a writer.

There had been no news from Markish, so I decided to take my chances and try to get through to Moscow, which had been cordoned off, without a laissez-passer. Together with two other women, the poet Margarita Aliger and Sofa Mazo, the first wife of the poet Evgeni Dolmatovski, I left Chistopol by boat for Kazan. There, we were fortunate enough to obtain from the authorities special papers allowing us to proceed to Moscow. The travel warrants were not issued in our names, and if there had been a verification, we would all have been arrested. In wartime, if a person was discovered with false documents, he exposed himself to the direst consequences.

Traveling by riverboat—we couldn't get on a train and, besides, it was more dangerous to go by rail with false papers—we reached the limits of Moscow Province. If we had gone any further, our papers would surely have been checked, so we went ashore about fifty miles outside Moscow. There was a reasonable chance of reaching the city by hitching rides in passing cars and using suburban trains.

It was the end of September when I finally walked into the entrance of our apartment house and took the elevator to the fifth floor. Markish was there working, sitting on the couch with his typewriter on a chair in front of him. He was in a sea-service uniform, the two stars on his epaulettes indicating his rank of commander.

Someone high up had gone through the lists of those

113

in the People's Volunteer Corps and, knowing that the volunteers would be decimated by Hitler's top divisions in the battles near Moscow, had struck Markish's name from the rolls. Markish was then ordered to present himself to the war-fleet general staff, given the rank of commander and, for the time being, granted leave. He was allowed to return home and devote himself to his writing.

Markish's comrades, the Jewish writers Meir Vinner, Godiner and Rosin, all serving in the ranks of the Volunteer Corps, fell in the defense of Moscow.

Markish had been granted authorization to accompany his family to the evacuation center at Tashkent. We left Moscow for Kazan, where we joined dozens of other writers and their families to wait for the convoy that would take us on the final stage of the journey. Later on, some of the writers went to the front, and some remained in Tashkent. As for Markish, he returned to the army.

The convoy train was crammed full. We managed to obtain a compartment for four in a first-class car, and the seven of us squeezed into it: Markish and I, our three children, my mother, and Yura, a nephew of Markish's. Just as the train was about to pull out, we saw a young man and woman running frantically along the platform; the man's eyes were wild with fear.

"We'll have to take them," Markish decided.

The train was already moving when the two clambered aboard. Since our compartment was already crowded, the couple, with a glance full of gratitude, scrambled up onto the baggage rack.

The man was Alexander Chakovsky, a Jewish anti-Semite, who today is editor-in-chief of the *Literary Gazette,* the weekly newspaper of the Union of Soviet Writers.

Traveling in the car next to ours were German writers and antifascists who had fled Hitler's Germany and taken refuge in the USSR. From the first, there was no doubt that they intended to keep their distance from the motley assortment of voyagers on the evacuation train, to completely snub us as if we didn't even exist,

114

as if we all were not pulled by the same locomotive to a common destiny. Thus we "Soviets" had nothing to do with the "foreigners." One particular incident established the impossibility of any contact with them whatsoever. It happened that the train came to a halt at a God-forsaken halfway station. Since it was a fine day, the passengers in our car, most of whom were women and children, got off the train and went to warm themselves in the sun. One of the German writers stepped out on the platform of the car, stretched his arms as he squinted into the sun, and then, as if completely oblivious to our presence below, slowly unbuttoned his fly and proceeded to urinate. We couldn't believe our eyes: so this was a European—and an intellectual to boot! For a moment we were speechless, but then we exploded with outrage. The writer remained imperturbable, calmly finished what he was doing, and returned to his compartment. To be quite honest, we were so indignant over his behavior that we put all the Germans in the same category, even though they didn't all act so shamelessly.

Markish imposed strict discipline on the life of our compartment. In the morning the children went out to walk and play in the corridor, the Chakovskys disappeared God knows where, and Markish worked. He had no intention of changing his work habits or wasting his time in idle chatter such as went on in all the other compartments. Writing was for him a vital necessity. Indeed, while traveling on the evacuation train, he composed the whole cycle of verses entitled "Moscow—1941."

For the twenty-three-day journey from Kazan to Tashkent, the "Writers' House on Wheels" was a veritable "train of fools," with its scandals, tears, despair, torpor, and flirtations. It moved along the steppe far from war and death into an unknown future.

I think I can say without exaggeration that Markish was the only one on the entire train who continued his creative labors during the journey. All the hustle and bustle and confusion of the trek transformed cultivated and civilized people into neurotics and savages. But Markish was not affected by this flight into exile; he had been inoculated with the bitter experience of gen-

115

eration upon generation of his people, the externally exiled, the eternally wandering.

Scandals broke out often, on the slightest pretext. We were the butt of the most outlandish attacks. First, Markish was accused of evicting the other members of his "household" and obliging them to loiter in the corridor. Second—and this was sheer madness—it was repeated *ad nauseam* that "these Markishes are real operators! They've gone and packed their compartment with children and receive a daily ration of four whole teaspoons of condensed milk!"

This was so, because the train master allotted to every child one teaspoon of milk. But the fact that Markish's nephew, Yura, who was ill and whom we had taken in temporarily from the dormitory car, received his ration infuriated these people, who had sunk to the level of barbarians.

Finally the explosion occurred. It was the smart and intelligent Victor Shklovsky who kicked up a row. Again, Yura served as the pretext, although what exactly there was about him that rubbed Shklovsky the wrong way is hard to say. Shklovsky stormed through the corridor, shouting menacingly, "Markish! I'm not just going to beat you up, I'm going to kill you!"

He didn't explain himself further, but his cries grew ever more strident. Markish, who was sitting in front of his typewriter, couldn't make out what Shklovsky was kicking up such a fuss about, but the noise bothered him. So I stepped out in the corridor to give the raving Shklovsky and his colleagues who were egging him on a piece of my mind. Beside myself with rage, I shouted from the entrance to our compartment, "You, engineers of the human soul, you're all a bunch of shits!"

I had always been calm and collected until that moment, and when Shklovsky heard me utter such a profanity, he froze up, as if a pail of icy water had been poured over his head. He didn't know which way to turn.

The Yiddish novelist and short-story writer David Bergelson and his wife, Tsilya, occupied a compartment not far from ours. Markish and Bergelson were

116

linked by a curious friendship—or perhaps affinity is a better word to describe the feeling these two caustic individuals had for one another. It lasted throughout their lifetimes, right up to the day of their death, on August 12, 1952.

Markish first became acquainted with Bergelson in 1917, in Kiev. In 1921, they ran into each other again, this time in Berlin, where the cream of Russian Jewish writers had migrated: David Hofstein, whose elegies for the Jewish communities devastated by the civil war pogroms was published in 1922, with illustrations by Marc Chagall; Der Nister; Leib Kvitko, poet and novelist; Markish; Bergelson. . . . Bergelson was intelligent and refined, but at the same time corrosive and malicious. Markish, a kind and gentle man, could be as explosive as gunpowder. The rebellious temper of the young Markish riled Bergelson, a sophisticated "European," and, as is so often the case, his personal feelings colored his judgment of Markish's writings. Thus the stage was set for the polemical battles they waged in the Yiddish press.

The Bergelsons returned to Russia from the emigration in 1934, and after that Tsilya and I became fast friends. We did whatever we could to restrain our respective husbands from clashing with one another, and were delighted whenever things went well between them.

It was in the thirties that an American woman who had come to live in the USSR decided to open a Paris-style literary café in Moscow that would attract writers, painters and actors, and those who sought their society. The National Café was a success. People enjoyed sitting and chatting, drinking coffee laced with brandy, and tasting the specialty of the house, American-style apple pie. (The National still serves apple pie today, but that is the sole vestige of the old days. Its former habitués were either arrested and died in the camps—the fate of the American woman—or simply are no more.) In 1937, the café fell on hard times: people were afraid of talking even in their own homes, much less in public. After World War II, the old habitués started trickling back—Mikail Svetlov, Yuri Olesha, Vladimir Bugayevsky, Mark Shechter—

117

but the MGB (Ministerstvo Gosudarstvennoi Bezopasnosti—Soviet Ministry of State Security), which was
engaged in ferreting out "liberals," installed a network
of microphones in the salon of the National and
obliged the waitresses to collaborate with Lubyanka,
the MGB headquarters.

Bergelson, who came from a well-to-do family and
had received a European education and upbringing,
jokingly called Markish an Asiatic, because he preferred staying home to sitting around in cafés. But
Bergelson did succeed in dragging Markish to the
National a few times a year, teasing him all the while
about his predilection for poppyseed cakes, which had
been regarded as a delicacy in Markish's native *shtetl*.
Bergelson, who had grown up in comfort, was somewhat shocked by Markish's plebeian tastes.

Marc Chagall and Markish had been friends in Russia before emigrating, and their reunion in Paris in
1924 cemented their friendship. I suspect that their
very different natures, as reflected in their art
(Chagall's melancholy serenity and Markish's blazing
intensity) was the essence of their mutual attraction. Because of their closeness, I had always been
anxious to make Chagall's acquaintance. Years later,
on a visit to France, I decided I would try to meet
him, but my French friends were not encouraging:
He is a busy man . . . He doesn't receive visitors. . . .
Still, very soon after I had dropped him a note saying
I was the wife of his friend Peretz Markish and was
in France, I received a special-delivery letter saying
that he expected me at his home on the Côte d'Azur.

The three of us—the artist, his darling wife, Vava,
and I—sat down together and talked. I had never
known much about Markish's life during the emigration. When Chagall told me that Peretz had been
something of a Bohemian in Paris and had drunk
heavily during that time, I found it quite incredible. I
could not remember a single occasion when Markish
had had so much as a glass of vodka—and excessive
drinking was rife among Russian writers. The effervescent Chagall was full of questions about Markish's life
in Russia after his return from the emigration. We

spoke in Russian or Yiddish; he seemed to enjoy using the languages of his youth.

Naturally, I was dying to see his new paintings, and the place where he worked. He obliged by throwing open the door to his studio. It was immense, sunlit, and bare. Not a single painting or drawing was in evidence. But meanwhile, Chagall had drawn back a sliding screen behind which had been laid away, as if in a steel vault, works from his cycle of paintings, "The War."

I left carrying a precious gift: Chagall's book *Monotypes*. On the title page he had sketched his portrait with the following inscription: "To my dear Esther Markish, in remembrance of the beloved friend of my youth, Peretz Markish. Wishing you happiness."

Though busy at work in our compartment, Markish nevertheless followed with an observant eye the life of the "train of fools." Later, in his novel *The March of Generations,* he would give an accurate account of that journey and the Jewish writers who were on that train.

Small bands of Jews who had fled from Poland were making their way over the steppe routes that ran along both sides of the wearisome railroad line. Nobody was taking them anywhere; they were fleeing for their lives from the advancing German troops. Whenever the train halted, they came up alongside and gazed with hungry eyes at the passengers. Markish and Bergelson gave them whatever bread they had. (In Israel, I came across one of those Jews whom Markish had saved from starvation at some Central Asian stopping place.)

One Polish Jewish refugee in particular made a profound impression on Markish. The refugee was traveling in the opposite direction—westward.

"It's no good for me here," he said. "Nobody cares about me. I am starving and unable to earn a crust of bread. So I'm on my way back to Poland. Don't tell me the Germans are going to eat me up!"

A short time later, the man was apprehended and "just to be on the safe side" was sent away to prison.

After the war, he was released; prison had saved him from Hitler's ovens. We came across quite a number of people like him that year, 1941.

As the train neared the end of its journey, the steppe became yellower, and the heat more intense. Arguments broke out with increasing frequency. At long last, after almost a month on the road (the trip ordinarily takes five days), we reached Tashkent, *terra incognita*.

11 / High Life in Tashkent

WRITERS AND THEIR FAMILIES arrived in the evacuation center of Tashkent in several waves; ours was the second. Among those who preceded us and whom we found on our arrival there were Alexei Tolstoy (our neighbor on Gorky Street) and the family of Maxim Gorky (his widow Yekaterina Peshkova, his granddaughters, and his daughter-in-law Nadezhda, whom Gorky had given the pet name of Timosha). My old friend Joseph Utkin was also living in Tashkent. He had lost the fingers of his right hand at the front and was now trying to be returned to active duty as a war correspondent.

Thus there was a whole colony of writers leading a precarious existence in starving, wartime Tashkent, and more were living in Ashkhabad and Alma-Ata.

We, the second wave, were housed in the two-story public library, at 6 Khorezm Street. Today, neither the street nor the building exists; the whole area was devastated during an earthquake.

The large Markish family was installed in the library's reading room, a rather spacious chamber divided into two unequal parts by a high counter with a small window through which books were formerly given out. The day we moved in, the children invented a quiet game that was to become their favorite pastime: one of the children would stand on one side of the counter and act the role of librarian, while the others would press close to the delivery window and ask for books.

We were, accordingly, the happy occupants of a two-room dwelling with the adjoining corridor at our disposition. We later set up folding cots in the corridor, mostly for the use of homeless Polish Jewish writers who had come to the Markish "house" for help.

Our quarters were not, of course, palatial, nor as comfortable as an ordinary city apartment, but they were quite satisfactory. Our next-door neighbor was David Bergelson, and living on the floor above was the Yiddish writer Der Nister, who arrived just after we did from Namangan, a small provincial town not far from Tashkent. He had been evacuated there first in accordance with the Table of Ranks that had been set up by the Writers' Union. But, thanks to the "German revolt," he obtained a small room in our house. This is what happened:

The German, antifascist writers who had fled Nazi Germany—Johannes Becher, Friedrich Wolf, Erich Weinert and others—had arrived in Tashkent along with us. The house on Khorezm Street was not at all to their liking: no hot or cold running water, no baths or showers, no toilet. Unaccustomed to such Spartan conditions, the Germans registered a vehement protest with the Central Committee of the Uzbek Communist Party, demanding immediate transfer to another house, failing which they all threatened to commit suicide in a spectacular manner.

There was no question, of course, of acceding to their demands, but the authorities lost no time in getting rid of these troublesome Europeans by shipping them off to Kuibyshev, where they would be closer to civilization and could fend for themselves.

As a result, Der Nister and a number of other Soviet writers, who were used to just about everything,

121

moved into the small rooms and cubicles that had been vacated.

The days and months passed by. The war was far away. The older children, Simka and Lyalya, went to school. I got a job on the radio committee, in the French monitoring service, where I listened to broadcasts from the Middle East and prepared transcripts. I didn't receive much money, but it was enough for us to make ends meet. Our room gradually took on a homey appearance: out of some plywood boards we put together a clothes chest, someone gave us a chair, and from somewhere we picked up a folding bed.

Our younger son David caused us some anxiety: for days on end he walked about in the yard dressed in prewar red boots and a red cape, and the Uzbeks, who kept feeding him bread and occasionally meat, tried to persuade him to go off with them. The Uzbeks were very fond of children, and David was very fond of bread and meat.

On one occasion when Markish had managed to tear himself away for a few days from Moscow or the battlefront and come to visit us, the Jewish writers, mostly those from Poland, came to see him the moment he arrived. They were in worse straits than the others, and needed advice and protection. One man showed up looking like his own shadow; he was all skin and bones, dressed in rags, a tattered military overcoat tied at the waist with a piece of string. Markish did not recognize him; he turned out to be Keitelman, a Jewish writer from Poland. He was on his last legs from hunger and despair. Markish gave him his clothes and some money and took him around to see the authorities. After Markish left, Keitelman lived with us for some time, and then went away somewhere and vanished. I lost all track of him until I reached Israel, where his widow (Keitelman had died only a short time before) got in touch with me and told me how he had spoken often of his meeting with Markish in Tashkent and how he owed his life to him. Many Jews passed through the Markish house in those days— more than one can remember. Many of them survived and have gone to Israel. Even today I frequently come across people whose faces I fail to recognize, who tell me Markish helped them during the war, bolstered their spirits, and saved them for life, for Israel.

Solomon Mikhoels and his family lived not far from us in the Academy of Sciences building. Mikhoels looked in on us often, signaling his arrival by a shrill whistle.

A major event in our life in Tashkent was the lottery organized by the Committee for Aid to Children of Soldiers at the Front. One day, Timosha Peshkova, Gorky's daughter-in-law, came around to ask me to work with the committee. I was only too glad to accept; I'd do anything to brighten up the humdrum existence of the evacuation zone—especially something that would help people who were in a worse situation than we were. The first meeting of the committee took place in Timosha's place. All the ladies from Tashkent's high society were in attendance, and it was there I met Irina Trofimenko, wife of the famous General Trofimenko, who was at the front. Irina lived in Tashkent with her two small sons in a splendid, roomy private house. We took a liking to each other immediately and soon became friends; it was a friendship that was to endure.

Drinking sugarless tea in old Meissen teacups, we discussed the arrangements for the lottery. All receipts, naturally, were to go to the aid fund for children of soldiers at the front. We decided to organize several concerts with the participation of well-known Moscow artists, and to make the lottery the high point of the entire affair. The first prize, it was agreed, would be a live sheep. Not only was the prize an unusual one, but it held out the major attraction of providing the winner with nearly forty-five pounds of meat. The second prize would be a torte, the third, a small cake; additional prizes would be wearing apparel, shoes, and so on. Naturally, we had none of these things—neither a sheep, nor tortes, nor shoes. So we decided to ask the government of Uzbekistan to provide us with those items. In our letter of request, we agreed to assume responsibility for the organization and conduct of the lottery: it would be up to us to locate the sheep, to

123

number and fold the lottery tickets, to sell them, and to make arrangements with the artists.

After the letter was drafted, I left Timosha's in the company of Irina Trofimenko, and we agreed that the next meeting would be held in her place. In reply to our letter the authorities informed us of their support for our project and promised to provide us with a sheep. The literary wives accordingly assembled at Irina's house to work out further details, this time with some of the husbands present. Irina laid out a regal feast for those wartime days: sandwiches, cakes, wine. . . . Thereafter, it became the custom for the impoverished writers to drop in at Irina Trofimenko's regularly: it was a pleasure to pass the time in her magnificent and relatively well-provided-for home to reminisce about the past and make plans for the future. The habitués were somewhat apprehensive that the general and master of the house might turn up; to judge from the newspapers, which carried a great deal about him, he was a fearless swordsman, a harsh despot, and God knows what else. Would a combat general have any use for a literary salon? Might he not want to "liquidate" it, in the natural order of things?

Happily these fears proved groundless: Sergei Trofimenko did not return from the front until the end of the war, and when the majority of the habitués of the "salon" finally made his acquaintance in Moscow, they discovered a fine man who treated them with tact and respect.

The lottery preparations were now going ahead full steam. We knocked on the door of everyone of any importance in Tashkent, selling tickets for the concert. Academicians, military men, Party workers—we didn't miss a trick. The tickets were expensive, we obtained the use of the auditorium free of charge, and the actors, of course, received no fee.

The benefit took place at the Tashkent Opera House. The *pièce de résistance* of the evening was a short play written especially for the occasion by Alexei Tolstoy, who acted in it along with Mikhoels. The lottery was held the following day. A ticket office was set up in the municipal park, and all Tashkent came to view the coveted sheep peacefully grazing on the lawn of the park under the vigilant eye of a guard. To raise as much money as possible, we wanted to have three separate drawings, which would mean we'd have to get another two sheep. We knew that was impossible, but we also knew that if we saved the sheep for the third and final drawing, no one would buy tickets to the first two.

And so we hit upon an innocent subterfuge: the first two evenings, one of our "own" people—a member of the committee—would draw the winning ticket. This was just what happened. Amid the good-humored but disappointed moans and groans of those whom fortune had passed by, the stubborn sheep was led away on a rope. Within an hour after the public had dispersed, the sheep was returned to the grazing place. On the third evening, some lucky Uzbek really won the prize, and fresh meat undoubtedly garnished his plate of *plov,* the traditional Uzbek meat and rice dish.

The Uzbek's good fortune was the sheep's misfortune, but our own lot was none too enviable either. We were living from hand to mouth. I became obsessed with the thought of a casserole of fried potatoes. Little David—and he was continually being punished for it—would go around to the neighbors begging for food. He devised a rather ingenious system: he would go to Der Nister, for example, and assure him that the night before, at his place, he had not eaten all of his boiled beet peelings and that he now had come to pick them up; or he would try to persuade the wife of the critic Isai Lezhnev that the round of smoked sausage she guarded so lovingly was tasteless, simply horrible, and that he, David, would be happy to take it off her hands. . . . Little by little we grew accustomed to the constant gnaw of hunger until we accepted it as something quite natural.

And lo and behold, one day, on returning home from work, I discovered a whole casserole of smoking fried potatoes on the table! It was like a miracle, a dream come true: just the night before I had told my mother how silly it had been of me, only a year and a half earlier, to turn up my nose at fried potatoes.

Seeing how delighted I was—I couldn't conceal my

feelings—my mother smiled contentedly. I was not fool enough to imagine, however, that some kind person or heavenly angel had brought me such a treasure. And then my mother explained what had happened. On a nearby street, there was a store that purchased gold and other valuables. My mother had gone there and sold the gold crown from one of her teeth, and that was how the fried potatoes appeared on our table.

In our wretched and starving existence, old friendships and new were sorely tested. Our old doctor friend Yakov Bruskin, the professor of medicine, lived opposite us. He was the chief doctor of a large, rear-echelon military hospital, and as such received special food rations. They were by no means large, but still a bit more substantial than the civilian rations. It was March 1942, and we invited the Bruskins over to celebrate the birthday of our elder son Simon, who had just turned eleven. That morning Simon went off to the bake shop to pick up a ration of black bread for the party. He returned empty-handed.

"Where's the bread?" I asked.

Simon looked down guiltily at his hands, as if astonished to discover that they were empty.

"I must have eaten it up absentmindedly," he muttered.

We were in a fix; there would be no bread for the guests. Bruskin learned of our plight through his wife, to whom I had told the story. When they came that evening, he triumphantly drew out of his briefcase the finest gift that money could buy: two chunks of black bread. It was an act of true friendship, for the Bruskins were left without any bread for themselves.

The rumble of war was scarcely audible in faraway Tashkent, and we heard only occasional echoes, but echoes that were sometimes painful. A letter arrived: my beloved Uncle Naum, my mother's brother, had fallen at Sevastopol. Two cousins of mine were also lost.

Meanwhile, my brother Shura continued to languish in a far northern camp, powerless to offer his life in the struggle against German fascism, but liable to be cut down any day by his fellow Russians or perish from starvation and disease. I received news about Shura from someone who knew him in prison. The letter, which had been smuggled out from behind the barbed wire by some kind soul and dropped in a mailbox, said that the camp was in the throes of famine. The inmates were receiving no rations and eating grass and roots, and, if they were lucky, the meat of horses, dead of glanders, that they dug out of the ground. Political prisoners were not being released even if their term was up; orders had come through to extend their sentences—Shura had been given an extra ten years on top of his original term of eight. He was accused, as I mentioned earlier, of planning to build an airplane in his barracks and desert to the enemy!

Word reached us from Lyalya's mother in Potma—she was sick and starving. We in Tashkent didn't know whether we would ever again see our relatives who were in the camps, or whether the fate of the troops at the front was awaiting them.

In January 1943, Irina Trofimenko decided to join her husband at the front, and she agreed to take me along to Moscow so I could see Markish. General Trofimenko's orderly, Petrenko, came to pick us up in Tashkent and accompany us on our journey westward.

Moscow creaked and groaned under a bitter frost; the buildings were without heat. I found Markish at home, living in the kitchen, the only room where there was a bit of warmth. Wearing his naval officer's coat with a blanket thrown over his shoulders, Markish sat at his typewriter by the gas range, which emitted a weak bluish flame. He slept on the bed of our loyal servant Lena Khokhlova, which was in the kitchen, and Lena, who was small and hunchbacked, slept on the stove.

The war had receded westward, far from Moscow, and Markish agreed that I should return home with the children. In a few days, he managed to scare up the necessary papers, and I went back to Tashkent to pack up. I sold the last of my valuable possessions, a karakul coat, and with the money I bought sugar, rice, flour, and dried raisins. There was enough to get us through our first weeks in Moscow.

Markish met us at the station with a small truck—

there were no taxis, and he hadn't been able to get hold of an automobile. It was April and the cold was subsiding. We had hope in our hearts as we threw open the doors of our apartment on Gorky Street— perhaps the war would soon be over, Shura would be released, we would begin to live like normal human beings. . . .

Could we ever have imagined then that the victory over Nazi Germany was to usher in the most terrible period in our lives?

12 / "Jews Excepted"

WE SET about refurnishing the apartment. The rooms looked strange, the objects unfamiliar—all except the antique secretary that we had acquired from the Rohrs, which gleamed with its warm, mahogany glow.

Markish's naval officer's uniform became him; he seemed more slender than before, and taller. He didn't wear his officer's dagger, but kept it in his desk drawer out of reach of the children. (Someone we knew had been placed under house arrest for the loss of his personal arm—his dagger had been stolen in the subway. Markish had no desire to be confined, even if only under house arrest.)

The problems connected with the moving, the spate of domestic concerns, Moscow's dank weather after the sunny warmth of Tashkent—it was all too much for me. In those days, Markish enjoyed special privileges, and as a member of his family I was admitted to the Kremlin hospital. After years of wartime privation, the "Kremlyovka" was like paradise. The patients received the same rations as Kremlin officials, and the food was excellent and abundant. I did not feel quite right about it; Markish and the children had long since forgotten what ham, caviar, salmon, and many other things looked like. Visitors were permitted in the Kremlyovka two days a week, and I set aside some of the food I was served for visiting days, passing it on to Markish or my mother. This touched Markish and he was even a bit proud of me. One day he sent me this humorous message:

Ever so charitable Esther!

The family of the impecunious writer Peretz Markish expresses its gratitude to you for providing it regularly with products of first necessity, made possible by your steadfast love and capricious arteries.

We promise to trade in your capricious arteries for a ravenous appetite.

Your family thanks you all the same for relieving it of its anxieties.

Markish.

Life in the hospital was like that in a sanatorium in peacetime, although one day there was an air-raid warning and we were all rushed to a bomb shelter. The nurses ran from one floor to another comforting the nervous Party members and their panic-stricken wives.

We were already settled in a comfortable bomb shelter when the door opened and in walked Litvinov. I was reminded of my meeting with the famous diplomat long before the war in connection with the Stavisky Affair. Litvinov was not looking too well, and he had aged.

"Hello," Litvinov said to all of us. But I was the only one who acknowledged his greeting.

The man sitting next to me—the secretary of some provincial Party committee—registered astonishment. "Why, do you know him?" he asked. "That's Litvinov!"

From a Party boss's point of view, to acknowledge the greeting of someone you didn't know was shocking.

Litvinov, intellectual that he was, visibly sensed the deep chasm that existed between him and the "new generation" of leaders—the bureaucrats, the technocrats, and other such *apparatchiki*.

No matter how pleasant it was for me to fatten up my family on the largesse of the Kremlin, I had no desire to prolong my stay in the hospital. The older children had to go to school, and I was terribly lonesome for my younger son, David. So I returned home from the hospital.

While I was away an incident had occurred that shocked and distressed Markish. He had submitted one of his war poems to *Pravda*. When some time had passed and the poem had not appeared in the paper, Markish decided to phone Pospelov, the editor-in-chief, and ask what the reason was for the delay. Instead of answering him, Pospelov invited Markish to come to his office and discuss it.

After a few empty words and some beating around the bush, Pospelov got down to business.

"To publish the Jewish poet Peretz Markish in the central organ of the Communist Party is a matter of high policy," Pospelov declared.

That was in 1944. *Pravda* never again published Markish. Stalin, it must be supposed, had already begun drawing up his plans for the throttling and destruction of Jewish culture and the persecution of the Jews.

On the evening of May 9, 1945, Markish and I met Mikhoels in the Yiddish Theater. Before the curtain went up, the actor Zilberblat came out on the stage. He struggled to hold back his emotions, and there was a long moment of silence. Then, his eyes filled with tears and he cried in a heartrending voice, "The news has just come over the radio: the war is over! The Germans have capitulated!"

With all due apologies to the author, the name of whose play I've forgotten, I must confess our minds were elsewhere. The actors didn't have their heart in the play either; they just wanted to get it over with as soon as possible and take off their makeup and costumes. Here and there in the auditorium, people were talking; ripples of laughter were heard at the most incongruous moments. After the first act, a good half of the audience left and headed for the theater buffet, where they sat drinking, weeping, laughing, and raising toasts to the victory. The future looked as bright as a warm sunny day.

A few days later, Irina Trofimenko telephoned to tell me that she was leaving for Hungary to join Sergei—his army unit was at Lake Balaton—but that they would be back shortly because her husband would be participating in the victory parade in Moscow. Irina asked how we were getting on and promised to call on her return.

On May 23, the telephone rang and it was the general himself. "This is Trofimenko speaking. Thank you for your kindness to my Irina in Tashkent. All she talks about is you, and she also told me about Solomon Mikhoels."

"Well, come now," I said, not knowing how one speaks to a famous general, "Irina and I are, after all, very good friends."

Just like a military man, Trofimenko came straight to the point. "I have a request to make of you. Tomorrow is the parade, and afterward we would like to celebrate in an appropriate manner. I don't have to tell you how impersonal restaurants are. Irina tells me you have a large apartment. Would it be all right if we came by with a dozen generals? I trust your friends won't mind sitting down at the same table with us," Sergei joked.

"Of course, of course, we'd be delighted," I said, wondering frantically where I would be able to find the food and wine.

"Then it's all arranged," the general concluded. "Tomorrow morning I'll have everything delivered to your house, and you can expect us in the evening. Now, here's Irina, she wanted to ask you herself, but I took the bull by the horns."

The next morning, army orderlies appeared at our door bearing baskets filled with German sausage, American ham, Italian wines, and French brandy. The sight of this parade of food drove our son David wild —he had never seen such abundance before. The thing that fascinated him more than anything else was

131

a tall bottle of liqueur—it was as tall as he was—inside of which a shrub seemed to be growing.

Toward evening, the guests started to arrive: generals in full-dress uniforms, their chests covered with medals from shoulder to waist. They were simple people of modest upbringing and, like all simple people, they conducted themselves with marked respect toward the writers who were with us that evening: Vsevolod Ivanov and his wife Tamara, Mikhoels and his wife, Alexei Tolstoy's widow Lyudmilla, Gorky's daughter-in-law Timosha, and so on. The dinner was lively; we ate a great deal and drank still more. We talked about the war, the generals reminiscing about their wartime experiences, and we honored those who had fallen in battle. I watched Markish—as usual he wasn't drinking, but he was listening intently. I could see from the involuntary twitching in his cheek muscles that he was on edge, and I knew the reason: he was waiting for someone to say something about the millions of Jews who had been exterminated during the war. But nobody said anything.

When the round of toasts had come to an end, Markish filled his glass and rose to his feet. A hush came over the gathering, and then he spoke: "I want to raise my glass to the hospitality that the Russian people have given to my people, the Jewish people."

There was a moment of silence and then Vladimir Sudets, a general in the air force, exclaimed, "Come now, Peretz Davidovich, what hospitality are you speaking of? Why this is your home!"

Markish stubbornly shook his head and repeated, "I drink to your hospitality. . . ."

There was another victory toast that I will never forget as long as I live. That same day, at a solemn reception following the victory parade, Stalin raised his glass and said, "I drink to the great Russian people!" His words were interpreted as a clarion call to action.

Postwar times were almost as grim and disorganized as the war period had been. For the "chosen few," however, depending on their position in the Soviet Table of Ranks, special centers—closed to the general

132

public—for the distribution of food and consumer's goods were established. Markish, a holder of the Order of Lenin, was placed in Category A and had the right to purchase products in the distribution center that opened up in our apartment house. (The same distribution system is still in force today for the Party and governmental élite.) One could purchase, with coupons and in very limited quantities, sugar, candy and bakery products. Oils and some meat products were also available. These rations could be supplemented on the black market, but that required a lot of money, which was a problem. At the beginning of the war deposits in savings accounts were frozen, and after the war only a very small sum could be withdrawn each month.

We never sent our children to the distribution center, or *limitny* store, as it was also called. If, God forbid, our ration book was lost, that meant a whole month without provisions.

One day, though, Lyalya inadvertently went off to the *limitny* store with seven-year-old David. His eye was taken by a gorgeous ball of chocolate in the window. It was wrapped in silver paper and tied with a red ribbon, and it had a surprise inside. There was no way of dragging David away. Lyalya clutched the ration book tightly in her hand as she listened to the arguments of her younger brother. David was quite a smooth talker and he managed to persuade Lyalya that the surprise inside the ball of chocolate would cover the cost of the coupons spent on the ball itself. To make a long story short, Lyalya let herself be taken in by her brother and the ball was bought. The upshot was that we were without sugar for a week; the surprise, a small porcelain fox figurine, ate up the coupons of one week's ration. There was no use scolding David; it wasn't the chocolate that delighted him, but his success in carrying off the operation.

All of these everyday problems, with their joys and sadness, passed Markish by. He secluded himself again in his sparsely furnished study, which contained a desk, a couch, an easy chair, and a few bookcases, and worked from morning to noon, as before. Lena Khokhlova, who idolized Markish, used to prepare a

133

special treat for him: every week she baked him a shortcake, using ingredients she diverted from essential food supplies. The cake had its traditional place on a bookshelf in Markish's study and there awaited its inevitable fate.

No one entered Markish's study in the morning hours to disturb him. Such was the law of the house known to family and friends alike. If the children were at home, they walked in the corridor on tiptoe. But there was one exception to the rules: at around ten o'clock in the morning, little David would scratch at the door of his father's study waiting for the official command to come in. David thereupon would enter, greet his father and say, "I've come for my literary ration." Markish would get up from his desk, take the cake down from the shelf and give his son a slice. The delivery of his "literary ration" became a tradition in the house, and David, not without reason, came to regard it as his special privilege.

After overcoming Markish's resistance to innovation, I insisted on renovating the apartment. For two weeks, the workmen turned the place upside down. They made a terrible mess, drinking vodka all the while and making lots of noise. Finally, they finished the job and the rooms glistened with their fresh coats of paint. But only a few days later I discovered that the wall in the children's room—the largest of all—was covered with pencil marks.

"Who did that, you, David?" I asked, certain I was not mistaken.

David did not deny it. "I was drawing a horse," he said, sensing the coming storm.

He was not wrong, and he was put in a corner for a long time. Taking pity on the youngster, Lena Khokhlova brought him food. David gradually accustomed himself to the new condition and was feeling himself again, so much so that one time when Lena came with his plate of food, she discovered him, pencil in hand, busily at work on the desecrated wall.

"What *are* you doing?" she scolded in a loud whisper.

"I'm finishing up the horse's tail," he proudly answered.

For a long time after, Markish told his friends about the incident. I don't think he was the least bit sore at his son for his stubbornness. Markish had undergone a considerable change during the past ten years. He had become more mellow, and more considerate toward me and the children. In the summer of 1945, we rented a dacha in the outskirts of Moscow and Markish occasionally took walks with the children. Once, returning with David, he said to me, "Your elder son will bring you much happiness. He will be a wise and learned man. But don't expect any joy from your younger son; he's going to be a writer."

"But what makes you think so?" I asked.

"Dashka [his pet name for David] just told me something about butterfly wings. . . ."

Markish was right.

The two years after the war showed no promise of a change for the better. Zhdanov's condemnation of a group of Leningrad writers and of the magazine *Zvezda* ("The Star") in August 1946 caused disarray in writers' circles.* The review was shut down, an act that was taken by the leadership of the Writers' Union as a call to action against all manifestations of free thought in literature and art.

Markish meanwhile was finishing his epic poem "The War," which was twenty-two thousand lines long on completion. At the same time he wrote some lyric poems of inspired, limpid beauty. He hoped to publish them in a book, but this wish was not to be realized during his lifetime.

"The War" was assailed by a group of Jewish rhymesters who hated Markish for his talent and cowered before his strength.

Markish treated literature with the consideration

In the Soviet Union, during the period immediately following World War II, Andrei Zhdanov, a Politburo member and leading spokesman on doctrinaire questions, was responsible for the imposition of the socialist-realist style on the arts and for the attack on Western influence in the arts and scholarship. It was the *Zhdanovshchina*, or, loosely, "period of Zhdanov."—Ed.

that a great master always manifests toward his art. When literature was at stake, Markish shed his characteristic goodness and compassion; considerations of friendship and propriety were of no account. He was brutally frank and caustic. And, as might be expected, people who were devoid of talent could not forgive him. They openly—though more often, anonymously—accused Markish of Jewish nationalism, at that time the worst possible indictment. They even accused him of "writing too much," thereby depriving others of the possibility of writing and publishing! The fact is that when Markish published "The War," he refused a part of his royalties in favor of the publishing house so as to enable it to purchase new printing presses and type.

The first tangible anti-Semitic blow was struck by the prominent Russian writer Nikolai Tikhonov (who is now chairman of the Soviet Peace Committee). In the summer of 1946, he wrote an article entitled "In Defense of Pushkin" (*Sovetskaya Kultura,* No. I), which took issue with Isaac Nusinov's treatment of Pushkin in his book *Pushkin and World Literature* (1941). Calling Nusinov "a vagabond without a passport," and "an Ivan who has forgotten his roots," Tikhonov blasted Nusinov's conceptions about the Western precursors of Pushkin. He turned himself inside out to "protect" the Russian Pushkin from Western culture and, simultaneously, from the Jew Nusinov. The article had strong anti-Semitic overtones.

A scapegoat had been needed, and was readily found among the Jews, a "foreign body." The first was Isaac Nusinov.

Nusinov answered the attack with his article "In Defense of the Truth," but the literary authorities refused to allow it to be published. The writings of the great Russian poet were beyond the competence of a passportless vagrant like Nusinov; only Russians could write about Pushkin.

Nusinov decided to take up the matter with Aleksandr Fadeyev, general secretary of the Writers' Union. Fadeyev read the article and promised to help, but he was powerless to do anything about it. He did not enjoy undisputed authority.

Nusinov held his ground for a long time, but finally

his resistance was broken. At a closed meeting of the Writers' Union, he recanted—recognized his errors and promised to make amends for them. Nusinov wanted to live, and he knew that if he didn't buckle under he would end up in prison.

Markish was present at that closed meeting, and he came home depressed and disheartened. He didn't condemn Nusinov; he merely tried to analyze in good conscience what had happened. And he understood only too well where it was all leading.

The "campaign against the pernicious influence of the West" went ahead full tilt. The protagonists vied zealously with each other. One fine day the candy American Nuts was renamed Southern Nuts; French rolls became city rolls; Jewish sausage, dry sausage, et cetera. People were afraid of dressing in foreign clothes or reading foreign literature: it could get you into considerable trouble or even land you in jail.

In tsarist Russia, restricting the rights of Jews had been a matter of legislation, the statutes always carefully denoted with the phrase "Jews Excepted." Now the restricting process would take the form of a campaign against "cosmopolitanism," a euphemism for Semitism. It began on a nationwide scale February 2, 1949 (five days following Markish's arrest) with an article in *Pravda* entitled "Concerning One Anti-Party Group of Theater Critics." It was unsigned, a sure indication that it emanated from the highest authority. The article called to account a number of critics who allegedly refused to recognize the singular achievements of contemporary Soviet drama. Some of the critics bore unmistakably Jewish names, and for most of the others, "parentheses were opened up," as the saying went at the time: alongside his Russian pseudonym the individual's real name was given in parentheses—for example, "Yakovlyev (Kholtsman)." There could be no mistake not only about the anti-Semitic tone of the article, but also about its directive nature: Jews are incapable of loving and appreciating Russian culture, the highest culture in the world, the source of all major discoveries in science and in the arts. Anti-Semitism thus fit in neatly with the theory of Russian primacy in all fields of knowledge (everything in the world, from the wheel to the splitting of the atom, was invented or discovered by the Russians); and it was this theory that crowned the edifice of chauvinistic isolationism that Stalin had already begun to erect during the war.

The *Pravda* article set the stage for anti-Jewish purges in all branches of the economy and culture throughout the country. The "rootless cosmopolitans" (the Yids) were driven from their posts with no hope of finding other suitable employment, and in many cases were sent to prison. Strange as it may seem, especially to a Western reader, those whom the press covered with mud and filth were rarely sent away to prison, whereas practically no mention was made of those who were imprisoned or would eventually be.

The press played up the story of two microbiologists, the Russian Klyuyeva and the Jew Roskin, to whom she was married. They had been working on the problem of the early diagnosis of cancer and had developed a preparation called "KR." News about KR filtered through to the West, where scientists naturally manifested interest in the work of their Soviet colleagues. In no time at all, Klyuyeva and Roskin were practically accused of being spies. "Letters of workers and peasants," which have long been a permanent feature of the Soviet scene, flooded the central press. The correspondents condemned the "traitors" and demanded that they be dealt with mercilessly. (Similarly, in the post-Stalin period, Soviet citizens wrote in to condemn Pasternak after he was awarded the Nobel Prize, and more recently the same procedures were used against Sakharov and Solzhenitsyn.)

Faced with the threat of arrest, Klyuyeva and Roskin made a public recantation. The question of how anyone could possibly conceal from the world a breakthrough in the fight against one of mankind's most fatal diseases never came up.

One writer, Alexander Shtein, who was, by the way, of Jewish descent, made his career out of the Klyuyeva-Roskin affair. He slapped together a play called *The Court of Honor*. The Party lavished praise on the author and millions of spectators throughout the country flocked to see it. Shtein even received a Stalin Prize.

As soon as our life returned more or less to normal, I had decided to resume my postgraduate studies. The subject of my thesis was "Linguistic Particularities in Molière's Dramatic Works and His Literary Entourage." I had already begun working on this subject while I was a student at the IFLI. Now that it was closed down, I had to make other arrangements, so I went to the Chief Administration of Educational Establishments to discuss my problem. Friends told me that I was sure to encounter difficulties in the realization of my study plans, because postgraduate work was practically closed to Jews. But I myself had not yet come up against anti-Semitism of this kind and refused to believe them.

The deputy head of the chief administration, a man by the name of Gusev, received me in his office. The first thing I noticed was that he had a complete set of stainless-steel teeth; his mouth shone like silver tableware. Gusev looked hastily through my documents. My family name, Lazebnikova, sounded Russian enough, but it seemed to intrigue him. He kept repeating it aloud, over and over again as if it were causing him some doubts.

After I had explained my project, Gusev smiled broadly, baring his steel teeth, and said, "But Molière, who needs him? Who's interested in him? Now suppose you dealt with someone like the great Russian playwright and scholar Ivan Fonvizin!"

To suggest that I, a graduate of the Faculty of Romance and German Languages and Literatures, do work on such a minor literary figure—at least, compared with Molière—was either plain mockery or sheer ignorance on his part. I was terribly disappointed.

As it happened, that very same evening, Nikolai Gudzy, a brilliant scholar and literary specialist, paid us a call. He had formerly been the head of the Faculty of Russian Literature at the IFLI and now held the same chair at Moscow University.

When I told him about my visit to Gusev, Gudzy said, "You'd better forget about your doctoral studies. They have orders not to accept Jews. I'm a Russian and I'm ashamed to have to say this to you."

As Markish listened in silence, there was a nervous twitching in his cheeks. It was only after Gudzy had left that he spoke. "This is in the same vein as my conversation with Pospelov. It's state policy. . . ."

Markish withdrew increasingly into himself, working more feverishly than ever, as if there were no time to lose, on his epic poem "The War," his big, thousand-page novel *The March of Generations,* and his collection of lyric poetry. He seemed to accept, almost with a sense of relief, the fact that he was gradually being eased out of Jewish public activity. The person responsible was the Yiddish poet Itzik Feffer, who had received one of the lesser awards at the same time Markish received his Order of Lenin, in 1939. Markish regarded him as an intriguer and troublemaker, phony and doctrinaire.

Feffer came from Kiev after the war and settled in Moscow, bringing along several of his cronies, one of whom was the poet Gontar, who is poetry editor of *Sovyetish heymland,* the unique Yiddish-language journal published today in the Soviet Union. (The journal's editor-in-chief is Aron Vergelis, who docilely gratifies every whim and fancy of his masters, the pogromists of the KGB and of the Propaganda Department of the Party Central Committee.)

Markish had nothing to do with the split in the ranks of the Jewish writers into two camps, the Markishists and the Fefferists, but such a split did occur. Very few remained in the Markish camp, but this was not at all surprising: the Jewish Antifascist Committee held the power and the purse strings, and Feffer was its deputy chairman. (It is worth noting that at the beginning of the end, sometime in 1948, many Fefferists, especially those of the younger generation, including the notorious Aron Vergelis, sought a rapprochement with Markish.) Feffer "the Pure" (unlike the majority of Jewish writers, he had not been in the postrevolutionary emigration), disdained neither intrigue nor denunciation to make his way to the top. He was abetted in his enterprise by the executive secretary of the Antifascist Committee in which Feffer, as deputy chairman, occupied the role of "commissar." The first test of strength was Feffer's trip to America during

140

the war. Originally Mikhoels and Markish, as cochairmen of the Jewish Antifascist Committee, were to have gone, but this decision was reversed in favor of the "iron man of the Party," Feffer.

Unable to vie with Markish in the field of poetry, Feffer continued to impede him. As it happened, Markish, who was in charge of the Yiddish broadcasting service, had hired a hapless Jewish writer from Minsk by the name of Katsovich. In the panic and chaos of the evacuation, Katsovich had lost—in the literal meaning of the word—his two children, and he never found them again. He was a conscientious though not particularly gifted worker. Once a week he came to see Markish on radio matters. One day, when Markish was sick (he was often troubled by throat infections), Katsovich appeared. Since Markish was unable to speak, he wrote down his instructions on a piece of paper. His visitor was visibly ill at ease—in fact, he seemed paralyzed. Katsovich finally broke his silence: "Markish, I've come to take things over from you. I've been named to your post."

It's worth saying a few words here about the organization of the Yiddish broadcasting service that was set up after the outbreak of the war. The broadcasts were transmitted by short wave and were destined for Jewish listeners in the United States. The emphasis was on news and propaganda, and the broadcasts were intended to acquaint Jews in the West with the situation in Russia while playing on Jewish national sentiments. Moscow was only too well aware of the influence wielded by the American Jewish community and hoped to enlist its aid as far as possible. While Markish was in charge, the broadcasts concentrated on the common struggle against fascism, and he brought in several Jewish writers to serve as editors, among them, David Vendrov and Samuel Halkin.

Following Markish's dismissal, the work of the editors took on a more distinct political coloration. In the postwar drive against Jewish culture, the Yiddish radio was shut down, and many of its collaborators were arrested. It is interesting to note that Yiddish-language broadcasts have now been resumed and are engaged in violent, anti-Israeli propaganda. One of the stalwarts of the editorial desk is *Sovyetish heymland*'s editor, Aron Vergelis, who had also worked in the Yiddish broadcasting service toward the end of the forties. When it was closed down, however, he came through unscathed and no action was ever taken against him.

Once, during a meeting, Markish disputed Feffer's contention that a distinction should be made between Polish Jews, Russian Jews, et cetera. He considered it improper and misconceived: there was a single Jewish people throughout the world. A formulation such as Markish's was "suspect" and "dangerous" at that time: the war was over and, in the eyes of the authorities, Jewish solidarity in the struggle against fascism was becoming a "conspiracy of the Elders of Zion," an "instrument of imperialism," and so on.

Relations between Markish and the Feffer group became even more strained, and in late 1947, Writers' Union Secretary Fadeyev asked his friend Markish to come and see him on a matter of the utmost urgency. Fadeyev informed Markish that certain individuals had sent a denunciation of him to the Central Committee, accusing him of Zionism and Jewish bourgeois nationalism. Substantiation for these charges was supposedly to be found in "A Conversation with the Devil," one of the chapters in Markish's poem "The War." The denunciation had been referred to the Writers' Union with instructions that they should examine the incriminating chapter and send their recommendation to the Central Committee. With a wave of his hand, Markish dismissed this fresh attack as utter nonsense, but Fadeyev told him that the matter was very serious and that both Feffer and Shakhno Epstein had signed the denunciation.

Returning home after his meeting with Fadeyev, Markish asked me to sit down at the Russian typewriter. Nervously pacing back and forth, he began dictating an interlinear translation of "A Conversation with the Devil." The chapter dealt with the millions of Jews who had perished during the war and with the future of the Jewish people.

Markish submitted the translation to Fadeyev, who defended the chapter before the Central Committee.

Thanks to his intervention, the chapter was published in the Yiddish edition of "The War." (In the Russian version, translated by our son David and published after Markish's rehabilitation, this chapter, as well as a few others, was not included; it was also deleted by the censors from all later posthumous editions of Markish's works on the same grounds as those cited in the original denunciation.)

Around the same time a group of leading Jewish public figures, headed by Mikhoels and Feffer, were summoned by Vyacheslav Molotov, secretary of the Party's Central Committee, and Lazar Kaganovich, vice-president of the Council of Ministers. Markish was not among those summoned, so he learned the substance of the conversation at a meeting of the presidium of the Jewish Antifascist Committee. The "summit" meeting had discussed reviving an idea that had already been proven a fiasco—the idea of Birobidzhan, the Jewish Autonomous Province that Markish and a group of other writers had visited in 1934. Molotov and Kaganovich proposed that the Jewish Antifascist Committee send a letter to Stalin requesting that the Crimea be transformed into a Jewish republic. The letter had been drafted and Markish was now asked to sign it.

Markish refused to have anything to do with the proposal. It was the Tatars, he maintained, who had a right to the Crimea, and he regarded the proposal as a gross and blatant provocation. He thereupon drafted a letter of his own in which he suggested that the Jews be given the territory of the former Republic of the Volga Germans, with Engels as its capital. Such an act, Markish wrote, would be of the "greatest historical justice" after all the Germans had done to the Jewish people.

Markish's letter received no support—no one dared oppose the Molotov-Kaganovich proposal. Markish stood by his opinion, however, and continued in his refusal to endorse the original proposal.

On another occasion, Markish returned home from a meeting of the Antifascist Committee more dejected and dispirited than ever. He had learned that thousands of Jews who had survived the war were addressing letters to the Committee asking it to facilitate their emigration to Palestine. These letters were being forwarded to the Ministry of State Security, and Markish was sure that Feffer was behind it.

This was the last straw. Markish refused to have anything further to do with the Antifascist Committee. He now avoided contact with people engaged in "cultural policy," and even went so far as to refuse to participate in an evening celebrating the jubilee of Sholem Aleichem, organized by the Antifascist Committee. It was held in the Hall of Columns of the House of the Trade Unions and had a markedly propagandistic character. At the last minute, however, I persuaded Markish to go; his absence on the presidium would be considered an affront and would undoubtedly have unpleasant consequences. Markish and I walked to the Hall of Columns and just as we reached the entrance, he stopped. "I can't do it, I won't go—all that band inside . . . " And we turned around and walked home.

On January 13, 1948, all dissension came to an end: Mikhoels was dead, the extermination of Jewish culture had begun, and the attempt to find, once and for all, "the final solution to the Jewish question" was under way.

On January 2, 1948, the Trofimenkos telephoned us from Minsk, where Sergei Trofimenko was commander of the Byelorussian Military District, to wish us a happy New Year and invite us to come and stay with them. Knowing that Mikhoels was leaving for Minsk to judge some plays that were being considered for the Stalin Prize, we decided to go along with him.

We had already bought our train tickets and only a few hours remained before our departure when Markish was compelled to cancel our trip: the page proofs of a forthcoming book required his urgent attention. I was terribly disappointed. So Mikhoels left without us, accompanied by the theater critic Golubov, who was also going to Minsk in connection with the Stalin Prize selection.

On the thirteenth I was giving a French lesson in

the studio of the Yiddish Theater, where I had been working since my return from Tashkent in 1943. Suddenly the door opened and Podryadchik, the studio's supervisor of studies, came rushing in to say that the director, Moisei Belenky, wanted to see me at once.

Something has happened to the children! was my only thought as I hurried to Belenky's office.

The director was sitting behind his desk. His face was ashen and there was terror in his eyes.

"What has happened?" I cried, sensing disaster.

"The old man is dead," he said. "He was run over. That's all I know."

Classes were dismissed; students and teachers left for home. I had hardly stepped into the apartment when I heard the intermittent buzzing of the telephone that announced a long-distance call. It was Irina Trofimenko calling from Minsk.

"It's all true," Irina said. "Mikhoels is dead."

The next day Markish and I went to the Dyelorusse sian Station to meet the train carrying the old man. Two zinc caskets were removed from the train bearing the bodies of Mikhoels and Golubov. The latter had been killed to dispose of an embarrassing witness.

Mikhoels's corpse was taken to the Yiddish Theater, where it was to lie in state beginning at noon. Crowds of people coming to pay their last respects to the great actor had been thronging to the theater since early morning.

Markish and I were waiting in the lobby. It was already past twelve when Markish clambered up the staircase leading to the auditorium, where Professor Zbarsky, who had embalmed Lenin, was working on Mikhoels.

A few moments later, Markish returned to the lobby, white as a sheet. "Don't go up there!" he said, pointing to the closed door of the auditorium. "It's not the old man any more!" And, after a short pause, "Now there's nobody left for me to have a real argument with."

Until five o'clock in the evening, Zbarsky worked on the crushed head of Mikhoels, trying to make it look human again. And then the crowds poured into the theater as if the floodgates had opened up.

"Find me a room someplace," Markish asked me calmly, "and don't let anyone in."

We went backstage and found a dressing room. Then I left.

There, in the dressing room, amid the dull thunder of thousands of tramping feet, Markish composed the first two quatrains of his ode "To Mikhoels—the Eternal Light"—lines that prefigured his own fate:

Dripping blood—that's the most authentic make-
up of all.
Even in death you are alive, and the stars shine
brighter still
Glowing proudly over your final curtain call,
And in the haze of dawn they scintillate applause.

To one of these, shimmering through the mist,
You'll offer up your pain, your anger, your human-
ity.
In the face of Eternity, of your wounds,
Of your torment, be you not ashamed. The shame
is Eternity's.

Mikhoels was given a lavish funeral.

Irina Trofimenko arrived in Moscow soon after and came to see me. Here is what she told me.

The day after Mikhoels's death, she had taken the children to music school. Halfway through the lesson, Sergei Trofimenko came into the classroom and beckoned his wife to the corridor.

"They killed Mikhoels!" he said. "Go home and send a telegram to Solomon Mikhailovich's wife in Moscow."

Sergei returned to his headquarters, and Irina and the children went home. At dinnertime, Sergei asked his wife if she had sent the telegram yet. She had not. "Then don't send it! I had a call from the Central Committee. They categorically advised me not to send a telegram."

In 1956, after my return from exile, I met Irina Trofimenko again. She was now a widow. That evening

146

she invited me to a gathering in her home of Sergei's former comrades-in-arms, including a highly placed general who had served under Trofimenko in Minsk. He told me why Sergei had been forbidden to send a telegram of condolence to Mikhoels's widow:

"In the MGB, they knew very well that Trofimenko was a friend of Mikhoels. They knew Mikhoels had spent his last day at Sergei's and from there had gone to the theater, after which he had been killed. They also knew by whom the murder had been organized . . . and that it was on instructions from Beria, who was acting under orders from Stalin. The only thing they didn't know was how the 'top leadership' would react to the murder, and for that reason they advised the commander of the district to refrain from sending a telegram."

"But," I asked, "how did they know that Sergei was planning to send a telegram?"

The general smiled. "And are you naive enough to think that the commander's chauffeur didn't transmit everything he heard to the MGB? Sergei must have spoken to Irina about the telegram in the presence of the chauffeur. . . ."

13 / Arrest

IN 1948, Markish and I spent our last summer together in Ilinki, not very far from Moscow. We shared a dacha with Der Nister and his wife; they occupied the second floor and we the first. Der Nister was by nature reserved and not very talkative; but that summer he became quite expansive. Markish and he would spend long hours together before sundown talking endlessly. And they were not happy conversations.

Neither Markish nor Der Nister now harbored any illusions about the future of Jewish culture and of Jewry itself in the Soviet Union. The period of postwar anti-Semitism had set in, with all its distinctive features and characteristics. Artificial barriers were placed in the way of Jewish boys and girls seeking higher education. Once again the Soviet Union fell back on the traditional Russian practice of blaming the Jews for everything that went wrong in the country's internal life: the shortage of food and consumer goods, the accelerated tempos in industrial enterprises, the miserable wages, the complete and utter absence of civil liberties. The State did nothing to counter this dangerous evolution and that do-nothing policy only served to fan the flames of anti-Semitism.

Our elder son Simon had just completed his high school education and decided to take the university entrance examination for admission into the Department of Romance and German Studies. It was a hazardous step, since it was common knowledge that Jews stood almost no chance of being admitted. Simon realized that, and he therefore asked his father to have Fadeyev put in a good word for him so that he would be given the same chance as any Russian applicant. After carefully listening to what Simon had to say, Markish told him this:

"You, the son of a Jewish writer, are asking me to help you, a Jew, while other Jews must fend for themselves. That I won't do. You'll have to share the lot of your fellow Jews."

Simon passed his exams so brilliantly that even the university professors were amazed, but he had no great hopes of being accepted. While he was waiting for the decision of the admissions committee, he stayed with us at the dacha. And then one day, out of the blue, the postman brought a telegram from Nusinov, who was still associated with Moscow State University. The telegram was addressed to "Simon Markish, Student at Moscow State University. . . . "

At that time, Markish's daughter, Lyalya, had already been living in Kiev for a year. Her mother had

148

Peretz Markish at 16, 1911. He had already begun to write verse.

Ten-year-old Esther with her mother, Vera Markovna Lazebnikov, and brother, Alexander, Constantinople, 1922.

*Peretz Markish, Paris, 1924. The poet was one of many
intellectuals who had left the Soviet Union for the French capital.*

*Markish, writers David Bergelson and Izi Kharik, and actor
Solomon Mikhoels at soiree honoring Kharik, Moscow, 1935.
Thirteen years later the Soviet campaign to exterminate Jewish
culture would begin. Mikhoels would be one of the earliest
and most prominent victims.*

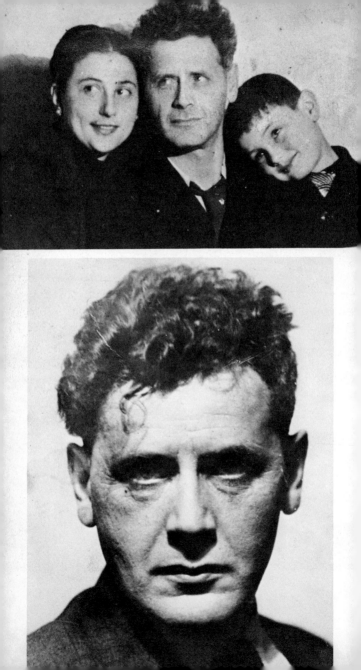

*David with his brother, Simon, and Lena Khokhlova, whose
official function was nursemaid, but who became a beloved
member of the Markish family.*

Opposite, above: *Esther and Peretz Markish with David,
the younger of their two sons, 1946.*

Opposite, below: *Peretz Markish, 1948. He was arrested
the following year.*

Simon, Yura, Markish's nephew, and David in exile village of Karmakchi, Soviet central Asia, 1953. Peretz Markish had been executed the year before, but his family would not be informed until 1955.

decided to settle in a small town in the outskirts of Kharkov. Lyalya, who had just finished high school and had a penchant for design, joined her there and entered the Kharkov Technical Art Institute; at the end of her first semester, she transferred to the Kiev Art Institute.

Markish rarely left the dacha to go to the city that last summer. He finished his novel *The March of Generations* (its original title was *Yevra*) and his book of lyric poetry and submitted the manuscripts to the Yiddish Publishing House, Der Emes. The work had taken a lot out of him and, moreover, he had aged considerably in the course of this terrifying year. That fall, I urged him to get away for a rest at the sanatorium in Kislovodsk. He was lukewarm to the idea, but I managed to persuade him. I saw him off at the station; as usual, he had his briefcase in one hand and his portable typewriter in the other.

Markish was in Kislovodsk when the authorities shut down Der Emes Publishing House on November 17, 1948. The staff had come to work as usual in the little old house on Staropansky Lane. The new linotype machines, which Markish had helped to buy, were humming away. The chief editor Moisei Belenky was in conference with Strongin, the director, when, without a word of warning—as in a movie about Nazi Germany—trucks filled with State Security agents pulled up in front of the house. Soldiers in civilian clothes burst into the printing plant and disconnected the machines. Everything came to a standstill; all was silence.

"Your publishing house is closed down!" one of the pogromists bellowed.

They then proceeded to the second floor, sent the editorial staff packing, and gave orders to Strongin and Belenky to prepare an "act of closure."

Markish learned about all of this on his return from Kislovodsk, when, cursing Stalin and his band of henchmen under his breath, Belenky told Markish the whole story. Strongin had saved Markish's two manuscripts from confiscation, and he now returned them.

Markish lost all hope. He realized the end was near,

149

that it was now only a question of time—days or, at best, months.

Markish had returned from Kislovodsk with a few new poems—serene, meditative lyrical verse. But now he practically stopped writing anything new; he sorted through his archives, rereading the yellowed pages of manuscript without retouching them. One day he showed me some long, narrow, handwritten pages and observed, "This is 'The Forty-Year-Old,' the best thing I've ever written."

Until that moment, Markish had never so much as mentioned this poem to me or published a single line of it.

"I started writing it at the beginning of the twenties," Markish said, as he lovingly rustled the papers before putting them aside.

Shortly thereafter, Markish wrote his last poem. It was fitting and prophetic.

> How much time is left
> Until the bitter end,
> How much time is left for grieving! . . .
> Fill your glass with wine!
> Let's lift our faces to the stars—
> And may our destiny be done!

The month of December 1948 rumbled with the approaching storm. People were afraid to make any contact with one another. The Yiddish Theater was on tour in Leningrad and Zuskin, who succeeded Mikhoels as artistic director, was sick in hospital—for the past several weeks he had been undergoing a sleeping cure. Only a few actors and administrators remained behind in the theater in Moscow.

In the last week of December, Feffer made an unexpected appearance at the theater. He was not alone. The second most feared man in Russia after Stalin, Abakumov, the minister of State Security, accompanied him. Together they proceeded directly to Mikhoels's former office, which had been temporarily turned into a museum. They locked the door behind them and went about their business—searching for something, sorting through papers and documents.

150

You couldn't, after all, expect the minister of State Security to be able to read Yiddish! Moreover, it was not important what Abakumov was looking for or what he did in Mikhoels's office; what was significant was the fact that Itzik Feffer was at his side.

On the night of December 24, the first one to be arrested in his Moscow apartment was Itzik Feffer. He was the first to be taken just because he was their man, a "loyal, tried and true" Party man. The State Security agents could count on his comprehension and cooperation. That same night they picked up Zuskin, whisking him away from the hospital in his sleep wrapped in a blanket. He woke up in Lubyanka.

Long before the night of December 31, we had accepted an invitation to celebrate the New Year outside of Moscow, at the dacha of marshal of the Signal Corps Ivan Peresypkin and his wife, Roza. We had no intention of sitting at home that evening, waiting for a stranger to knock at our door, trembling every time the elevator shut. Peresypkin rang us up at five in the afternoon and said, "My car will be at your door at twenty-one hundred."

And so we went.

Not long after the war, on the day Selikh, the former editor of *Izvestiya,* brought Roza Peresypkina to our apartment, he telephoned Markish and said, "Markish, there's a woman who is dying to have you take a look at her poems. Do me a favor and see her."

An hour later, Selikh showed up with a young woman, a bit on the plump side, but possessing a languorous Semitic beauty heightened by clear, deepblue eyes. Selikh introduced her: "The wife of Marshal Peresypkin of the Signal Corps!"

"You look more like a *rebbetsin* [a rabbi's wife] than the wife of a marshal," Markish ventured.

"I come from Proskurov," Roza explained.

Markish proceeded to tear her poetry apart, but this did not distress her in the least. She had no delusions about her talent. What interested her more than anything else was the chance to meet the famous poet Markish. This was the beginning of our friendship

151

with Roza, who had managed to preserve her Jewishness among the top echelons of the Soviet military and Party hierarchy. Her husband, Marshal Ivan Peresypkin, was a man of courage and integrity who had not been contaminated by the bacillus of anti-Semitism.

Shortly after the close of the Civil War, the cavalry regiment in which Ivan Peresypkin was serving as a private was quartered in the Jewish village of Proskurov. It was there that "Vanya" met Reizl (Roza) and realized he had found his life's partner. Reizl felt exactly the same way about Vanya, and she announced the news to her parents, adding that she planned to go off with him and get married. When her father, an orthodox Jew, heard this, he called down a curse on the head of his daughter, who dared to think of marrying a *goy*. The outcast climbed onto the saddle of her beloved Vanya's horse and together they galloped away from Proskurov.

Vanya was a clean-cut youth of worker and peasant extraction. He quickly made his way up the ladder of success and he and his Jewish wife lived together in harmony. In time, Roza's father grudgingly removed the curse from his daughter and recognized her husband. During the first days of the war, when the Germans were approaching Proskurov, Peresypkin sent an airplane for his wife's parents and the old couple was saved.

"Our Vanechka!" Roza's mother would say later. "He's a *goy* made out of gold! He delivered us from the jaws of death!"

Marshal Peresypkin was not the least bit embarrassed or shocked by the provincial Jewish appearance and Yiddish accent of his parents-in-law, which provoked the mockery and ridicule of the Soviet riffraff.

Roza's mother died and was buried in Moscow. Returning from the cemetery, Roza's father tore his clothes and, in accordance with Jewish law, sat *shivah* in one of the rooms of the elegant Peresypkin apartment. Sharing the affliction of his father-in-law, Peresypkin poured out two glasses of vodka and went to the old man. But he refused to touch the vodka or leave his place on the floor to sit down to the traditional Russian funeral repast.

152

"Well, Papasha," the marshal said, "if that's the way it is, then that's the way it is. You won't mind, then, if I join you on the floor for a while." And he sat down beside him.

On one occasion—it was before Mikhoels had been murdered—Roza came by to see us. Taking me aside, she whispered in my ear, "Please, I implore you, take care. Don't have anything to do with foreigners!"

"What's wrong?" I asked.

"I can't say any more, but I know what I'm talking about. Difficult times lie ahead."

The Peresypkins' dacha was situated in the "government zone" just outside Moscow, on Nikolina Hill. The moment we arrived, I took Roza aside. "Last night, they arrested Zuskin and Feffer!"

"Oh, my God!" Roza exclaimed. "Don't say anything to Vanya. . . ."

The Peresypkins' guests, for the most part, military men, welcomed the new year in boisterously. There was lots of drinking but, as usual, Markish didn't touch a drop.

"Whenever I talk to you, I feel ten feet tall," Ivan told him. "Pity, though, you don't drink."

We got home at daybreak. Near the window on our landing were two State Security agents; they had been posted at our door. Other MGB agents were detailed to shadow Markish. When, for example, he and I went to see a documentary film—on January 10, I think it was—our watchdogs went along and sat on each side of us.

In the middle of January, Markish went to a meeting of the Writers' Union for the last time. They were holding elections to the board. The absence of one of the candidates, Boris Gorbator, was explained when a member of the presidium asked for the floor and read a letter from him in which he asked that his name be removed from the ballot; he declared himself ineligible in view of the fact that twenty-four hours earlier his wife had been arrested.

On January 19, the telephone rang. "N—— is sick," a voice announced: people were afraid to say "arrested" over the phone, so they said "sick." All the rest of that day, people telephoned to inquire if Markish was in good health.

On the morning of the twenty-third, the poet Mikhail Golodny was buried. He had been run over—or run down—by an official car on a Moscow street.

That night others were arrested, among them David Bergelson and Leib Kvitko. The net was closing in. Markish asked Simon to pack up the manuscripts of his novel *The March of Generations,* his last book of poems, and "The Forty-Year-Old." Simon did so, marking the packages with the words "My Archives." I fell sick and took to my bed. There were no meals prepared and the house went unattended.

On the evening of the twenty-seventh, Markish put the packages containing his manuscripts in his traveling briefcase.

" 'The Forty-Year-Old' is the best thing I've ever done," he said again. "I want you to take special care of it."

At about nine that evening, one of my mother's cousins dropped in. I kept to my bed in Markish's study, and Markish went to the kitchen with my mother and her cousin to have some tea. I was feeling very groggy, but could only doze off intermittently; ever since the watchdogs had stationed themselves outside our door, all of us had difficulty in getting to sleep at night.

A few minutes before twelve Markish brought my mother's cousin to the study and silently handed her the briefcase with the manuscripts. She immediately left the apartment with it. The elevator was occupied so she took the staircase. She had just gone down one flight when the elevator stopped at our floor.

Our bell had been out of order for several weeks—it gave off a scarcely audible buzz—and no one had thought of calling an electrician and having it repaired. Markish had returned to the kitchen, where the feeble buzz of the bell could not be heard. I did hear it but did not have the strength to get up. And then they started banging on the door.

Markish went and opened it. I heard the shuffling of many feet in the vestibule. A moment later, Markish appeared in the study, already dressed in his coat, scarf and hat. Seven officers followed him in, their uniforms hidden by their civilian coats with gray karakul collars. On their heads were *shapkas,* trimmed with the same gray karakul. The outfit was itself a uniform familiar to every Soviet citizen, for it identified the wearer as an agent of the MGB.

When I saw them there, standing behind Markish, I screamed.

"Come now, no need to get excited," one of the officers said. "Our minister just wants to have a talk with your husband."

Markish peeked into the room where David was sleeping and then went to the vestibule. Simon and I ran to his side.

"Take it easy, get hold of yourself," one of the officers said. "So you won't feel nervous, one of our men will stay behind with you. Your husband will be back in no time."

Weeping bitterly, our faithful housekeeper Lena Khokhlova threw herself on Markish, but they pulled her away. Six officers led Markish away, the seventh remained behind. He settled into a chair in Markish's study and just sat there in silence for a while. Finally he spoke. "Get everyone together in this room!"

"Our younger child is sleeping," I said.

"All right, no need to bother him. Let him sleep."

Three hours must have passed when the elevator door on our landing closed with a clang, and there was a loud and persistent banging at our door. This time four new MGB agents barged into the apartment with an order for Markish's arrest and a search warrant; they made no effort to reassure us, nor did they stand on ceremony. The first thing they did was to close the shutters tight so that from the street it would appear that we had retired.

I found out much later that, with one exception —Lina Stern—none of Markish's "confederates" was arrested under such strange circumstances. Markish was taken away a few minutes before midnight on January 27, for "talks" with the minister; the order for his arrest was served three hours later and was dated the twenty-eighth; and finally, Markish was the only one not ordered to remove his belt and tie before leaving home.

The search party, led by a lieutenant colonel, attacked the bookcases first. The books were scattered on the floor and each one carefully scrutinized, even to the point of leafing through the pages one by one. Next the household objects: every item was thoroughly probed, shaken down or ripped open. One member of the search party, still a young man, showed particular zeal: he unscrewed bulbs from their sockets, disassembled the table lamps, and even went through the pots and the kettles in the kitchen.

When David, who had just turned ten, woke up the next morning and saw strangers in military uniforms, he asked no questions.

Soon the telephone was ringing. We were not allowed to take calls; it was the lieutenant colonel who took the receiver and answered, "He's not in" or "She's not at home."

By noon everything had been examined except Markish's personal papers. The lieutenant colonel dismissed two of his men and stayed behind with an aide. The apartment had been turned upside down, but the lieutenant colonel kept wandering from room to room as if he were still looking for something. Finally, in the bathroom, he discovered a valise with old papers, among them, materials from the First Congress of Soviet Writers. His face lit up with joy when he came upon a copy of Radek's report at the Congress. He put it aside. He also put aside a fragment of Markish's ode "To Mikhoels—Eternal Light," in Boris Pasternak's translation, as well as a copy of Markish's letter proposing cession to the Jews of the former Republic of the Volga Germans. These documents were packed separately from the others.

A scenario by Markish from which a film had been made before the war caused the lieutenant colonel deep perplexity.

"And this, what is it?" he asked. "A play?"

"It's a scenario for a film," I replied.

"What's that?"

I shrugged my shoulders; my answer couldn't have been more explicit.

"But how should I record it?"

"You can put it down as a film story," I tried to explain. "It comes to the same thing."

The lieutenant colonel drew the confiscation inventory toward him and, breathing hard, wrote down *kenopovist* (a distortion of *kinopovest*, "film story").

From time to time he telephoned a superior, always informing him that "everything was in order."

In the course of the day, several friends and acquaintances dropped by. They were all admitted into the apartment and detained until the perquisition had been completed, which was about midnight. It goes without saying that their papers were checked and the particulars entered into a report. The MGB term for this practice of holding people for questioning is, I think, "mousetrap."

In the evening, the lieutenant colonel informed me that seals would be placed on three of our four rooms and that all of the beds were to be moved into the one remaining room.

"I object," I said. "Leave us two rooms. After all, there's a whole family involved."

He referred the matter to headquarters: "I want to seal three rooms, but she protests and insists on keeping two."

Headquarters apparently agreed to leave us two rooms, and the lieutenant colonel and his aide began transferring into the two back rooms the cartons containing Markish's personal papers and books. After completing the job, he locked the doors and affixed the seals.

"If the seals are broken," he warned, "you'll get at least ten years."

Then the aide went downstairs to get witnesses—the house superintendent and the caretaker—and in their presence the procès-verbal of the perquisition and seizure was signed.

By then I was in a state of nervous collapse. My mother asked the lieutenant colonel for permission to call a doctor. With a smirk on his face, he refused.

At midnight, twenty-four hours after Markish had been led away, the perquisition was over. The lieutenant colonel and his aide left, taking away with them certain papers of Markish's, notably Radek's report, the ode to Mikhoels, and the copy of the letter about the Republic of the Volga Germans.

By one o'clock, those who had been caught in the "mousetrap" were released and we were alone: the children, my mother and myself. The house was in a shambles. Without even undressing, we just collapsed into bed. For the first time in a long time I slept like a log. No longer did we live in mortal terror that Markish would be arrested; what had to happen happened, and all of us, including Markish, had seen it coming.

Early the next morning the telephone rang. Simon got up to answer it. It was Roza Peresypkina.

"Sima," she inquired, "is Papa there?"

"No, Papa isn't here, but Mama is."

"I see," she said, and she hung up.

I neither spoke to Roza Peresypkina nor saw her again until we returned from deportation. I don't hold it against her. After Markish was arrested, many of our "friends" rushed like mad to burn his books, but Marshal Peresypkin kept his copies with Markish's dedications.

Roza's phone call woke us all up, but we didn't stir: we had no desire to get up or do anything in this new life of ours.

"Mama," I called out, "let's open up the gas and be done with it all."

Before my mother even had time to answer, little David had rushed over to my bedside. His face was white as a sheet.

"Mama!" he cried, "I want to live!"

"Did you hear that?" my mother asked. "There you have your answer."

During the day, rumors began to reach us. They spread through the house, sparked by the superintendent or the caretaker's wife or simply by people who delighted in rumor-mongering: Markish was an important American spy—during the perquisition a big sack of dollars had been turned up as well as a radio transmitter that had been concealed in a wall. A few months earlier the same rumor had been started when one of the tenants in our apartment house, the test pilot Farikh, had been arrested. In fact, whenever anyone was arrested in those days, the story was identical.

We had practically no money except for a small sum in Markish's bank account, which he had recently made over to my name. There was a sizable sum of money in Markish's name in the Department of Royalties, but these assets were seized. I made up my mind not to touch the money we did have; it could come in handy later for sending Markish parcels or visiting him if he were sent to a camp.

There was not a soul to be found who had the decency to lend us a helping hand. Our neighbor who lived one floor above us in Alexei Tolstoy's old apartment was a certain general who used to fawn before the "famous Markish" on the rare occasions that my husband dropped by his apartment in response to his repeated invitations. The general was now scared out of his wits. He avoided me like the plague; when he did happen to run into me in the staircase, even though nobody else was in sight, he became panic-stricken.

Fate did not spare him. His daughter married an actor from the provinces and they came to Moscow, where the general got his son-in-law a job in the Red Army Theater. The couple moved into the general's apartment and in no time, the actor began leading a dissolute life. His drinking caused him to sell every last thing in his room. By that time, his wife had had the good sense to move out. She got a divorce from her husband because of his ungovernable temper, but Soviet housing legislation being what it is, there was absolutely no way of getting him evicted from the apartment. The actor holed himself up in one of the rooms, padlocked the door, and proceeded to wreak vengeance on the general's family. He stripped down the room, not even sparing the parquet flooring, which he removed square by square, and exchanged everything for vodka until only a single object remained: a concert grand piano that the general had looted in Germany. The black hulk of the piano lay on the floor (the actor had unscrewed the legs and sold them for drink), where it served as a table and a bed. The only

159

thing that saved the piano from the fate of all the other objects was that it was too bulky to pass through the door and be carried away. After all but driving the general's family out of their minds, the happy-go-lucky actor finally moved out. On the eve of his departure, he hacked the piano to pieces with an ax.

Another neighbor of ours, whom we occasionally met on the staircase, seemed to us a malevolent spirit. We had never, in fact, been introduced to him, but we knew he was Lieutenant General Reichman of the MGB. He was Deputy Minister of State Security for Extraordinary Affairs and later became Beria's deputy. He was tall and well groomed and always wore civilian clothes. Although he was imprisoned twice, he served only short terms. During the second—after Beria's execution—his wife, a ballerina named Lepeshinskaya, abandoned him. On his release, he was stripped of his rank; he now works as a legal adviser in one of the bureaus. He would singularly embellish the prisoner's dock in some Soviet version of the Nuremburg Trials if ever the KGB,* like the Gestapo and the SS, were brought to justice. Among the KGB tormentors, Raikhman is perhaps the most important figure alive and flourishing today.

A few days after Markish's arrest, I went to the MGB's reception bureau on Kuznetsky Bridge. I wasn't the only one; there was a long line in front of the information booth where an uncommunicative major was installed.

"No news," the major said in reply to my question. "The investigation is under way."

"Are parcels authorized?"

"No."

"Money?"

"Inquire at Lefortovo Prison."

The prison of Lefortovo is a city in itself, a cluster of brick buildings enclosed by a high stone wall. Again there was an information booth and a long line of people. I began talking with an aged Jewish woman

* After Beria's death, in December 1953, the state security and police powers were reorganized and the new formation was called the KGB (Komitet Gosudarstvennoy Bezopasnosti —"Committee for State Security").—Ed.

who was standing in the queue. There were the usual questions.

"Who are you coming for, your husband?"

"That's right. And you?"

"For my husband, too. . . ."

It turned out that the woman, Masha, was the sister of the president of Israel, Chaim Weizmann. Apparently, the MGB found it embarrassing to put the sister of the president of a sovereign state in prison, but they had no qualms about arresting her husband, a full-blooded Russian, for the sole reason that he was the brother-in-law of the president of Israel. The experience did not, however, turn him into an anti-Semite; after Stalin's death Masha's husband was freed and they went to live in Israel.

The queue in front of Lefortovo Prison buzzed with rumors about the possible fate of our loved ones: the terrifying conditions in Lubyanka or the still more terrifying conditions in Sukhanovka, a prison in the Moscow suburbs where people often succumbed to the torture inflicted on them.

I was given permission to transmit a small sum of money once a month or, if I preferred, the same sum in four equal weekly installments. I decided on the latter, since it would enable Markish to have more frequent news of me. (The naiveté of the Soviet citizen is indestructible, while the perfidy and baseness of the Soviet regime know no limits. It would never have occurred to me at the time that Markish would never see the money I sent—after all, didn't the major at the information booth show me the register certifying that the money had been received, and even give me a receipt? Right up to February 1, 1953, the day we were sent into internal exile, I received such receipts regularly, notwithstanding the fact that Markish had been executed five months earlier—on August 12, 1952. They didn't have the courage to notify widows of the fate of their husbands. Or perhaps they were afraid that the news would leak out to the free and civilized world, which shared the same planet with a group of fascist bandits.)

A few days after Markish's arrest, we were surprised by a visit from the old Jewish writer David

Vendrov. He was already over seventy, yet he managed to preserve a wry sense of humor and maintain his equanimity.

"How ever could you have taken the risk of coming to see us?" I asked him after we had silently embraced.

"Everybody tried to dissuade me," he said, chuckling bitterly, "but, between you and me, I'm no spring chicken, you know. So I figured the worst thing that could happen would be that I might be arrested a few days sooner."

And, as a matter of fact, Vendrov was arrested not long after. It was not until the end of 1954 that he was released from the terrible prison of Vladimir.

Unfortunately, at the very end of his long life, Vendrov succumbed to the inexorable pressure of the Kremlin's lackey, the Jewish poet Aron Vergelis. The ninety-year-old Vendrov, shortly after the Six-Day War, signed his name to a letter vilifying the state of Israel.

With Markish gone, I had to give some thought to the problem of earning a living. (I was, of course, now prohibited from doing any more translation work.) It was then that I remembered an old hobby of mine, knitting. My loyal companion Lena Khokhlova and I set about unraveling all the woolens we could find in the house and started knitting new things, like women's hats with matching scarves, which were very much in fashion at the time. David would make the rounds of the watch shops and persuade the watchmakers to give him broken alarm-clock springs, which we inserted into the borders of the hats. I knitted sweaters and dresses, too, which sold rather well. But this was a hazardous occupation, since it was illicit to engage in private enterprise. If anyone reported me, I could end up behind bars. What I really needed was a stable, officially recognized position that would allow me to have a work permit and legalize my status. But what personnel department would take on the wife of Peretz Markish, a convict?

I learned quite by accident that the All-Union Scientific Society of Microbiologists, Epidemiologists and

Virologists was looking for a secretary. The society was a voluntary organization and therefore not under the jurisdiction of the Department of Employment, which subjected every applicant to the most thorough examination. I went immediately to see the president of the society, Professor Victor Victorov.

"I would like to work for you," I told Victorov, "but I am the wife of Peretz Markish."

Victorov shook his head glumly.

"I go by my maiden name, Lazebnikova," I added.

"Well, that puts things in a different light," Victorov said. "But remember, you said nothing to me about your husband. Now, let's talk about your future duties —I cannot spell them out with any precision, since they are so broad and varied."

"I am ready to do anything that's needed," I said.

"That's fine." He tapped the ends of his fingers together. "You see, my wife is an invalid—she's blind. For four hours of the day you are to read aloud to her, take her out for walks, discuss the news with her—I have in mind the achievements of our national economy, of our socialist culture. The other four hours you will devote to the affairs of the society: correspondence, answering the telephone, getting out bulletins and reports. I'm referring to scientific reports."

"But I don't have any experience," I objected.

"Well, you'll just have to acquire it," the professor declared. "And before I forget it, you'll also have to take care of some of the household chores, although of course I do have a housekeeper."

"Do you mean to say I'll have to go out and shop for potatoes?" I asked somewhat impertinently.

"Why potatoes!" Victorov tossed up his hands. "Potatoes, no, but you'll be responsible for buying the candy."

"It's a deal," I said.

Simka, who was now nineteen, also started to earn his living. He gave English lessons and tutored students in all subjects of the school curriculum. Happily, he had not been expelled from the university following his father's arrest. But Simka realized full well that the Department of Romance and German Studies of the Faculty of Philology was not meant for the son of a

Jew who had been imprisoned. Even if he were graduated from that department, he wouldn't be able to find any work, so he decided to transfer to a "neutral" department, classics. While continuing his studies of philology, he took up Latin and Ancient Greek, disciplines that were remote from the "ideological front" and the "struggle against decadent Western art." In transferring to the classics department, he was guided not so much by considerations of professional advancement, but, rather, by a desire to have nothing to do with the modern period.

One by one, our old acquaintances drifted away. The last to abandon us was a Jewish family of writers and musicians who had been our friends for a number of years. They invited me over to their apartment to explain: they could no longer have any contact with me, since it would expose them to the direst consequences, including arrest. They were afraid to associate with me and they said so frankly. When I was about to leave, one of my hosts got up and said he would see me to the trolley stop. But another member of the family restrained him. "My dear, apologize to Firochka, but you know you can't get away now. You were supposed to give us a hand with something, and it will take you an hour or more before you're ready."

I put on my coat and walked out into a blizzard. The trolley was a long time coming, perhaps a quarter of an hour. And, lo and behold, whom should I see coming toward the trolley stop but the writer who had offered to accompany me; he must have thought I would have already left. I turned away and walked on. I would have been embarrassed to confront him.

I have no feeling of animosity toward these people today. After I returned from internal exile, we met again and resumed our relationships. In 1971, when I filed my application for emigration to Israel, and "courageous" friends of mine once again forgot the way to my house, I decided I would not place the family of writers and musicians (I was very fond of them) in an awkward position. I therefore decided to call on them myself and say good-bye, perhaps for the last time. But the eighteen years that had passed since the death of Stalin had wrought a change in that family, too.

"Under no circumstances," my friends declared. "We were your friends and are still your friends. You'll continue to come to visit us and vice versa. We have only one big favor to ask you: Don't mention the name 'Israel' out loud . . . better to say, well, 'Exlandia.' You know we have a maid, and why tempt the devil?"

14 / On the Eve of a Pogrom

SHORTLY AFTER MARKISH'S ARREST, the Jewish Section of the Writers' Union was liquidated. A Jew, Alexander Bezymensky, the "komsomol poet," was charged with the formalities. He summoned the Jewish writers who were still at liberty and informed them that enemies of the people and traitors to the motherland had been "unearthed" in the Jewish Section and that it had been decided to close it down. Many of those present "enthusiastically" approved the shameful decision, Oyslender and Khenkina among them.

The spectacle of the extermination of Jewish literature was to be reenacted a few days later in a more solemn setting: at a general meeting of the Moscow Section of the Writers' Union. On this occasion, the inglorious role of hatchet man was given to the Jewish poet A. Kushnirov, who had been a front-line officer and had lost his son during the war. Kushnirov, who knew only too well what was expected of him, was literally dragged onto the podium. Before he could utter a word, however, he burst into tears and was led away.

After such a fiasco, Kushnirov was sure to be arrested; it was merely a question of time. But fate dealt kindly with him: he died very soon after the Jewish Section was closed down. His wife, however, was arrested and sent away to a camp.

My work at the Society of Microbiologists continued. I read to Victorov's blind wife, Nina Borisovna (and managed to knit scarves and hats at the same time), drew up the monthly reports and bulletins, collected membership dues, and so on.

I discovered that my boss, Professor Victorov, was a rather strange man. Once, he asked me to put in order his card file of "friends and acquaintances." There were several hundred cards, each with an individual's name, date of birth (for congratulations), license-plate number, home and office address, maid's name, and even the names of any pets. If ever they decided to put Professor Victorov in prison, the cards would have been a veritable treasure trove for the MGB. No doubt, he would have been indicted under the provisions of the redoubtable article covering a "counterrevolutionary organization," and all of the people in his card file would have been prosecuted.

Another remarkable element of Professor Victorov's archives was his "Stomach Book," tidily bound in red leather and containing a record of the family menus for the past twenty-five years. Two other carefully preserved volumes labeled "My Health" and "Nina Borisovna's Health" contained several decades' worth of blood, urine and stool analyses, cardiograms, and prescriptions.

Of course, I refrained from expressing any opinion about the idiosyncrasies of my employer.

One Saturday evening as I was preparing to leave for my day off, the professor called me into his study and solemnly declared, "I have decided, my dear Esther Yefimovna, to restore the good name and reputation of the unjustly forgotten Russian microbiologist Professor Gabrichevsky."

Victorov paused and looked at me expectantly. I hoped my face showed that I fully shared his concern,

166

although this was the first time I had ever heard of Gabrichevsky or of his contribution to science.

"After the most painstaking labors," Victorov continued, "I have tracked down two photographs. One of them shows the professor lying in his coffin, the other, a section of the railing around his grave." With that, he handed me two worn and yellowed photographs.

"Yes, I see all right," I murmured. "And when did the professor die?"

"In 1912," Victorov told me. "He was buried here in Moscow, in the Pyatnitskoye Cemetery. I am entrusting you with a responsible and noble assignment: Tomorrow you are to go to the cemetery and try to locate the grave of Professor Gabrichevsky. Our society will see to it that the grave is kept up and will erect a monument."

The following day I set out for the cemetery with David. It was cold and the cemetery, which was in a sorry state of neglect, lay piled high with snow. As my son and I trudged through the drifts, I cursed the noble initiative of Victorov. We were passing by a freshly dug grave when we stumbled on a hoary gravedigger who was warming himself with vodka. He looked as if he came straight out of Shakespeare. When I explained to him that I was looking for the grave of a certain Gabrichevsky who had died nearly forty years before, he didn't seem at all surprised. After scrutinizing the photographs, he told me he remembered very well the day the professor was buried, the more so as it was he who had dug the grave. Encouraged by a token of my appreciation, the old man agreed to show me the spot.

We roamed around for half an hour before he pointed to a mound that was practically level with the ground. "Here it is."

"But where's the headstone?" I asked. "And the railing?"

"They were stolen," he explained. "The good people stole everything. They sold the marble slab and they transferred the iron railing to another grave."

With the location of Professor Gabrichevsky's grave

firmly fixed in mind, I proudly went off to report to Victorov on the success of my mission.

He listened in silence and then asked, "I presume that you noted down the name, patronymic and surname of the gravedigger as well as his home address?"

"No, somehow I didn't think of it," I said, feeling as if the ground had opened under me.

"My, my, what a pity," Victorov muttered. "That is of the utmost importance. You should have done so."

Victorov had begun sending me more and more often to various medical research institutes as his personal secretary. I became a familiar figure and people started calling me "Doctor Lazebnikova." Besides Victorov, there were only two other microbiologists who knew who Doctor Lazebnikova really was; they sympathized with me and would never have revealed my real identity. Had they done so, I would surely have lost my position.

On one occasion, Victorov sent me to the Institute of Highly Contagious Diseases. A few days later, I was feeling under the weather. The doctor who came to see me was unable to diagnose the trouble but treated me for the grippe. My condition worsened steadily; I lost consciousness and became delirious. When that happened, Lena Khokhlova, who had seen many people die of typhoid fever during the Civil War, made her own infallible diagnosis, "Why, she has typhus!"

I had a severe case, and it lasted quite some time. But as soon as I could stand on my feet, I went back to work. My doctor "colleagues" were rather puzzled as to how a "doctor" could have risked a visit to the institute without having been vaccinated.

Since there wasn't enough money to make ends meet, I began giving knitting lessons in the evenings. My students were mostly wives in comfortable circumstances who wanted a distraction to make the time pass. They came recommended to me and, of course, had no inkling that their teacher was actually a "criminal."

I received one group in the apartment of one of my students in the center of Moscow, on Sadovoye Koltso. It was made up of my student's neighbors, whose husbands were officials. I had no idea what their exact positions were; nor was I especially interested. But once, on the eve of November 7, I received a telegram from that group sending me their best wishes for the anniversary of the October Revolution. One of the students signing the telegram was a woman by the name of Yevstafeyeva. When I learned from the friend who had recommended her to me that she was the wife of the deputy minister of State Security, I became panic-stricken—surely now I would be arrested on the grounds that I had attempted to infiltrate the entourage of the deputy minister, to assassinate him, or whatever.

I decided that the best thing to do was come clean with the *zamsha* ("wife of the deputy") and await my fate. On learning who I was, the *zamsha* evidently became very scared herself and immediately informed her husband. When he realized that the lessons were after all being conducted in a neighbor's apartment and not in his own, he heaved a sigh of relief. Nevertheless the lessons were discontinued.

I learned later through a friend that the chief of the MGB's Investigation Branch, M. D. Ryumin himself, had visited the deputy's home and, over a glass of vodka, revealed to the *zamsha* and her husband that the MGB had just completed a serious, difficult investigation of the Jewish Antifascist Committee. According to Ryumin, the committee had been infiltrated by spies and traitors to the motherland who were bent on detaching the Crimea from Russia and turning it over to Israel. The families of the traitors, Ryumin went on, would be arrested and sent into exile.[*]

But even when we heard this news, we continued to hope, although without any foundation. We lived like people in a leper colony, and while there were some exceptions—those who would stop and exchange a few words—it would have been better had they ignored us. Once, I ran into Konstantin Finn in the company of the Russian writer Nikolai Bogdanov. After asking whether I had heard anything new about

---

[*] Ryumin was arrested shortly after Stalin's death, on charges of having used "forbidden methods," and was soon shot.—Trans.

Markish, Finn said to Bogdanov, "They surely won't touch you or me, Kolya! After all, you're a Russian writer, and I'm a great Russian writer! No, they wouldn't touch us, would they?"

"When it comes to prison or poverty, Kostya," Bogdanov replied, "there's no insurance."

Finn is still flourishing today.

Fortunately, there were other encounters during this difficult period of my life. Two of them I will never forget. On one occasion, I literally ran into Vsevolod Ivanov on the street. Chastened by experience, I pretended not to notice him and quickly passed by. I could hardly believe my ears when I heard him call after me, "Fira!"

Ivanov caught up with me. "What do you mean avoiding me like that!" When I explained to him that I didn't want to put him in an embarrassing position, he laughed wryly. "Don't think badly of all of us. Why, life isn't worth living that way. . . . You know what? Go get the children and come to stay with us, either at our apartment or at our house in the country. Okay?"

I thanked him and said that I would, but I couldn't bring myself to take advantage of Vsevolod's civic courage. God only knows what would have happened to him if we had taken up his invitation.

On another occasion, I met the writer Alexander Borshchagovsky, who had been stigmatized as a "maleficent cosmopolitan" and expelled from the Writers' Union. Left without a livelihood, Borshchagovsky was compelled to work in a factory to earn a crust of bread. When this became known, three fellow writers and friends came to see him: the Kievan Victor Nekrasov, the Kharkovian Vladimir Dobrovolsky, and the Muscovite Konstantin Simonov.

"Don't be crazy," they told him. "Give up your job in the factory—you're no longer a twenty-year-old. Now, take this money and stay home and write."

As I heard this, I smiled somewhat bitterly. It did not escape Borshchagovsky's notice, and he turned to me and asked, "Tell me, do Markish's friends come and see you?"

"No . . ."

"But they do help you out with money, don't they? If they're afraid to do so openly, they can still send it to you by mail under an assumed name."

"No . . ."

"But 'X' for example?" Borshchagovsky mentioned the name of an important Jewish theatrical director, a friend of Markish's, a man of means.

"No . . ."

Toward the end of 1952, the net began to close around us more tightly. On the eve of December 5, the anniversary of the Soviet Constitution, the wives of three Jewish personalities were arrested. Knowing the predilection of the Communists for preholiday arrests, I paid an evening visit on one of my childhood friends and stayed with her until daybreak. On my return home, I saw the silhouette of my mother through the window. She made a sign to me, which, as it turned out, I misunderstood. I thought they had come for me, and I took off as fast as my legs could go, driven by a visceral fear and heedless of the absurdity of my action. I returned home a few hours later to find that my fears had been unwarranted; it was not yet my turn.

In connection with the dissolution of the Jewish Antifascist Committee, only Feffer's wife was taken, shortly after the arrest of her husband. What exactly were the MGB's motives for that, it is difficult to say. But Itzik Feffer's fate is most revealing. In 1950, his daughter, who was still free and only later was sent into exile, at the same time we were, was ordered to deliver a parcel for her father: a pin-striped suit, a checkered tie, and a few delicatessen items. When the news became known it was interpreted as a favorable sign, and caused a considerable stir among the wives whose husbands had been arrested. It meant that Feffer was alive at least, since no one but himself could have been so specific in requesting a particular suit, a particular tie, and the Jewish salami he had such a fondness for.

It was only a few years later, after my return from exile, that I learned the story behind this parcel. The information came from an entirely reliable informant whose name I cannot reveal. In 1950, the famous American black singer Paul Robeson, whom Feffer had met in the United States on his wartime tour there, came to Moscow for a series of concerts. By that time, rumors had already begun reaching the West about the fate of Jewish writers in the Soviet Union, and Robeson was anxious to verify them. He asked his hosts to arrange a meeting with Feffer, who was then brought from prison to Robeson's hotel. It can be safely assumed that Feffer said nothing to his American friend about prison; he dutifully performed the role that the MGB had given to him. This did not, however, alter his fate: he, too, was shot, a victim of the postwar Stalinist purges.

On December 16, 1952, my mother telephoned me at work and asked me to try to come home a bit earlier than usual. When I got there, I discovered that my older son, Simon, had been gone since ten that morning, when he had been called to the district branch of the Ministry of State Security. There had been no news of him.

Simon returned home late that evening. He had been interrogated—they wanted to know, among other things, the names of Markish's friends whom we continued to associate with. Finally, he was made to sign an agreement that he would not leave the confines of Moscow. Moreover, I was ordered to appear at the same office at ten that same evening.

Simon took me aside to say that he had noticed on the interrogator's desk a blank with the heading "Questionnaire Concerning Members of the Family of a Traitor to the Motherland." And then it dawned on both of us at the same moment: two years before, "in response to the demands of Soviet workers," the death penalty had been introduced for "traitors to the motherland."

An illiterate MGB officer by the name of Mukhin interrogated me from ten in the evening until three in the morning. I, too, was forced to sign a pledge not to leave the city.

"What's the meaning of this?" I asked.

"It's in your own interest," Mukhin explained,

"and in your husband's interest. Some additional information on his case may be urgently required and this will enable us to contact you immediately."

As always, the MGB didn't have the courage to tell the truth. By December, Markish had already been dead for five months, although I did not know it.

On the morning of January 13, 1953, the newspapers announced that our indefatigable and valorous organs of security had uncovered a doctors' plot. It was alleged that the doctors, "agents of Zionism and American imperialism," all of whom worked in the Kremlin's hospital service and attended top Party and government officials, had conspired to murder their patients. Except for one or two Russians, all of the arrested doctors were identifiably Jews. (Long after the death of Stalin and the rehabilitation of the doctors, I heard from a number of people that the MGB had, in fact, arrested a large number of non-Jews, but that the press had publicized only those names and surnames that served their purpose.) The chief of the conspiracy and the man who served as liaison between the conspirators and their foreign masters was identified as "the well-known Jewish bourgeois nationalist Mikhoels." (No mention was made, of course, of the fact that Mikhoels had perished five years before.)

It now became unmistakably clear that this was the end of the road for us. The fact that we had been "assigned to residence" in Moscow left no room for further hopes or illusions: one month before this measure was taken against us, there were the Prague Trials (described in Arthur London's book *The Confession*), which had an unequivocally anti-Semitic character, and one month after, the Jewish doctors' plot, a throwback to the anti-Semitism of the Middle Ages.

A prepogrom atmosphere reigned in Moscow. It was dangerous for Jews to venture out into the streets, and Jewish children were beaten in school. My younger son, David, was not spared: he told me (with a certain degree of pride) how some hooligans had pursued him with shouts of "Clear out and go to that Israel of yours!" And my neighbor, an elderly Russian lady, told me a terrifying story. She had gone to school to pick up her grandson. While she was waiting for him at the entrance, a Jewish boy suddenly came running to her crying, "Auntie, tell them I'm your grandson! They want to kill me because I am a Jew!" My neighbor took the boy home with her.

It is particularly distressing to recall how normally intelligent people—and there were even some Jews among them—were ready to accept the MGB's murderous slander as the truth. It was Hitler all over again: the lie had to be so grotesque that nobody would dare to call it into question.

But, as always, the voice of nobility, courage, and integrity would not be silenced completely, and for us, the outcasts and helpless victims, it rose above the howls of the rabid mob of pogromists. I will never forget one brief encounter in the corridor of the Faculty of Philology of Moscow University. Simon, who was in his fifth and final year, decided at all costs to defend his graduation thesis. Now that he had been assigned to residence, he understood that our days of "freedom" were numbered and that he had only a little time to defend it before we would be arrested. He succeeded in persuading his department head to give him permission and not wait until the spring term as university regulations required.

I accompanied Simon to the university to be present at the defense, which looked as if it might very well be the last happy event in our family's life. We were met at the entrance to the auditorium by Justina Severinovna Pokrovskaya, the widow of Academician Mikhail Pokrovsky, the eminent classicist and specialist in Romance philology. She herself was a teacher of Greek and Latin. In a loud voice that carried to the other end of the corridor, Justina Severinovna declared, "What a sorry pass we've come to! Why, it's even more horrendous than the Beilis affair.* Then,

---

* Under the tsarist regime at the beginning of this century, a Kievan Jew, Beilis, was accused of ritual murders after the suspicious death of a Christian baby. He was acquitted after a long inquiry and trial that roused international public opinion.—Ed.

at least, you could speak your mind, but now no one says a word, their mouths are sealed!"

Only someone who lived through the black winter of 1953 with us can understand the incredible, fantastic courage of those words. They are all the more precious because they were spoken by a Russian.

I would like to mention one other brave and noble action. Simon had a close friend and classmate by the name of Alexander Syrkin. His father, Yakov Kivovich Syrkin, a prominent chemist and corresponding member of the Academy of Sciences, and his mother, Mariam Veniaminovna, offered to adopt Simon to save him from deportation. We refused, primarily because we didn't want to place these wonderful people in jeopardy.

Simon's defense was brilliant. The enthusiastic examiners (oh, these Soviet paradoxes!) even decided to recommend Simon for postgraduate study. That in itself represented a veiled challenge to the authorities and as such was fraught with danger for the sponsors, since they knew full well what lay in store for their protégé.

That evening, we went to a café to celebrate. According to Soviet university regulations, the defense of the undergraduate thesis takes place several months before the State examinations. Only after their successful completion is the student awarded his degree. Still, the successful defense of the thesis alone enables a student to work in his specialty, albeit at a lower level.

Expecting the arrival of uninvited guests, Simon and I were in no hurry to get home. (By then, I should mention, I had sent my other son, David, who had just turned thirteen, to stay with relatives in Baku, a futile precaution because when the time came, the MGB had no trouble in locating him.) So after we left the café, exhausted and full of forebodings, we stopped by to see some relatives and stayed with them until the early hours of the morning.

But our apprehensions proved unjustified; our nocturnal visitors did not come for us that night either.

15 / "Where Are Your Abrahams?"

SIMON AND I ARRANGED to spend the last night prior to our arrest—and we were persuaded that this would be the last night—away from home. As usual, he went over to see his girl friend and classmate, who later became his wife and followed us voluntarily into exile; I spent the night with a friend who never faltered in her loyalty or feared associating with me. When, on returning home, I turned the key in the door and stepped into the apartment, Simon came rushing over to me. From the excited expression on his face, I knew at once that something was wrong.

"We've been ordered to appear at the district branch of the MGB tomorrow at 10:00 A.M.," he said as he handed me the summons. "It's all over for us now!"

Simon was not mistaken. The night before, they had arrested Bergelson's family, and the day before that they had taken in Eda Zuskina, her daughter, and Kvitko's wife, one day prior to their arrest. Now our time had come.

Despite the lateness of the hour, Simon and I left for the long-distance telephone office to call my mother in Baku and say good-bye to her. My poor beloved mother! The pain in her voice when she asked, "Won't I have time to come and see you off?" Then we called Lyalya in Kiev. Her passport had already been taken away; it was a sure sign that her arrest was imminent. We returned home, got together only whatever was absolutely essential and packed our bags.

Early the next morning, I went downstairs to the public telephone—our private line had been disconnected soon after Markish's arrest—and called a few close friends to say good-bye. They couldn't hold back their tears, but I was calm and collected and displayed no emotion. Around nine o'clock, Markish's nephew Yura, a mature and self-reliant young man of twenty-four, joined us at our place. He had also been summoned to MGB division headquarters: he was registered at our address and was in the same boat with us for the simple reason that the MGB needed to take over this four-room apartment, located in the center of Moscow.

It is difficult for a Westerner to understand the complexities and absurdity of the Soviet administrative system, so I shall say a few words about it. Every urban resident in the Soviet Union possesses a "passport." I put the word in quotes because it is not a passport in the ordinary sense of the term—proof of citizenship and a prerequisite for travel abroad—but an identity card for internal use without which an individual has no legal existence. The collective farmers have no passports and, accordingly, no right to move about freely even within the confines of the Soviet Union. The passport must bear a seal certifying the holder's permanent place of residence. In order to obtain the right of domicile in Moscow, it is mandatory to have nine square meters (thirty square feet) of living space per capita, the minimum required by sanitation standards. Otherwise, you cannot get a job. But if you do not have a job, you cannot obtain a residence permit.

Yura had a job but his rented room was not the requisite nine square meters, and for that reason he was registered in our apartment. He showed up at our place in time to leave with us to keep our appointment at MGB headquarters. The three of us appeared at the already familiar, quaint-looking little house with white curtains, situated in a quiet lane on Sadovoye Koltso, a few minutes after ten. The MGB officer who opened the door ushered us in gruffly—"You've kept us waiting. You're five minutes late."

"Things being what they are, there was no particular reason for us to be in a hurry," I retorted.

Mukhin appeared; he was the same officer who had

177

interrogated me on December 16 and ordered me not to leave the city. He was accompanied by a few soldiers. They took us in tow and hustled us into the courtyard, where a freshly painted van, marked with the word Bread, was waiting. The van dropped us off at Gorky Street and we proceeded under escort to the apartment that had been our home for so many years. The head of the detachment, a colonel in the MGB, noticed that our suitcases were already packed.

"Why, you've packed up already?"

"We are responsible Soviet citizens," I said.

"So much the better," he observed.

As he looked around the apartment, he was surprised at the emptiness of the place—not so much as a table or chair. After we had been ordered not to leave the city, I had disposed of everything that had not been impounded at the time of Markish's arrest, and for the past six weeks Simon and I had lived in an empty apartment.

"Tell me, where's your furniture?" the colonel inquired.

"I sold it all. We had to subsist some way," I answered.

The colonel's eyes searched for some place to sit. I pointed to the only stool that remained. He sat down and proceeded to read out the decision of the Special Session, which had handed down its verdict *in absentia:* "Ten years exile in the remote regions of Kazakhstan with confiscation of all property as members of the family of a traitor to the motherland." The name of thirteen-year-old David also figured on the list of those condemned. Remarking his absence, the colonel demanded to know his whereabouts so that a soldier could be sent after him. No matter how reluctant I was to involve my relatives in Baku, I had no choice but to give their address. But the colonel was not content with that; he demanded a photograph of David—to guard against the possibility that some other young "criminal" might be substituted!

Then, after checking to make sure that the seals on the doors that had been locked up had not been violated, he ordered us to get ready to leave and commanded our loyal nanny, Lena Khokhlova, to pack up and clear out of the apartment. And so the poor homeless soul was thrown out like an old rag onto the landing of the fifth floor.

My sons had a cat to whom they had given the Yiddish name of Shifra. While the colonel and his cohorts were fixing the seals to the entrance of what was now our former apartment, Shifra managed to slip out of Lena's arms and squeeze through a crack in the door. We implored the colonel to stop the sealing of the door until the cat had been retrieved, but he remained deaf to our pleading and Shifra was immured alive in the sealed apartment.

As we went down the staircase, we ran into some of our neighbors; a number happened to be at home that Sunday morning. The more courageous ventured to acknowledge our farewell; others hurried past. The "bread" van pulled away. The colonel urged the chauffeur to hurry; that day he had a long list of people who had been condemned by the Special Session, and undoubtedly he wanted to take advantage of as much of his day as possible to spend with his family.

The van made its way through the snow-covered streets of Moscow. I remember that wintry February 1, 1953, as if it were yesterday. Simon and Yura peered through the window as they followed the route of the van. "Mama, take a look at Moscow; it may be for the last time," my son said to me. But I was lost in my unhappy thoughts.

I turned to the colonel and asked, "How are things with my husband? Where is he?"

"That is something you'll never know," was his reply.

Suddenly, Simon grabbed me by the hand. "Look, Mama," he said, motioning toward the window. For the first time since we had left home, I glanced outside, and saw a railroad yard. "A prison train," Simon said.

It came as a complete surprise to me. I had naively believed the colonel's assurances that we would be traveling to our place of exile in a regular train. The van halted at the railroad embankment alongside the tracks. We stepped out. The colonel and a few officers led us to a car with barred windows. It was only then that I realized that we were going to travel under escort—prison, or perhaps several transit prisons, lay in store for us on the way to our final destination.

The commander of the convoy of the "prison on wheels"—my first prison ever—an insolent young second lieutenant, roared, "Get a move on, queen, pick up your belongings." My nerves cracked. Up until then, I had made a herculean effort to keep my composure, but it vanished in a flash, and I began to shriek hysterically. I was shaking all over.

I categorically forbade my son and my nephew to execute the lieutenant's order. "Go carry our things yourself, you snake!" I thundered. Apparently, my angry outburst and boldness came as such a surprise to the colonel that he ordered the lieutenant to transport our belongings from the van onto the platform of the prison train. The next thing I knew, I was behind bars in a compartment of the prison car together with a few other women. Simon and Yura were led away to the far end of the corridor without even having been given a chance to say good-bye to me. There was no light in the compartment, but once my eyes grew accustomed to the darkness, I saw that the bunk alongside mine was occupied by Maria Yuzefovich, the wife of a prominent labor union official and member of the defunct Jewish Antifascist Committee who had been arrested at about the same time as Markish. Maria's little ten-year-old daughter clung to her mother's hand and kept repeating in a muffled voice, "Mama, why have they done this to us?"

And her mother would gently answer, "Because of Papa."

But the child persisted. "And Papa, what did he do?"

"I don't know, my child." And again and again, the same questions, the same answers, without respite.

Our compartment kept filling up with more and more "passengers." In the pitch black, the eerie silence was broken only by the occasional scraping of the bolt as the door was opened just enough to let pass new companions of misfortune, who were counted like cattle. Eventually, when there were at least twenty of us crammed into a compartment that our jailers themselves admitted was meant for only fourteen, the women began to voice their discontent. In the adjoining compartment, for male prisoners, they stuffed in as many as thirty-two—I heard the guard shout out that number as he shoved the last man in, with the aid of his boot. By the next day, it was clear that the most intrepid of the female prisoners were the criminal elements—the thieves and prostitutes.

A severe penal regime was in force in our prison on wheels: reveille at 5:00 A.M., toilet visits limited to twice a day (if you happened to be sick and had to go more often, well that was just tough luck; you could even die, but regulations were regulations). Round-the-clock guards were posted at the door to the compartment—young, beardless soldiers from the detachment of the Ministry of State Security. One such guard displayed an unusual interest in a large table clock that—God only knows how—one of the prisoners had managed to take along with her. The clock methodically ticked away the hours. My bunk, as it happened, directly adjoined the compartment door (to be more precise, a tall grill that extended from floor to ceiling), and I would sit and peer stonily out into the corridor of our car. Now and then, the guard would turn to me and ask, "What time is it?" Every half-hour I would patiently tell him the time; evidently he couldn't wait to be relieved. Gradually this contact developed into a sort of friendly relationship, and finally I ventured to ask him about my boys. You can imagine my joy when he suggested that I write a note, which he offered to take to them immediately. Moreover, he reassured me, they were "with the politicals." I scratched a few words on a scrap of notebook paper that I found in my handbag. I also asked the soldier if he would mind taking a bit of food I had with me along to my boys. Naturally I didn't have a knife, so I sent them the key to our old apartment to cut the sausage with. It wasn't long before the soldier returned with a note from Simon. The happy tears that I poured over that message! Simon and Yura buoyed up my spirits, assuring me that they were traveling under reasonably good conditions.

Forty-eight hours after our departure from Moscow, the train pulled into Kuibyshev. A Black Maria—or "Black Crow," as it is known in the Soviet Union—was there waiting for us. We were disembarked one by one. I waited to catch a glimpse of my dear boys. It was a bitterly cold day. I climbed into the van. It was pitch dark inside; the short winter day was drawing to a close and the only light in the railroad yard was from a dim lantern. Simon and Yura, nevertheless, still managed to make me out in the darkness, and from the innards of the Black Crow they called out to let me know they were there. My mind at rest now, I somehow found room for one leg and stood as best I could in that position until the van came to a screeching halt. Once again we were counted out one by one and unloaded from the Black Crow. And now, for the first time since leaving Moscow, I caught sight of my boys. Gaunt and unshaven, they seemed to have grown older by several years. Sima, hailing me from afar, removed his *shapka*. To my horror, I saw that my son had gone gray! As we looked around, we realized that we were standing in front of a prison, one of the oldest, in the ancient Volga city of Samara, which the Bolsheviks had renamed Kuibyshev to honor the memory of Valerian Kuibyshev, one of Lenin's comrades-in-arms.

The gates of the prison opened up before us, and we were soon standing before the warden, a short man who tugged nervously at his sparse red whiskers. He personally interrogated each of the transit prisoners.

Turning to me, he inquired, "Under what article?"

"I have no idea. All I know is that I have been exiled as a member of the family of a traitor to the motherland."

"Under no article, then," the warden concluded.

He put the same question to Maria Yuzefovich, to my boys, and to the old woman with the table clock, who, I learned later, was a Bessarabian who didn't know a single word of Russian and who was again on her way to exile after escaping once at the end of the war. This time, instead of getting only ten years, as before, she was being sent away for life.

As we were being led away to a prison ward, the boys passed in front of me and disappeared somewhere in the far reaches of the prison corridor. A heavy door, with a lock dangling from a thick transversal bolt, swung open before our small group of frightened women and we were momentarily blinded by the glare of a powerful, unshaded electric light that hung from the ceiling. Before we even had a chance to enter the huge ward, which resembled the waiting room of some provincial railroad station, the inmates, leering like apes, assailed us with shouts of "Sarahs, Sarahs! Where are your Abrahams?" Young or old, they all ranted and raved, accompanying their vociferations with indecent gestures. We stood frozen at the threshold, afraid to budge. Amid the torrent of abuse, the likes of which we had never heard before, two of the more enterprising hellions swooped down on us with cries of "Let's shave their heads! Let's clip their locks!" Poor little Marinochka! As if it were only yesterday, I see your eyes before me—the beautiful, clear blue eyes of a child frightened to death and shielding her head with her hands in mortal terror. Marina had the most striking silken-blond tresses.

We started shouting and pounding on the door. Finally, with a scrape of the bolt, the door opened and the chief warder, a huge hulk of a man, stood there towering over us. "Why the racket?" he asked.

"For God's sake, please get the warden," Maria Yuzefovich begged.

Our tormentors, under the encouraging gaze of the chief warder, continued their vituperations and antics. The warden was not long in coming. Maria rushed up to him and implored, "Comrade warden, please have mercy on my child." But the "comrade" cut her short and did not let her continue.

"You are not to call me comrade. For you I am citizen warden."

Holding back her tears, Maria continued, "Citizen warden, please have pity on my child. You are surely a father yourself and can understand a mother's feelings. Please transfer us to another ward."

"I don't have another women's ward that's heated. It's thirty-six degrees centigrade below zero outside. All I can offer you is an unheated ward. Moreover, all the politicals will have to be transferred together," he said as he pointed toward me and the old woman with the clock.

"It's all right with me," I said. "For the child's sake,

I'm prepared to go to the unheated ward. It's all the same to me."

The poor old Bessarabian lady dutifully followed behind us, clutching her unique and prized possession, the clock.

The warden had not misinformed us: the ward was unheated—and the windowpanes were broken. In a half-hour, we were all freezing; Marinochka was sobbing fitfully, her arms and legs stiff with cold. We had no choice but to return to our tormentors.

We expected to be subjected to a new storm of abuse and filthy invective, so you can imagine our surprise when we were met with a warm and cordial welcome. With the same enthusiasm and gusto they had displayed in unleashing on us their full panoply of obscenities, the *filles de joie* now began to pour out their affection on Marinochka, who was chilled to the bone. They vied with each other in plying her with tea and the miserable sweets that were on sale once a week in the prison store. I won't even attempt to explain the brusque change in behavior of these prostitutes and thieves.

One of the girls interested me a great deal. Her name was Vera. She was twenty, nice-looking, and there was something attractive about her. Vera was the ward's ringleader and the star performer in the wild spectacle that we had witnessed upon our arrival. She had now changed completely. Gentle and tender, she made a place for me on the bunk beside her and asked me to sit down. Then, as she brought me a bowl of tea, she began the usual prison conversation: "What are you in for? How much did they give you? Is it your first time?"

"Because of my husband," I answered.

At that, she began abusing my husband for failing to shield his wife from the "affair," a woman like me, et cetera. I explained the story to her as best I could, and she listened with rapt attention and sympathy. "Well," she said when I had finished, "there's something terribly wrong when a wife and children have to answer for a husband and father."

Then she told me about herself in vivid, humorous terms. She was sent up, you see, because of her love

184

for . . . geography. That passion had led her to travel far and wide over the vast expanses of the Soviet Union in search of new places and discoveries. But she failed to get a passport, as is required of every Soviet citizen on reaching the age of sixteen. She was, therefore, guilty of "violating the passport regime," an offense punishable by one or two years of prison. So Vera, owing to repeated violations of the passport regime and to robberies committed on trains, had been cooped up for four years. "But now," Vera went on, "I've had it! I got caught, but as soon as my time is up, to hell with them, I'll get a passport, go back to my hometown, and study to become a geography teacher!"

She then proceeded to describe in glowing terms the place I would be exiled to, where huge melons grew in profusion, where I would know no sadness because I was still a young woman and would "catch the fancy of the top man himself, and live like a lady." It would have been pointless for me to try to explain to her my grief and affliction, my yearning for Markish, my hatred toward those who destroyed or banished wholly innocent people—she would never have been able to understand.

It was thanks to Vera that I managed to get into contact with Simon and Yura. Considerably experienced in the ways of prisons, Vera was able to communicate with the other cells but her method was different from the one so often used by convicts: instead of tapping out the message on walls, she set the metal tea mug on the radiator and spoke into it. The heating pipes conveyed her message to the next cell and so on. In this way she located my boys.

One morning, when the warden made his usual stop at our cell, he was accompanied by one of his aides, a trusty. This wasn't just an ordinary day for me; it was my birthday, the first I had ever spent away from my loved ones. I happened to feel quite ill, and when the warden asked the routine question "Are there any complaints?" I reported it and asked permission to go and get some medicine from my suitcase, which was in the storeroom. The warden agreed that I could go after roll call had been completed. A short time after, his aide reappeared. I dragged myself out of bed and followed him into the corridor, at the end of which was a small, dank chamber where the prisoners' belongings were stored. The aide unlocked the door and accompanied me inside.

Before I even had a chance to look around, Simon and Yura threw their arms around my neck. It turned out that the trusty had been present at the roll call in the men's ward where my boys were held and had called them out, saying there was some sort of job to be done. What he really had intended was to arrange our get-together. I was speechless with gratitude and also curious to know why he had been so kind to us. He told me that the day before the arrival of our prison train, the families of Bergelson and Zuskin had been shipped out of Kuibyshev. Before leaving, Tsilya Bergelson and Eda Zuskina, expecting our arrival at Kuibyshev any day, had asked him to pass on their regards to the Markish family. My dear friends also let it be known that they, too, were on their way to Kazakhstan, but, as it turned out, their place of exile was far north of the region where we finally ended up. So, thanks to the kindness of this man, my birthday was enhanced by a joyful reunion with my boys.

That evening a new contingent joined us. My attention was caught by one young woman who seemed to hold herself somewhat aloof from the boisterous band of aggressive, brazen convicts who were welcomed like old friends by the other inmates. The majority of these women were habitual criminals and had old friends and "colleagues" from previous stopovers in transit prisons. I went up to the young woman and offered her a spot next to mine. The poor girl had nothing on her feet but a pair of rubber overshoes worn on top of some old, thin woolen stockings, no protection against the bitterly cold February weather. Arranging ourselves as comfortably as we could on the hard bunk, my new companion and I talked almost all through the night. Her name was Betya, and she was a native of Kishinyov, in what was Bessarabia until 1940, when it was "liberated" by Soviet troops (it is now the Moldavian Soviet Socialist Republic). While still a young girl, she had joined the Zionist

Youth Organization and, like many Jewish youngsters in the Diaspora, she had dreamed of her ancestral home, studied in the Hebrew gymnasium, learned the poems of Byalik by heart and made grand plans. But her whole world collapsed when she and all of her compatriots were united with the Soviet Union. The Zionist organization was dissolved and all its members arrested, but because of her youth she was spared. The years passed. Betya became a university student, she met the man of her life from whom nothing in the world, it seemed, would ever separate her. But one night they came for her and whisked her off to the MGB. After long and torturous interrogations, a Special Session of the MGB decided to sentence her to a term of eight years in exile for the Zionist activity she had "engaged in" as a schoolgirl. (At that time, the end of 1950, the liquidation of anything that could be even remotely classified under the category of Zionism, "bourgeois nationalism" or simply Jewishness was going ahead full speed.) Now, after having spent two years in the Potma camps, she was being shipped off to an unknown destination. The camps in the Potma area came to be known as "women's camps," by virtue of the fact that the vast majority of inmates were women who had been imprisoned because of their husbands, men who at one time had enjoyed high status in Soviet society.

One early morning in February 1953, the good and cheerful Betya vanished from my life forever and was never to be heard from again.

I still have a memento of her—a small, embroidered collar. The women in the camps found solace, as women have since time immemorial, in handiwork, contriving to use old scraps of material and threads stripped from the tattered remnants of their "free" clothing.

One prison succeeded another, new cell mates succeeded old ones, as we made our way to our final destination. Maria Yuzefovich and her daughter Marinochka were shipped out by stages to someplace at the other end of Kazakhstan. But it was always the same prison regime wherever we were, the same *parasha,* or waste bucket, you never got used to.

And so it went until one fine day we found ourselves in Kzyl-Orda, the chief city of Kzyl-Orda Province in West Kazakhstan. We were driven to the city prison in the early morning, this time not in a Black Maria but in a dirty coal truck. The sun was shining and it was uncustomarily warm after the freezing temperatures of Russia. The same prison routine, the same routine questions from the warden, except this time the warden was a slant-eyed Kazakh who looked like a descendant of Genghis Khan. To my tired imagination, the resemblance appeared even more striking when I noticed the long clanking saber that dangled from his waist. I found myself alone in a cell. Simon and Yura waved to me and then were led away by the chief warder, but the sound of their voices continued to reach me in my cell for a rather long time; they made a point of talking as loud as possible in order to prolong the contact.

In the cell were a bare bedstead made of iron slats and cobwebs in every corner. Even though it was a sunny day, I felt chilled by the dampness and gloom. Suddenly, the *kormushka*—the aperture in the cell door through which food is passed—opened noisily, and a few inquisitive guards peered brazenly through to give me the once-over. I tried my best to keep my composure. Then came the usual barrage of tiresome questions: "What are you in for?" "How much did they give you?" "Where are you from?" One of the guards asked me my name. I told him. And then something totally unexpected happened. "Lazebnikova,"—the Kazakh guard repeated after me, astonishment in his voice. "Tell me, did you have a brother Ruvim Lazebnikov?" And thus I learned from him the fate of my first cousin, the only son of my uncle in Baku with whom my David had hidden out. Ruvim, who had been reported missing, had been killed near Brest on practically the first day of the war while defending the frontier fortifications with other young and inexperienced Soviet soldiers, most of whom were fresh out of school. As I mentioned earlier, my youngest and beloved uncle, Naum, had fallen at Sevastopol;

my first cousin Mark, a student at Baku University, had perished while clearing a mine field. Yet the vile tale still circulates in the Soviet Union that "the Jews, you know, were doing business in the Tashkent bazaar while the Russians were shedding their blood at the front."

I sat on my bare iron bed mourning the loss of my loved ones. Images of my shattered life passed before my mind's eye like a moving picture. . . .

The sound of reveille at five o'clock the next morning brought me back to reality. A new guard appeared and led me through long, damp corridors. On the way I tried to speak at the top of my voice in hope that my boys were somewhere behind the locked doors we passed and would hear me. And then I heard them calling to me from behind one of the iron doors. That was all I needed—to know that they were nearby. The guard conducted me into a room where another descendant of Genghis Khan was sitting behind a desk. Courteously and with a touch of embarrassment, he explained that he had to take my fingerprints—those were the regulations. I felt sorry for the poor "Genghis Khan"; he took my hand clumsily, straightening each finger one by one and placing it on a blackened slab of window glass. The man was pleasant, even kindly. He began asking me questions. When he discovered the children and I had been sentenced to ten years' exile in the remote regions of Kazakhstan, he was taken aback: "Why, they sure threw the book at you! Members of the family don't get more than five years! But don't be disheartened. Many things can change in ten years. Why, look at me: I was taken as a child from the Far East when all Koreans, without exception, were deported to this region. And now, you can see for yourself, I am an officer of the MGB!"

His words were, of course, no consolation. I had no desire to see my children become MGB officers even in the far distant future. However, his human consideration for me buoyed up my spirits somewhat, the more so as he promised to do whatever he could to have us remain in the "center," that is, in the city of Kzyl-Orda itself, where there was a terrible need for teachers of foreign languages; Simon and I could help to alleviate the shortage.

After this final word of encouragement, he left to discuss the matter with the higher-ups. In the meantime, Simon and Yura had been brought out to have their fingerprints taken, and so the three of us went to the sunny prison yard to await the results of his efforts in our behalf. But, alas, the day was already coming to a close; we were hungry and tired from the interminable wait and wanted only to crawl back to our hard bed and rest. Just then, our good genius reappeared. It was at once obvious from his expression that his mission had not been successful. One concession had been made, however: We would not be sent to the region of the Aral Sea, where there is no drinking water. They agreed to let us settle in Karmakchi, a small village some one hundred and ten miles to the north of Kzyl-Orda, on the railroad line.

We were happy even over this result as three young soldiers escorted us aboard a third-class train on the Tashkent-Kuibyshev line. The Korean officer had been sincerely sorry that his mission had failed and waved good-bye to us until the train was no longer in sight.

With a whole section of the car to ourselves because our escort had taken the precaution of getting rid of the other passengers, we heaved a sigh of relief. For better or worse, we were at least on our way to our final destination, to a life of some sort where we would, perhaps, enjoy a certain amount of freedom. In any case, we would no longer have guards and jailers on our tail, or so we thought, with no previous experience of exile, to guide us.

It was late at night when our train halted at a snow-covered halfway station called Dzhusaly. We had one minute to unload our belongings and jump from the high platform into a snowdrift below, but we managed.

We found ourselves standing in pitch darkness alongside our miserable bundles of clothing waiting to see what now lay in store for us. But our escort seemed as perplexed as we were, since there was no transportation in sight and they had no idea how to get us to the KPZ, the provisional detention ward, in Karmakchi (the village where we could expect to spend the next ten years had no prison). The immediate problem seemed to be where to put up criminals as dangerous as the family of the traitor to the motherland Peretz Markish! But our military escort, under the command of Sergeant Ivan (he did not, of course, divulge his family name), had warmed up to us during our five-hour journey together. They had even ventured to eat with us—despite the fact that they had been warned not to forget that we were "politicals"! Ivan, on his own responsibility and using the prerogative of a soldier engaged in an important mission, flagged down a passing truck. It was carrying a full load, so we climbed into the back and stood exposed to the icy winds as the truck sped forward toward Karmakchi.

16 / The "Assassins" Are Rehabilitated

AT THE KARMAKCHI *komendatura,* or commandant's office, where we would have to check in every ten days, Major Akhmetov, the lord and master of all the exiles in the district, gazed in wonder on his new wards, the likes of which he had never laid eyes on before: A well-dressed woman, and two intelligent-looking young men wearing coats of good quality—and kidskin *shapkas* to boot, the last word in Soviet style. After giving due consideration to the matter and by virtue of the high authority vested in him, he granted us permission to spend the night in the "hotel," a euphemism for the large dormitory room with several rows of iron cots that was used to accommodate men and women sent on official business to the area. My bed, covered with a worn, faded sheet and a cheap blanket, seemed to me like the height of comfort. I was happy to be able, at last, to stretch out on my own bed, free of the necessity of sharing my bunk with fortuitous prison "comrades." For the first time in weeks, we took off our shoes and stockings and outer clothing. The room was warm. There was a large kettle boiling on an electric plate for tea, a definite luxury for us.

More than anything else we wanted to get to sleep, but this was not to be—everybody in the dormitory began to ply us with the same old tiresome questions. They were a motley group of men and women, some young. On learning that we were from Moscow, one of the guests, who figured we were Jewish, asked, "Have they begun deporting Jews then?" It turned out that even in this godforsaken hole, there were newspapers and radio to give news of what was going on in the world. They knew about the "doctor-assassins in white coats," who had conspired "to poison and do away with the best sons of Russia." Two brothers named Kogan had been implicated, and the name had become a synonym for "Jew." We had enormous difficulty in convincing our interlocutors that our name was not Kogan, that my husband was not a doctor, and that he had not "committed sabotage in the Kremlin."

On our first night in exile, we made the acquaintance of a wonderful young man, a Jew, who had voluntarily gone into exile to be with the girl he loved. Izya Tubis was his name. He lived in Kzyl-Orda and often came to Karmakchi on business. Born and bred in Kishinyov, he spoke fluent Yiddish, was well read in Yiddish literature, and had deep respect and affection for the name of Markish. He had studied Markish's poetry in the Jewish gymnasium in Kishinyov (formerly in Bessarabia), and when he discovered that we were members of Peretz Markish's family, tears came to his eyes and he threw his arms around us.

Izya explained how things operated in the village. Our "freedom," alas, would be on a short rein—we would be under the constant and vigilant surveillance of the local *komendatura*, which was responsible to the chief of ROMGB, the District Branch of the Ministry of State Security. Tomorrow, the chief of ROMGB, "Citizen" Galliulin, would explain to us our

192

"rights and obligations." But for the time being, our new friend invited us to share his white bread—unknown in Karmakchi—which he had brought from Kzyl-Orda. And tomorrow, he would help us find a place to live and give us a few pointers on our new way of life.

The only thing I dreamed of was to be able to wash in private. The prison bath remained fixed in my memory like an ugly nightmare: the degrading inspection by the prison matrons, the foul talk and obscene gestures of the hoydens. But things were not much better in Karmakchi—there was only a public bath, and it was reminiscent of a medieval engraving in a psychiatry textbook: the kind of place where at any minute you might see witches appear, who, with the aid of boiling water and switches, would try to exorcise the devil from the minds of the demented.

After we all had taken baths, our main concern was to get hold of some newspapers and find out the latest or at least recent news on what was happening in the world. It goes without saying that there were no newsstands in Karmakchi. But not far from our "hotel" there was a "Red Corner," a sort of reading room and library where the Moscow newspapers were available. The three of us decided to stop there before checking in at the *komendatura*.

The newspapers were not more than a week old. One issue of *Crocodile,* the satirical journal still published today by *Pravda* (the central organ of the Communist Party of the Soviet Union) contained the regular anti-Semitic feuilleton by Vasily Ardamatsky, an anti-Semite of the first water. The unbridled tone of this particular opus entitled "Pinya from Zhmerinka" left no doubt that the pogrom wave was still at its height in the capital and in the far-flung reaches of the Soviet Union as well.

In another issue of *Crocodile* we read an equally repellent article by Nikolai Gribachov on the doctor-assassins and their henchmen from the Joint Distribution Committee who had been unmasked by vigilant Soviet citizens, notably by a "true" daughter of the people and colleague of the "assassins," Dr. Lidiya Timashuk.

We felt terribly depressed as we left the Red Corner followed by the frozen gaze of the Soviet leaders whose portraits, framed in gold, adorned the walls of the reading room.

Our meeting with the chief of ROMGB was not as bad as we had expected. Galliulin, a Kazan Tatar and still a relatively young man, made no attempt at intimidation. He informed us that we were under the open surveillance of the *komendatura,* that we had to check in every ten days, that we were confined to a three-mile radius from the center of Karmakchi, and that neither housing nor employment was provided. In other words, you could go to the devil and die from hunger for all they cared. However, speaking off the record, Galliulin advised us not to be discouraged and to apply for a job in the village's one and only industrial enterprise, a rundown factory, in operation since the war, that manufactured spare parts for drills.

Our new friend and protector Izya Tubis was waiting for us not far from the *komendatura.* He treated us to some food and hot tea, and then we all set out in search of a place to live. A multitude of curious onlookers followed us as we walked along the broad streets of this steppe village, with its little clay houses, all of which were inhabited by exiles like us. The diversity of the population was remarkable. Was there any ethnic group that "Soviet justice" or the Special Sessions had overlooked? Volga Germans deported overnight en masse on the orders of Stalin himself at the outbreak of the war; Chechens and Ingushes who suffered the same fate in 1944 for allegedly having welcomed the German occupiers; Greeks from the Caucasian side of the Black Sea littoral and from the cossack village of Byelorechenskaya who were uprooted after the war, loaded on cattle cars and deported to these barren and arid steppes for the rest of their days. . . .

Later, after we got to know our neighbors better, we learned many horrible and appalling stories. A Greek by the name of Davidi (he worked in a plant producing carbonated water, something unknown in Karmakchi before the Greeks came) told us how the deportees in his car refused to disembark when they saw where they had been taken to. The train commander informed them that if they had not gotten off the train by the count of three, he would open fire. The courageous Greeks decided to resist. They held out for twenty-four hours, until a military detachment, sent from Kzyl-Orda, arrived. Under a hail of machine-gun bullets, they jumped from the car while shielding their children with their bodies. In the tumult, they lost everything they possessed; many families were separated, some members being shipped further out into the steppes, others remaining behind. Because of the three-mile limitation on the mobility of exiles, the hapless Greeks found themselves separated from their loved ones for many years: husbands separated from wives, sons from mothers, brothers from sisters!

But the human spirit is indomitable. The pain of separation was dulled in time by the day-to-day struggle to survive, which overshadowed all other considerations.

Some fine Russian people gave us shelter, among them the Ustyugovs—Serafima Petrovna and Sergei Vasilyevich—peasants from the Volga who had also been exiled. They had been "dekulakized" because Sergei's father, alone of all the villagers, had by the sweat of his brow cultivated his own garden. At first I told my boys that for the next ten years I would not set foot outside the little house. I felt that life in this desolate and godforsaken land would be impossible unless you wore blinders against the ugly reality that confronted you. But life must go on; I realized I had to open my eyes wide to achieve a better awareness of the situation, to fathom the sense of my own life and the life of others.

Our immediate problem was finding work. We set out for the factory that Galliulin had told us about. The chief engineer turned out to be a virulent anti-Semite. The fact that we were Jewish produced such a violent reaction he didn't even want to speak to us, and he literally threw us out. In desperation, we decided to offer our services to the railroad, where, we were told, there was a demand for various kinds of workers. But word had already reached the railroad administration that some Jews had arrived in the village and that the father and husband of these Jews had "committed sabotage in the Kremlin." I simply didn't have the strength to try to convince these simpletons, who were so poisoned by fear and anti-Semitic propaganda, that the charge was just not true. Tired and dejected and with hatred in our heart, we went back home. Happily, the Ustyugovs were there to give us a warm and sympathetic welcome and to console us with their story of how, despite difficulties, they had become acclimated to the region and had even learned to love it—for the fact was that life here was better than in the hungry village they had come from.

News of the arrival of Jews in Karmakchi spread like wildfire. Before long we received the visit of two ladies who, until then, had been the sole representatives of our people in the village. One of them, Tsilya Gilkina, was a judge—or, as the villagers called her, a "defender." She was still in her prime, although her weather-beaten face was prematurely furrowed with wrinkles; her eyes were clear azure blue. She was slender and nimble, effervescent and alert. Soon after the outbreak of the war, she became stranded in Karmakchi when she and her two children were evacuated from Odessa to Kazakhstan. Her husband had been killed at the front, and she decided against returning to postwar Odessa, where, she knew, the atmosphere had become poisoned by anti-Semitism and it was exceptionally difficult for a Jewish woman to secure a position. So she had stayed on in Karmakchi, enjoying the respect of the local inhabitants, doing legal work. She moved about the steppes on camelback, which was the most practical means of transportation in this region. Tsilya advised us to try again at the factory the next day, this time going straight to the director, who had the reputation for kindness and consideration.

Tsilya's companion, Yevgeniya Isayevna, was, like us, an exile. She had been deported in 1940, that is, even before the German invasion. Her husband had come to the USSR from China, where he had worked as a bookkeeper in a movie house operated by the Chinese Eastern Railway, which had belonged to Russia until the USSR ceded it to China. Many Russian employees of the CER migrated to the Soviet Union and in 1937 were arrested and shot or sent away to a labor camp. Yevgeniya's husband had perished, and she and her children ended up in Karmakchi. After the war, her children were permitted to leave and they settled someplace in Russia, but she stayed on, working as the assistant to the financial director of the factory.

The next morning we did, in fact, see the director of the factory, Borodai. He was a good-natured, likable Ukrainian. When he learned that we were members of the family of a writer and had ten long years ahead of us, he treated us with the utmost consideration and even questioned the justice and rectitude of the sentence that had been meted out to us. "Do you mean to tell me that children are answerable for their father?" He was visibly embarrassed: how in the world could he offer "menial jobs to such educated people?" But I succeeded in persuading him any kind of job was preferable to dying from hunger. He offered Simon the job of apprentice to a planer, and Yura was assigned to the packing shop, where he would nail crates. Borodai didn't find a job for me, though. In his naiveté and simplicity, he felt sure that I could find something to do in the factory club where the workers had formed singing and dancing groups. But singing and dancing were the last things on my mind, and naturally I turned down the post, although I did appreciate his good intentions.

Thereafter, Borodai always took a great deal of interest in Simon, never failing to ask him about my health, offering to lend him money when the factory "gave out" some appetizing eatables on holidays. Whenever he passed the lathe where Simon worked he always asked, "Well, Marx, how goes it?"—in his misery, Simon had stopped shaving and had grown a long, thick beard that earned him the nickname.

After I returned from exile to Moscow, I tried on a number of occasions to locate Borodai (he left Kazakhstan shortly after we did) and thank him for all he had done for us, but my efforts were in vain.

The pittance that Simon and Yura received for

their labors was barely enough to keep food on our table. Winter is a particularly difficult time, since vegetables are nonexistent and food prices treble. Had it not been for the constant care of my mother, who sent us food parcels regularly, we would never have survived. Little by little I adapted myself to the situation, knitting sweaters and hats for the local ladies, the wives of officials; I even knitted a hat for the wife of that anti-Semite, the chief engineer.

My thoughts were constantly with Markish. How was he getting along? Was he still alive? Where was Lyalya? And what would happen to David if they found him in Baku? How would my mother manage alone? . . . One day, a letter arrived from my mother telling me David had gone back to Moscow, been picked up by the MGB and ordered to leave for exile immediately. Our ever-loyal nanny and friend Lena Khokhlova was traveling with him and we could expect them any day. And, indeed, the "juvenile delinquent" soon arrived. He had grown and matured, but this did not dampen his childish enthusiasm when he recounted his adventures to us nor diminish the pride he felt in joining us grown-ups in our suffering and sharing our common lot. He took a childlike delight in exile as something strange and exotic. It was this perhaps that protected him from the terrible ugliness of our new life.

I was anxious for David to resume his studies, for even here, in this backwater, knowledge could come in handy. The school was quite primitive; the children were left to their own devices, and the teachers not only commanded no respect, but were even afraid of their wayward charges. Still, there were a few good-hearted children.

At first, the children met David with hostility—a "city-slicker" and a Jew to boot, whose father had "sabotaged the Kremlin." They threw stones at him more than once, and I lived in perpetual fear. But one day David triumphantly announced that I need no longer be afraid, because he now had a loyal body-guard and protector in Kalu, a Chechen, who was a few years older than he. Kalu knew how to use his fists, and the other lads gave him a wide berth.

One day, early in March 1953, Simon came home

from the night shift with the news that Stalin was gravely ill. A hush fell over us. For a second we panicked—what would happen to us if he died?—but only for a second. We sat glued to the radio waiting for the next news broadcast. At dawn, March 6, the radio reported Stalin had died. Huddled about the loudspeaker, all of us, including the Ustyugovs, listened to the voices of the "orphaned" leaders speaking from Moscow. The speech of Molotov, swallowing his tears of fear (or joy?), the new appointment of Beria, the changes in the higher echelons—all attested to the disarray in the capital. Our landlady, Serafima Petrovna, sobbed fitfully. "What are you crying for?" I asked irritatedly. "Are you sorry for him? Don't you care what he did to you?"

Choking with tears, the frightened and unhappy soul answered, "I'm afraid things might get worse." Now, more than a quarter of a century later, I realize that we, too, were not exactly the picture of courage or fortitude, but also were filled with despair and a feeling of resignation: happen will what happen may! As luck would have it, March 6 was also Simon's twenty-second birthday. So while the loudspeaker poured forth the dolorous sounds of weeping and funeral marches, the mailman delivered a slew of telegrams from relatives and friends: "Congratulations!" "Congratulations and may the future be brighter," and so on. We were practically certain that this spelled trouble for Simon, since, naturally, all our mail was read. I accordingly got out his birth certificate so that I could readily produce it for the MGB agents when they came for the hapless hero of the day. But evidently the MGB had other more important things on their mind just then.

Meanwhile, the *komendatura* intensified their vigilance: not knowing what impact the new developments in the country would have on the "politicals," the commandant served notice on us that from now on we were to check in at his office every five days. To make sure we got this order, he sent a messenger to our house at a most ungodly hour.

The rumor spread like wildfire among the exiles that a plan was afoot to ship us all out to the back country, far away from the railroad line. Life seemed more oppressive than ever. Adding to the atmosphere of hopelessness were the letters I began to receive in response to my countless appeals to the highest echelons for information as to the whereabouts of Markish. Here is the most cynical one of all.

I hereby inform you that your complaint relative to the case of Markish, Peretz Davydovich, addressed to the Presidium of the Supreme Soviet of the USSR, was referred to the Procurator's Office for a decision.

Pursuant to the investigation, it has been established that Markish, P.D., was condemned by the Military Collegium of the Supreme Court of the USSR for having perpetrated grievous crimes against the State.

It has also been established that the verdict handed down in your case was valid and that there are no grounds for its abrogation or mitigation.

Your complaint is held null and void.

Military Procurator
Office of the Chief
Military Procurator
Captain of the Judiciary
(Kozhura)

At this time, the loving, heartening letters of our dear guardian angel, my mother, were our sole source of joy.

The Passover holiday fell in April. We decided to celebrate it in accordance with all the rules. It took some doing, but I scared up a chicken in the village. Our new friends Tsilya Gilkina and Yevgeniya Isayevna, whom I invited to the first night's Seder, brought along matzo that had been baked in the prayer house in Kyze-Orda. (The prayer house had been founded by the small Jewish community made up predominantly of Bessarabian Jews who had been exiled to this region immediately after their country had been "joined" with the Soviet Union.) The unprecedented delicacies—herring, dried fruits and sweets of all kinds —that graced our Seder table were provided by the painstaking care of my mother, who had sent us a parcel from Moscow. Among the other guests who came to celebrate Passover with us were the principal of David's school, the Korean Pak and his wife, who taught geography; Dr. Teimwiaz Dolidze, a Georgian exile, and his wife Zina Bernstein, a "free" Jewish doctor who had been assigned to this area after completing her training at Moscow Medical Institute.

On April 4, the country was rocked by the sensational news that the "doctor-assassins" had been rehabilitated. It now turned out they were completely innocent, that the whole story from beginning to end had been fabricated by saboteurs acting under the direction of Ryumin, deputy minister of State Security. At the moment when the governmental communiqué started coming over the radio, I was standing by the stove in the passageway preparing lunch for my boarders—Simon and Yura—whom I expected home during the noontime break. I could hardly believe my ears. It was Ryumin who, one year after Markish's arrest, had come to our apartment with a party of MGB officers to search for "material evidence" of Peretz Markish's guilt. I trembled as I listened to the radio speaker repeat over and over again the text of the communiqué. Good God! There was no time to lose; I must get to the *komendatura* at once—I possessed information on the activity of Ryumin. I remembered every word one of my knitting students in Moscow had told me about him. I would save Markish! I would save his friends and colleagues! I rushed out of the house and was heading for Galliulin's office as fast as my legs could carry me when I ran into Simon and Yura. They, too, had heard the broadcast, but their reaction was more reserved, and they cooled my excitement. We decided the best thing was to discuss the situation calmly and try to come up with some effective plan. That same night I sat down and wrote a letter. I decided I would bypass the *komendatura* (through whom official letters and complaints had to be channeled) and send it off on the postal train that came through Dzhusaly station in the morning.

At daybreak, after a sleepless night, I read the letter

201

to my children and then left for the station. Located next to Dzhusaly station was the Tashkent Railway School. It happened to be recess time, and the children were playing and shouting in the school yard. When they saw me, they came running with cries of "kike, kike, on a rope he swings." This was more than I would stand. God knows where I got the strength, but I grabbed two of the ruffians by the scruff of the neck and dragged them off to the teachers' room. The teachers gazed in stupefaction at the "notorious" saboteuse. "Why, you don't listen to the radio?" I exploded. "Enough of your mockery. You'll answer to me for everything, for everything!" I was so beside myself with rage that they became frightened and began assuring me that they would explain to their students that the doctors—and, therefore, the Jews—were innocent.

Drained by my outburst, I dragged myself to the station. When the train stopped, I tossed my letters in the mailbox—the original was addressed to the Central Committee of the CPSU, and I sent a copy to my mother. I still have the one I saved for myself:

Karmakchi,
April 5, 1953

Respected Comrades!

I, Lazebnikova, Esther Yefimovna, the wife of the well-known Jewish poet Peretz Markish, implore you to read this letter and give it your due consideration.

To this very day, I know absolutely nothing about the fate of my husband, arrested in January 1949. Throughout the long period of the investigation (January 1949–December 1952), he was in Moscow in the Ministry of State Security. My attempts to track down his dossier or to obtain a copy of the verdict have been of no avail.

On the first of February 1953, my entire family and I were exiled to Kzyl-Orda Province, Kazakh SSSR for a term of ten years with confiscation of property as members of the family of a traitor to the motherland. That cruel verdict was handed

202

down by the clique of Ryumin with the knowledge and assent of the former Minister of State Security Ignatyev. Now that the traitorous "activity" of the adventurer Ryumin, who deliberately tried to stir up national hatred, has been exposed, the arrest and conviction of my husband are eloquent proof of his nefarious aims. To what monstrous crimes was Peretz Markish compelled to confess, to what inhuman methods must he have been subjected to wrest a confession from him so that after almost a four-year investigation the terrible verdict of TRAITOR TO THE MOTHERLAND was inflicted on him! After this ruthless action against the person of Peretz Markish, a Special Session presided over by former Minister Ignatyev, which never so much as confronted a single member of our family, decided our fate *in absentia* and, in violation of Soviet legality and of the Soviet Criminal Code that fixes the penalty for families of a traitor to the motherland at *five years exile,* and impelled by the visceral hatred of the unmitigated racist, with a flourish of the pen condemned wholly innocent people to *ten years exile in the steppes of Kazakhstan.* Here, the local administration of the MGB did not authorize us to live in the provincial capital where we could be useful in our specialities, but sent us to the village of Karmakchi, one hundred miles away. Here we are subjected to a climate of hostility on the part of the population, and of distrust on the part of the local authorities. Our Jewish origin seals our miserable fate—we are taken for the family of one of the doctors who were accused, at the time, of being murderers and spies. This incites the bestial hatred of the children of the local inhabitants, who pursue us with savage cries of "Abraham, Jew, the sooner you croak the better," etc. We are refused work everywhere. We are doomed to moral and material extinction.

We beg you, respected comrades, to come to our aid. Look into the fate of Peretz Markish and let us know it, no matter how terrible it may be.

Help us to find out where he is and whether he is alive.

E. Lazebnikova

Time dragged on painfully. We were waiting for a miracle that was not to happen. But my mother reassured us in her letters that she was sparing no efforts on our behalf, that "people were talking" about a change for the better, that in any case there was no reason to despair. Man is a believing animal. We wanted to believe that our life was not completely ruined. The rare friends that had remained steadfast in their loyalty to us helped by sending parcels—groats, sugar and other items. Other friends did not forget I was still a young woman who in a happier time enjoyed being well dressed, and they treated me to a new dress, face cream, perfume. To this day I remain grateful to my friends who didn't let me forget about myself and bolstered my spirits.

We finally learned of our Lyalechka's whereabouts from Nikolai Rapai, a fine young man and talented sculptor. Lyalya and he met at the Kiev Institute, and when Lyalya was exiled to the region of Krasnoyarsk following her arrest on February 19, 1953, Nikolai joined her. From Dolgy Most, her place of exile, Lyalya wrote that Nikolai had asked her to marry him and wanted to share her exile. After their marriage, he had returned to Kiev, hoping to obtain a year's leave of absence from the Art Institute so as to be with Lyalya.

The rehabilitation of the doctors gave me new determination, and I wrote to all higher Party and government echelons asking for information on Markish and trying to obtain a review of his case as well as of our own. Above all, I sought permission for the entire family of Markish to be reunited, on the assumption that there was a good chance such a request might be granted. I asked that my brother Alexander Lazebnikov, who had been sentenced to lifelong exile, be allowed to join his sister. We waited impatiently for a reply.

One day early in May, a messenger came from the *komendatura* and ordered me to appear at once before

Major Akhmetov. Usually, a summons from the commandant augured no good. With heavy heart, I left for his office accompanied by Simon and David. I had no sooner stepped into the room pompously called Major Akhmetov's "study," than I knew from the fierce expression on the face of our lord and master that nothing pleasant was to be expected from this visit. Akhmetov pounced on me, ranting and raving and causing such a rumpus that it was some time before I realized the complaint involved David, who, it turned out, had taken a boat with one of his friends and crossed over to the other side of the Syr-Darya and gone fishing. We exiles, as I mentioned earlier, were confined to a three-mile radius, and the boys had broken this rule. I was warned that if there was another violation by my son, I would be sentenced to twenty-five years in a labor camp! For the first time in my life in exile, I was so scared that I didn't dare antagonize Akhmetov. I signed a promise that in the future I would be responsible for the acts of my son. I was dismissed. Outside, David and Simon, who had overheard the violent outburst of Akhmetov, flung their arms around me, happy over the relatively satisfactory outcome of the altercation. But we walked home in silence, depressed by the whole episode.

I tried as best I could to explain to David that he was not a free man and was subject to the regulations of the *komendatura,* and that if he failed to obey them, I'd be in serious trouble. I felt sorry for him: at his age, it was hard to forego childish pleasures or see any harm in them. David, who in general was not very talkative, didn't say a word. He crawled onto the trunk that served as his bed and lay there all day and all night, his face turned toward the wall. We never raised the subject again; I was afraid of traumatizing the child.

The less hope we had of an early release, the harder it was for us to reconcile ourselves to the thought that we might never know what had happened to Markish. Then, one hot, sunny day, I was again called to the *komendatura.* This time Akhmetov was with someone I'd never seen before, by all appearances, a Russian. Almost cordially Akhmetov began questioning me. The first thought that crossed my mind was that I was on my way to a labor camp for having bypassed the *komendatura* in dispatching my letter to the Central Committee. Just as I was mulling over this possibility, the stranger broke in and informed me that he had come from "the center," that my letter addressed to Moscow was being given careful consideration, and that he wanted to know something about our living and working conditions.

I asked him only one thing: to authorize us to transfer to the provincial center Kzyl-Orda, where we could put our knowledge to good use and begin to work in our specialty again, the teaching of foreign languages.

I positively flew back home because I was so anxious to share my hopes with my loved ones.

That was not all; notwithstanding the official decree, published shortly after Stalin's death, declaring an amnesty solely for prisoners who had been guilty of criminal acts, we were suddenly notified by the *komendatura* that our term had been cut by one-half. Thus, even before Khrushchev came to power, the first symptoms of de-Stalinization appeared. Encouraged by this turn of events, we began to write even more energetically than before to all echelons of authority in an effort to locate Markish and have his case reexamined. My dear mother came to stay with us to give us warmth and encouragement. Her arrival was a real holiday for us.

The summer was drawing to a close. It was particularly oppressive for us, accustomed as we were to the cooler climate of central Russia rather than the sweltering temperatures that rose as high as forty degrees centigrade on the barren steppes. News started filtering through from Moscow of new and favorable developments: this person had been freed, that one had been transferred from a labor camp into exile. There was talk that the Central Committee had set up a special commission to review the cases of labor camp internees. Our dear messenger from the free world, my mother, decided to return to Moscow at once in order to continue her efforts on our behalf. It was sad for us to see her go, but there was no one else to deal with our problems.

One day in August, Yevgeniya Isayevna rushed

excitedly to our house. The commandant had informed her that she was free to join her children. This was amazing news. It meant the "thaw" had begun. To be sure, the freeing of Yevgeniya Isayevna—who confused Malenkov, Stalin's chief deputy, with Marshall Malinorsky, who called Stalin "Stalinov"—didn't prove much of anything. She had been exiled way back in 1938, had never even dared to ask for the reexamination of her "case," and, the way it looked, the new commission had begun by taking up the oldest cases first. But still, although we tried to restrain our optimism, we celebrated this event. We even gave a party, to which we invited the *beau monde* of Karmakchi, and we discussed and assessed the changes that had taken place since the fall of Beria (he had been arrested in May). Again I wrote to Moscow recalling our difficult situation and soliciting anew our transfer to Kzyl-Orda, where we could work in our professions.

At about this time, Simon's girl friend from the university came to join him. She had completed her studies, received a diploma qualifying her as a teacher of English, and had requested a post in Kzyl-Orda.

Just a few days before the school year was to begin, we finally received permission to move to Kzyl-Orda.

17 / Tower of Babel in Kazakhstan

WE HAD SEEN Kzyl-Orda for the first time without an escort about six weeks before we moved there. During the first half of the summer Simon had fallen ill from a lung inflammation, and it was absolutely essential for him to have a chest x-ray. Our friend, Dr. Teimuraz Dolidze, issued the medical certificate required by the *komendatura,* and we were given leave to spend one week in the provincial capital.

After the barren wastes of Karmakchi, we were overwhelmed by Kzyl-Orda, with its forgotten charms of civilization: two-story houses, paved streets, a decent bathhouse, a motion picture theater, stores, and marketplace. But what overjoyed us more than anything else was to see trees again, majestic poplars lining the irrigation canals. We looked with envy on the pedestrians who, for the most part, were exiles like ourselves, but who, thanks to the munificence of the authorities, enjoyed the incomparable advantages of this verdant paradise.

Teimuraz Dolidze had referred us to the doctor of the province tuberculosis dispensary, Edi Pokhis. Edi was a free settler, whereas her husband Yekutiel (or Ksil to his family and friends) was an exile. Ksil landed in Kzyl-Orda in 1940, at the age of eighteen. His father had been a shopkeeper in the small Bessarabian village of Bálc, or Beltz. When the Red Army, on the orders of Stalin and with the blessings of Hitler, occupied that part of Romania, Ksil's father, along with tens of thousands of other "bourgeois," was shipped to Siberia to rot in some concentration camp while his family was sent into exile. Ksil had worked at a variety of jobs—whatever was necessary to keep his mother and younger brothers alive. In the thirteen years he had been there, he had made a "brilliant career" until he was now the deputy director of the wholesale department of the Province Trade Division. The director was, as might be expected, a free man, a Party member and non-Jew, who did nothing but draw his salary, while Ksil Pokhis killed himself working night and day.

After we had officially moved to Kzyl-Orda, I came to know Ksil quite well, and I realized I had never met a man or a Jew like him before. He belonged to the "exploiting class"—i.e., in bygone days, to that village bourgeoisie for which Markish had such a genuine aversion and which was so thoroughly condemned by the Jewish revolutionary poets. But Ksil was the personification of goodness, tact and discretion, ever ready to come to the aid of anyone in distress. He was a merchant and, therefore, by our criteria and by Soviet criteria, he belonged to the most lowly of professions, supposedly distinguished by vulgarity, stupidity and chicanery.

Ksil Pokhis had only a high school education, and life in exile, of course, had not been conducive to the acquisition of intellectual baggage. He was, nevertheless, a genuinely intelligent and cultivated man, with a keenly perceived view of the world. As Ksil saw it, Soviet society, which never tired of proclaiming its lofty principles, was actually the most unprincipled society in the world: deeply held convictions had long ago been supplanted by the newspaper slogans of the day or, even more frequently, by fear or indifference. In the years since Markish's arrest, this was a lesson I had learned well.

At the core of Ksil's convictions lay an idea of Judaism quite different from the one Markish and his friends cultivated and nurtured. Far be it from me to judge how deeply Ksil believed in God (or perhaps he didn't believe in God at all), but Judaism with its rituals and traditions was to him an essential, inalienable part of Jewish life and of the Jewish idea. It was not fanaticism; it was not a hysterical allegiance to the letter and the law of the Old Testament that characterized Ksil's concept of Judaism. He saw it rather as an almost physiological necessity: without the Sabbath, the festive Passover week, the "awesome" High Holidays, the joy of Chanukah and Purim, Jewish national consciousness would not endure, would not survive.

On Yom Kippur, I went to the synagogue for practically the first time in my life—in any case, for the first time seriously. Seriously in the sense that I came not merely out of curiosity, to observe strange rites and prayers; I came to feel myself among my own people, people I needed and who needed me. We shared the same sufferings, the kinship and wanderings of the past and of the present, and the hopes for the future. To be sure, any member is free to leave that community if he so desires (though this freedom of choice is denied them by the Soviet authorities), but if he does so he takes away with him a particle of that future hope and, to that extent, it grows dimmer.

A cramped, squat house consisting of two rooms

divided by a corridor is all there is to the synagogue in Kzyl-Orda. One room is used by the "Bessarabians" (that is, all the European Jews), the other by the "Bukharans." (As I learned from Ksil Pokhis, this division was inevitable inasmuch as the Bukharan Jews not only speak their own language, a Persian dialect, but also have completely different rites.) But even though we were separated by a corridor, we all felt we belonged to a single community, to one people. As I looked at the aged rabbi dressed in a white *kittel* that resembled a shroud, and at the faces of the congregation, so different from one another, and when, at the end of the service, I cast a furtive glance at the Bukharans—stately old men with flowing white beards, youths with faces out of Persian miniatures, young girls of incredible beauty, and older women of unbelievable corpulence—as I looked upon all of this, I felt and I understood that the living Jewish society, with its cohesion and mutual concerns, was *not* the intellectual elite (writers, actors, artists), divorced and alienated from their people despite their love for them; *living* Jewry was the people in its totality, the scholars and the uneducated, the rich and the poor, the pious and the irreligious.

These realizations of mine came later, in October. But now it was the end of July, and Simon and I were sitting in the hospitable home of the Pokhises, looking at the kind face of Edi and at the ruddy face of Ksil, tanned and marked by the burning heat, the frosts and winds of Kazakhstan, at his small, serene, clear blue eyes. Perhaps what he said was nothing particularly new or original, but it seemed to confirm our innermost thoughts, to give our trampled and bruised life meaning and significance. In any case, we found ourselves hanging on his every word, as if we were listening to the voice of the people, of *Kol Yisroel* ("All Israel"), of which we were an integral part. We saw that our own episode had its place in the history of our people. The understanding and age-old wisdom that Ksil Pokhis gave expression to suddenly meant more than anything else to us.

Ksil's mother-in-law Baba Libeh (as everyone called her, and I must confess with some embarrassment that I never thought of asking her her full name) gave us solace and encouragement. Sprinkling her Russian with Ukrainian and Yiddish words, she tried to persuade us that everything would work out well in the end; we must just be patient. *Pamelekh* ("Give it time") was Baba Libeh's favorite expression. Baba Libeh also loved to reminisce about her youth in Kiev, a period that remained etched in her mind as one of great cultural refinement.

What we received that afternoon from Ksil and Baba Libeh was a reason to hope that the future, although it might not be one of unadulterated happiness, would at least be better than stagnating in Karmakchi. Our hopes were not deceived: the period of something less than a year we spent in Kzyl-Orda remains a bright spot in the memory of all our family.

The sun was rapidly setting by this time, so Ksil sent us on our way to our lodgings. The community that arose in this remote corner of the land through the evil design of the Soviet regime conserved the fine rural traditions of villages in Bessarabia, the Ukraine, Lithuania, and elsewhere. The local residents took turns giving hospitality to newcomers. This time it was the turn of a tailor whose name, unfortunately, escapes me. The tailor, a lanky, unusually taciturn man, came by the Pokhises' house to pick us up. He was accompanied by his wife, Klara, who, unlike her husband, talked nonstop. Before we reached their place, she managed to tell us not only the whole story of her entire family (exiled, of course), but a half-dozen other stories. Eventually, we entered a courtyard, went up a few steps and stood before a locked door. The tailor, after searching through all his pockets, blurted out in a squeaky voice in Yiddish, *"Klyare, vu iz dos shlisl?"* ("Where's the key?").

Those were the first words we had heard him utter.

The room was tiny. They gave me the bed of their daughter, who had gone to spend the night with relatives. Simon had to content himself with a place on the floor under the table. We hadn't dozed off yet when a shadow slipped through the open window and jumped on the couple's bed. Klara, who was already snoring, awoke with a start and shrieked in an ugly voice, "The cat!"

The cat became as frightened as Klara and made for the window. The tailor didn't budge. Perhaps fifteen minutes had elapsed when the same thing happened again, but this time it was Simon who yelled; the cat had brushed his tail against his nose. That his guest should be so discomfited was more than the host could tolerate. The tailor got up out of bed completely naked (it was a terribly hot night) and spoke for the second and last time in our presence: *"Klyare, vu iz mayn hemd?"* ("Where is my shirt?").

Leisurely slipping on a long nightshirt that reached to the floor, the tailor groped about in the darkness until he dragged out the cat from under my bed, where it had hidden. With the cat screaming all the while, he wound it over his head like a sling and flung it through the window for all he was worth. Apparently the cat lost his taste for any further mischief, and the rest of the night we slept in peace.

When morning came, we set out for the market, not because we wanted to buy anything, but simply to feast our eyes on the abundant variety of fruits and vegetables, the likes of which we had never seen in Moscow. The display reminded me of my early years in Baku, Tbilisi and Constantinople. But it was not the native Kazakhs who gave the market the aspect of an oriental bazaar; until recent times, they had been a nomadic people with no agricultural tradition. The Kzyl-Orda bazaar was started by the Koreans, the first ethnic minority to be sent into exile en masse by Stalin. In 1936 or 1937, fearing a war with Japan, Stalin ordered the liquidation of the Korean National District with its capital at Posyet (southwest of Vladivostok) and deported the Koreans, who were regarded as potential Japanese spies, to Central Asia and Kazakhstan, far from the Japanese threat. The consequences of such a forced migration are not hard to imagine. The abrupt change from a humid maritime climate to a rigorous continental climate took its toll of the very old and the very young. Life under open skies or, at best, in mud huts, was compounded by the cruel and humiliating treatment inflicted on these innocent people. The

Soviet regime recognizes only one kind of statistics—those demonstrating its successes and achievements (real or imaginary, it's all the same). But there are no statistics on the number of Koreans who perished. Those who did survive, though, estimate that between forty and fifty percent of the deportees died, for the most part from tuberculosis. And those survivors created the richest and most flourishing kolkhozes in all of Kazakhstan and Central Asia, producing bumper crops of rice and vegetables. During World War II, these kolkhozes contributed huge sums to the country's defense fund, and this earned the Koreans a pardon for sins they had not committed. After 1950, the Koreans were given passports (i.e., identity cards), and were allowed to settle wherever they wanted or even to be repatriated to North Korea if they so desired.

The Koreans from Posyet were not only an example of industry, tenacity and a lust for life. They were also the backbone of intellectual life in Kzyl-Orda. With the liquidation of the Korean National District, the Posyet Pedagogical Institute had been transferred and was reestablished as the Kzyl-Orda Pedagogical Institute. Even in 1953, nearly one-half of the institute's faculty was Korean, to say nothing of the fact that a considerable number of Koreans taught in the many high schools of the province. The latter were, of course, Russian schools: Korean schools for the free population were as unheard of as Chechen, Greek or other ethnic schools for the exile population. In this respect, as in so many others, the Stalin regime did not differentiate between the free population and the exile population.

In 1949, the indefatigable Soviet authorities, in part to help out the Koreans, in part to supplant them, sent in Turks from Transcaucasia to engage in vegetable growing and horticulture. Rumor had it that although they had been living in Georgia, they had retained their Turkish nationality. Whether this was actually so, I cannot say, but I do know, because I saw them with my own eyes, that there were real Turks in real Turkish fezzes at the Kzyl-Orda marketplace. They sold wonderful carrots, cabbages, apples, and even pears, competing successfully with the Koreans.

Simon and his new wife were the first to leave Karmakchi. Authorization for our transfer to Kzyl-Orda came through at the end of August, just a few days before the school year was to begin, so they had no time to lose. Simon's wife had been appointed to a post in the "railroad school," which was under the direct administration of the Special School Department of the Ministry of Transport, instead of under the Municipal or Provincial Department of Education. As such it provided special benefits to the teaching staff.

Simon did not put much store by rumors of a crying need for foreign language teachers in Kzyl-Orda. Therefore, he too was anxious to be on hand before the school year commenced. While his wife was greeted with open arms, Simon received a cool reception. Krikbayev, the superintendent of the Municipal Department of Public Education, a young, by no means stupid (and, therefore, cynical) Kazakh, immediately told Simon first, that the Kzyl-Orda schools had no need of his services, and then, in the same breath, that if comrade so-and-so, adviser of the Party Province Committee, were of another opinion, there would be no lack of work for Simon. He casually added that the principal boys' school in the city, the Lenin School, was without a teacher of English.

Simon did not miss the point: a final okay—or *dobro*, as they say in Soviet Russia—from the Province Committee was a must. Needless to say, Simon left immediately to seek out the committee adviser, who listened with a sympathetic ear (among other things Simon said to him: "If exiles are not deprived of the right to vote, why should they be denied the right to work?"), and then called up Krikbayev and gave his *dobro*. Simon was named to the Lenin School.

It bears mentioning here that getting along under the conditions of the Stalinist terror was above all connected with the fact that the notion of law and order is alien to the Russian character. It is one factor that favorably differentiates Soviet from Nazi totalitarianism. If German punctiliousness and methodicalness had ever superimposed itself on "socialist" bloodthirstiness, life would have been a real nightmare.

Places of exile differed as much in the opportunities they offered as they did in climatic conditions. Kazakhstan had the reputation of being a paradise—especially Southern Kazakhstan, where it was our good fortune to be—but not only because the region was bountiful in potatoes and radishes, watermelons and melons, produce unknown in Siberia or in the far north of European Russia. What was really important was that the exile did not feel like an outcast or renegade, like a creature from some lower order. This was especially important to people in intellectual professions. In Siberia, in Dolgy Most, the village in the region of Krasnoyarsk where our Lyalya had been sent, for instance, not a single exile was permitted to engage in any intellectual pursuit. So at first Lyalya was a dairy-maid, and later, a plasterer; no other work could be found for her. Nor did the exiles' relatives who came of their own free will to be with their loved ones have a right to work at anything but physical labor. In our area, on the other hand, I can't think of one person with an education who was forced to dig the ground or lay bricks. As far as I can recall, the same situation held true for all the members of the families of Markish's "accomplices" who were exiled to various regions of Kazakhstan when we were.

David, Yura and I arrived in Kzyl-Orda not long after Simon and his wife. Simon had rented a whole house (three rooms) from a Bessarabian, a rich man by Kzyl-Orda standards. He owned three houses, registered in the names of various relatives, and rented out two of them. The first time we met the landlord, Yura, despite being twenty-five, introduced himself by his diminutive name, Yura. Our landlord, a large and fat Jew who was over sixty, startled by such informality, likewise introduced himself by his diminutive, which he distorted in his own fashion, as Vulodya. And "Reb [Rabbi] Vulodya" he has remained in all our family stories.

It was apparent that Reb Vulodya's house had been empty for a long time, and the dogs from the vicinity had taken over the large yard behind it for their love-making and squabbles. Not a night passed without all hell breaking loose under our windows: howling, barking, growling. The pack of hounds remained impervious to our threats, refusing to budge from their territory. We stood it for a week and then started looking for other accommodations. So it was that in the log of our life's peregrinations, one more landmark appeared: our home at 46 Kazakhskaya Street: two rooms and a hallway that doubled as a kitchen, in a solid, well-built, one-story structure on a high foundation. It was here we lived for more than nine months, right up until the time we returned to Moscow.

Simon's teaching duties proved anything but simple, particularly at the beginning. Russian schools in Kzyl-Orda were like Noah's Ark: a melting pot of all languages and tribes, the consequence of Stalin's social and nationality policy. The first thing that the school's director, Yuryev (Simon still remembers him with warmth and gratitude), told Simon was this: "It's not easy working here. It's no Moscow. Twenty-two nationalities, and most of them exiles to boot."

Indeed, the national composition of the student body was a faithful reflection of successive waves of persecution or, to be more precise, of the numerous attempts at genocide that the devil of the Kremlin had made on the territory of Kazakhstan. Koreans, Moldavians, Bessarabian Jews, Germans, Chechens, Ingushes, Karachayevans, Balkars, Greeks, Turks—I have listed only the "peoples in disgrace," ten in all, and I'm not certain that I haven't forgotten a few. The list does not include the children from all corners of the Soviet Union whose parents came to Kzyl-Orda either by choice or, as was more often the case, by force.

The spirit of chauvinism and national discrimination so zealously propagated by the authorities from the outset of the war and accentuated in the postwar period could not help but poison the minds of the youth. The spirit (or, rather, the decay and putrescence) of exile had demoralized the children and disarmed the teachers.

In the sixth grade, for example, there was a "bad boy" of eighteen, a Chechen, who was doing the year over again. He didn't do anything in school (I'm not sure he even really knew how to read), and the only reason he had stayed on, going from one grade to the next, was because of the grotesque law (like so many Soviet laws) making education compulsory: for all citizens up to the age of eighteen, secondary education (seven grades) is mandatory. Whether you like it or not, whether you have the capacity or not, makes no difference. You're not eighteen? You haven't completed seven grades? Then sit in school. So the Chechen boy was sitting out his final year. Not only had he no desire to learn; he was also unruly and terrorized his fellow students and teachers.

Once, after class, Simon tried to have a heart-to-heart talk with him. "Look here, you're grown-up now and by no means a fool; you need the education."

The Chechen frowned. "Look, you're an exile too, right?"

"Right."

"Then why are you feeding me fairy tales? What good is an education to an exile, to a Chechen? They don't take us into the army, they don't let us go and study in another city. Live here, die here! If I had any ability, then maybe I'd become a teacher. But I'm just an ordinary guy. What possibilities do I have? Digging ditches or working in a slaughterhouse."

Was there anything you could say to that? Simon did not try, and the Chechen appreciated his silence: From then on, he caused no more trouble during the English class.

Children who, from the day they are born, fall under the official surveillance of the KGB, who, from the time they begin to walk, acquire their first lessons of social injustice, of the most barefaced, unconscionable Soviet mendacity and hypocrisy, their first lessons of national humiliation, could not but react to their teachers (whom they saw as their overlords) with anything except suspicion and antipathy, and could not let an opportunity pass to ridicule them. A person had to possess an uncanny pedagogical aptitude and unqualified love for these unhappy children to gain their acceptance and affection. Simon did not possess such qualities. Besides, he was still not much more than a child himself. Yet, he won his first battles with his students, leading to a sort of truce that was generally honored.

The bone of contention of these first battles was Simon's patronymic, Peretzovich. The Russian word *peretz* means "pepper." Accordingly, Peretzovich can be construed as "son of pepper." When Simon introduced himself to his class and wrote his name and patronymic on the blackboard, the class rocked with laughter. A chorus of voices went up with cries of "Peretzovich," "Gorchitzevich" ("son of mustard"), "Chesnokovich" ("son of garlic"), "Solevich" ("son of salt") and so on. The anti-Semitic overtones of this raillery were all too apparent. But Simon did not lose his composure. The director was alarmed and sought —unsuccessfully—to persuade Simon to discontinue using his provocative, Jewish-sounding patronymic in favor of something more bland. By the third or fourth lesson, however, even the most unruly students had reconciled themselves to "Peretzovich."

Simon made the acquaintance of the school's German-language teacher, a woman named Lotta Rautenberg. Lotta's husband, Dr. Louis Rautenberg, a radiologist, was a German Communist who had fled Germany after Hitler came to power. He and his wife went first to Holland, where the Dutch organization that dealt with refugees offered them the choice of going to either Mexico or the Soviet Union. They chose the "land of socialism."

Louis was given a post in one of Moscow's leading hospitals, but shortly thereafter, during the early months of 1937, he was arrested and condemned by a special session of the MGB to a term of eight years in the camps. Following her husband's arrest, Lotta, who at that time was teaching in the Moscow Foreign Languages Institute, fell into the category of "socially dangerous elements" (one of the numerous varieties of political crime that existed in the Soviet Union). At the outbreak of the war, she found herself in a forced labor camp in Siberia. After the war was over, both husband and wife were released. Since they were forbidden to reside in Moscow, the Rautenbergs decided to settle in Kzyl-Orda, where Louis had been offered the post of radiologist in the province hospital. But before they knew it, they had lost their status as "free settlers" and become exiles. After their release from camp, they were given identity cards, but in their ignorance of Soviet notions of nationality, they had declared themselves as Germans. When the Rautenbergs arrived, the "militia" or police authorities in Kzyl-Orda, whose experience of Germans was limited to those who had been deported from the Ukraine to Kazakhstan during the early months of the war and sentenced to lifelong exile, withdrew their passports at once and placed both of them under the jurisdiction of the *komendatura*. For a number of years, the Rautenbergs tried, unsuccessfully, to prove they were, in fact, Jews. They applied to a variety of official agencies, including the Bureau of Records of the city of Kaliningrad (formerly Königsberg) and the Committee on Religious Affairs of the USSR Council of Ministers. For a person to try to prove, at the beginning of the fifties, that he was a Jew, seemed like insanity or a bad joke! In 1956, the Rautenbergs returned to Germany (East Germany, of course), rehabilitated by the Soviet authorities, but still unsuccessful in their efforts to convince them they were Jews and that, in all the rest of the civilized world, a Jew is not a racial category but a religious one.

The Rautenbergs, who were childless, became very attached to my sons. What was just a simple acquaintance at the start grew rapidly into a fast friendship. Lotta and Louis became frequent and welcome guests in our home. They had a house of their own which they had bought with the help of Louis's sisters, who lived in faraway America. Lotta, who was an excellent cook, treated us to her homemade pies.

Another resident of Kzyl-Orda was Mikhail Davidovich Romm, in his day a noted athlete and sports writer, the first-string goalkeeper of the Russian soccer team that played in international games even before World War I. (He was also first cousin to the late Mikhail Ilich Romm, the film director, who had the courage to refuse to take part in the anti-Israeli press conferences of the "trained" Jews that are so common in the Soviet Union. Declaring that he hated farce as a genre, Mikhail Ilich categorically refused to play any role whatever in the farce staged by the Soviet war hero Dragunsky and the critic Dymshits.)

Mikhail Davidovich worked as a legal adviser to the meat combine, one of the major enterprises in Kzyl-Orda. His first wife, an actress, had escaped arrest and repudiated him. Alone and forsaken by all, he married a simple and uneducated woman from whom he had been renting a room. Dusya was a person of unusual goodness and innate intelligence, and she understood her husband much better than his first wife had. Though he was rehabilitated some time in the late fifties, Romm was reluctant to leave Central Asia and began life anew in the capital, where it would have been an impossible struggle for him to resume his career at his age—he was past eighty. So he finished his days in Chimkent, in Southern Kazakhstan, where the Soviet Writers' Union had placed an apartment at his disposal.

18 / Farewell "Exile"-Orda

AT LONG LAST, in November 1953, our Lyalya received authorization to join us. She crossed the entire vast country—from the territory of Krasnoyarsk, in Siberia, to Kzyl-Orda, on the threshold of Central Asia —alone, producing a travel pass whenever necessary for verification of documents.

Now, almost the whole family was together again.

Lyalya found work in an "infant shelter," a home for foundlings and babies abandoned by their mothers in maternity hospitals. Her position carried the impressive title of "artist-decorator," but she earned only a miserly wage. Nevertheless, with our combined resources we were able to get by quite nicely. Lyalya was expecting a child, and it was not long before her husband came to join her.

We welcomed in the new year 1954 at our home on

Kazakhskaya Street with a number of new but already close and loyal friends. Despite the still impenetrable mystery shrouding the fate of Markish, despite our own condition of bondage, this new year was marked by serenity and joy—not only because we had the feeling the term of our suffering was coming to some sort of end, but also because Stalin's death almost a year before had brought some hope to the entire afflicted country. All told, we considered ourselves quite fortunate—to be in a city, to have work, and to be surrounded by bright, intelligent people and genuine friends. Deep inside, we harbored the firm conviction this new year would bring us our freedom. But none of us dared to speak this thought aloud.

Winters in Kzyl-Orda are severe; the land is swept by violent, almost hurricane-force winds that turn even a mild frost into a redoubtable enemy; you can get frostbite in a matter of minutes without even realizing what's happened.

At the end of January, Simon took over the German classes for a vacationing teacher at the Kazakh school in addition to his normal duties at the Lenin School. The Kazakh school was an easy fifteen-minute walk from the Lenin School, and during the long recess period Simon had time to go from one to the other. But once, on a very windy though relatively mild day (seven degrees below zero, centigrade), Simon went on his way as usual, proceeded directly to the classroom and, as was customary in the poorly heated building, didn't remove his coat. His ears and nose had already gone white, but in his haste to get the lesson under way, he didn't realize it. In the Kazakh schools, in contrast to the Russian ones, the pupils are very well behaved and never dare interrupt the teacher once the lesson has begun. It was only halfway through the lesson that Simon realized something was wrong, but it was already too late. His nose had swelled up to the size of a potato, and his ears were like thick pancakes.

The fact that the young Kazakhs were so well disciplined had no connection, of course, with any intrinsic quality or defect of their national character; it was the result of merciless beatings. When a Kazakh father

221

brought his son to school for the first time, he bowed deferentially to the teacher and pronounced the traditional, almost ritualistic phrase, "The flesh is yours, the bones are mine," meaning beat the hell out of him if you wish, but don't break any bones. The request was scrupulously honored. (There were beatings in the Russian schools, too, but they were administered on the sly, and with an eye to the parents, especially if they were Party bigwigs or, to cite a specific example, the director of the Kzyl-Orda prison—whose name, interestingly enough, was Palyuga, which means "scoundrel." But, even though they were wary, the teachers did resort to thrashings. Even the young Palyuga did not escape the hamlike fists of the physical education teacher, since that was, apparently, the language he understood best.)

The Kazakh schools were plagued by underage marriages, even though they were against the law. The girls' classes (the decree on separate educational facilities for boys and girls, issued by Stalin midway through the war, was not fully implemented in the majority of Kazakh schools where boys and girls continued to attend the same school but used different classrooms) lost nearly one half of their students in the fourth and fifth grades, when the girls were eleven or twelve years old. The law proved absolutely powerless against age-old tradition.

If I have dwelt at some length on the subject of schools, it is not just because the stories Simon told me have remained fixed in my mind, but also because the way of life in schools seems to me to be an accurate reflection of life as it was in general. This brings me to say something about two of Simon's pupils.

One February evening in 1954, we were surprised by a tapping at the window, at first quite gentle, gradually gaining force and momentum until the window pane shattered. We went outside to investigate a dozen times or so, but found nothing. The next evening eagle-eyed David noticed that a string with a stone attached was dangling above the window frame. He traced it to the branch of a nearby tree, where some unseen hand was causing the stone to sway back and forth until it succeeded in breaking the glass. On the third evening, we laid a trap. Yura, Simon and David posted themselves by the gate in the courtyard to wait for a signal from me. No sooner had the first, faint tapping been heard, than I gave the signal; the boys made a beeline for the tree and dragged down out of the darkness two adolescent boys, about fifteen. One of them turned out to be a student of Simon's, the other, a complete stranger. The boys hauled them off triumphantly to the "militia." Simon's student was crying and begged forgiveness, but the other fellow kept his cool and was even a bit insolent. It all became clear why at the station house. The sergeant on duty immediately discharged the stranger and made no mention of him in the *procès-verbal* on hooliganism that he drew up, citing only Simon's student. To the consternation of Yura and Simon, who could not hide their displeasure over such a miscarriage of justice, the sergeant explained, without the slightest touch of embarrassment, "Why, that other fellow is the son of the secretary of the Province Party Committee. I can't tell you the number of times we've complained to his father, but there's no stopping him. What a mischief-maker he is!"

The grandson of a drayman and the son of a Soviet district chief both broke the window, but the first is a hooligan, a juvenile delinquent, whereas the second is merely a mischief-maker, a harmless prankster. That's Soviet equity for you! Need anything more be said as to what the future holds for these two lads?

The other student of Simon's I would like to say something about was none other than Major Bikineyev, the head of the Section of Special Expatriates (*pereselentsy*) and Special Settlers (*poselentsy*) under the state security Province Administration, and the lord and master of all the exiles in the province of Kzyl-Orda.* Major Bikineyev was an external eighth-grade student who met with Simon once a week. He never missed a class, was always courteous and even gracious. Several years after our release,

* The term *pereselentsy* refers to people who have been exiled for an indefinite period, *poselentsy*, to either those like ourselves who have been exiled for a specific term or to former inmates of labor camps who have been sentenced to lifelong exile.

Simon and I bumped into him in a Moscow department store; he was in civilian clothes, and we did not recognize him immediately. But when we did, we greeted him like an old friend. He was just as glad to see us as we were to see him, and anxious to learn how we were getting along. The relations between the regime's victims and its agents did not always conform to official regulations or to the formulas of class struggle against "enemies of the people." This is another way, it seems to me, in which Soviet totalitarianism compares favorably with Nazi totalitarianism.

Spring was now fast approaching. The bats that swept by in the evening shadows were one of its harbingers. One evening, after we had all gone to bed, a bat flew into our house. It may have been as scared as I was; all I know is I was frightened to death when something cold brushed by my cheeks in the darkness. I jumped out of bed screaming, lit the lamp, and to my horror saw a bat flying under the ceiling. My cries woke up the whole house. Yura got up, put on his *shapka* (in Russia people believe bats entangle themselves in dark hair) and a pair of gloves, and chased after the bat until it finally found an open window and flew out.

The next morning we were all having a good laugh about it when suddenly someone remembered that bats were an omen of good news. "Well, Yurik, you can expect to hear from the *komendatura*. You, after all, were the hero of the night."

Our premonition was borne out. Just a few days later, the head of the special *komendatura*, Lieutenant Gavrikov (a portentous name: Secret Police agents are known in Russia as *gavriks*) called Yura into his office and informed him he was a free man. The Supreme Court of the USSR had upheld his claim that he had never been a member of the Markish household, but had simply been registered at our address. So, at the beginning of March, Yura left us. We were sad to see him go—we had grown very close during our year of exile—but at the same time we were happy about his "rehabilitation." (I place the word in quotes advisedly, because in his case, as well as in that of hundreds of thousands of others, the term is meaningless: "in the absence of any evidence of crime," the Soviet regime declares the innocence of a man who has never been accused of committing a crime but was nevertheless imprisoned or exiled for the fictitious crimes of another person to whom he happens to be related by blood or marriage, or with whom he is simply acquainted! Yura's rehabilitation was but one more straw in the wind auguring well for the entire family, Markish included—I still had a flicker of hope he might be alive.

It was about that time my brother Shura arrived, having been authorized to serve his term of lifelong exile with members of his family. This was another favorable omen. After fifteen years of separation there was much joy in our reunion. Shura found his journey from the Far North to Kazakhstan, under conditions of virtual freedom, an extraordinary adventure. He also found our Kzyl-Orda a fantastically beautiful city, with its irrigation canals, fresh vegetables and especially its beer, an inconceivable luxury in the Far North. (After Shura returned to Moscow in 1956, following his release, it was a whole year before he could pass an ice-cream vendor without treating himself to an eskimo pie, something he had dreamed of during his long years of prisons, camps and exile.)

Yes, the thaw had really started, even before the word had gained currency. It was used for the first time in this sense by Ilya Ehrenburg in his novel of the same name, the first literary work on the beginnings of de-Stalinization. *The Thaw* was published by the magazine *Znamya* in May 1954. But even prior to that, if my memory does not deceive me, I read an article in *Novy Mir* by Mikhail Lifshits. It was like a bolt of thunder. The subject as well as the title of the article seemed innocuous enough: it was nothing more than a review of Marietta Shaginyan's book *A Trip through Soviet Armenia*.

Mikhail Lifshits, a philosopher, aesthete and disciple of the celebrated Hungarian Marxist philosopher Georg Lukács (who lived in Moscow from 1933 to 1945), had occupied a lofty position in the Soviet literary establishment before the war but afterwards fell into disfavor for two reasons: he was a Jew and also an intransigent Marxist who rejected the transformations that Marxist thought underwent in the Stalinist epoch. Now, fired by the hatred and passion he'd been forced to hold back for so many years, Lifshits lashed into Shaginyan, who at one time or another had flirted with every modish literary, philosophical and theological school before "seeing the light" and "hewing to solid, proletarian positions."

Shaginyan's book was first published in 1950. In 1951, she won a Stalin Prize for it. Inspired by this solicitude of the leader (Stalin personally conferred the prizes), Shaginyan hurriedly prepared a second edition, strategically supplementing her travel impressions with the most adulatory (even for those days) panegyrics to the last work of genius ever to flow from the pen of the great leader and teacher, to wit, his brochure *Economic Problems of Socialism in the USSR*. Perhaps the dexterous old lady might have found further incentive for her facile and submissive pen had not the "immortal genius" proved to be mortal after all. In his review, Lifshits not only lambasted Shaginyan, but fired a broadside at Stalin—without, however, mentioning his sacred name—calling into question the deathbed revelations of the malevolent genius. That was the real intent of the article, which passed from hand to hand until the paper on which it was written fell into shreds.

It was a mystery to no one that the familiar, irresponsible gibberish of Shaginyan had served only as a pretext. But the pretext couldn't have been more successful. People at that time dubbed Shaginyan the "noble example" for a whole generation of literary time-servers reverently bowing before each and every idol that had been erected by the leadership. She was and still is an example. Today, with one foot already in the grave, she indefatigably burns incense before the ikon of Lenin, as she did yesterday before the ikon of Stalin.

Meanwhile, life continued with its daily share of troubles and joys. I became a grandmother of a boy

226

and a girl—a granddaughter born in exile, and a grandson born in freedom (Simon's wife had gone to Moscow to have her baby). Two weeks after his son was born, it was Simon's turn to leave for Moscow.

In the autumn of 1953, the daughter of Benjamin Zuskin, who had been sent into exile the same time as we but had been directed to another province of Kazakhstan, received permission to migrate to Karaganda so as to be able to continue her studies in a construction institute. When we learned the news from her, we all decided that it would be a good idea for Simon to take a similar course of action. Accordingly, Simon sent a letter to Khrushchev in which he requested permission to take the State examinations at any university that had a department of classical philology. He mentioned that he had successfully completed the university course of study and defended his undergraduate thesis, and that all he needed to fulfill the requirements for his undergraduate degree were three final exams, which could be taken within the space of one or two weeks. For a long time there was no reply, and we had all but forgotten about the letter, the more so since we had meanwhile learned from my mother, who had accompanied Simon's pregnant wife to Moscow, that our case was now being examined and that the outlook seemed promising.

One evening past midnight, there was a knock at the door. It was Special Commandant Gavrikov in person, and he had come to notify Simon to be at Major Bikineyev's in the morning when the office opened.

Obviously it was a matter of the utmost importance for the message to be delivered by a man like Gavrikov at such an ungodly hour. All that night we tossed and turned, mulling over the possibilities.

At eight o'clock sharp, Simon was waiting at the door to Bikineyev's second-floor office. I waited downstairs at the entrance to the building (since it was not I who had been summoned, the guard refused to let me in).

Simon came out a half-hour later looking terribly glum.

"Well?" I asked, rushing over to him.

227

He handed me a small sheet of official paper with lines of different colors. It was a printed form with the following text written in:

Travel Pass: The present certificate is issued to the exile settler Markish, Simon Peretzovich, pursuant to the decision of the Ministry of Internal Affairs of the USSR authorizing him to spend forty-eight hours in the city of Moscow for the purpose of taking State examinations at Moscow State University.

The pass was dated and signed by Major Bikineyev.

There was no need for Simon to say anything.

"It's all right," I said. "Don't be disappointed. No second thoughts. You're going. God bless Bikineyev, he didn't put any obstacles in your path. By the time you take your exams, you'll see, they'll have let us go, too!"

Before going, however, Simon had to give exams in his school. Fortunately, there weren't too many, and the director, who tried to be as helpful to Simon as possible, scheduled them at the very beginning of the exam period. Thus, at the end of May, Simon boarded the Tashkent-Moscow train. In one hand he carried a small suitcase; in the other, the *History of the CPSU* (the only subject that he had any concern about was Party history, which is an integral part of *all* State exams in *all* institutions of higher education throughout the Soviet Union). The book which Simon took along with him has been described as the most astonishing book the world has yet seen. No matter how many times you read it, the result is always one and the same: it's enough to read the first page to feel that you know it all by heart already, and this feeling stays with you until you've reached the final page. But no sooner have you turned over that final page than you realize that you don't remember a thing.

What was to be our last month of exile dragged on. I knew that the end was almost certainly in sight. Each new day seemed like torture. July is a very hot month in Kzyl-Orda, and with the ingratitude that is typical of human beings toward their lot, I became oblivious to the comfort provided by the shady trees, to the refreshing sprays of water splashing in the irrigation canals that had so delighted me less than a year before. All I felt or saw now was the withering heat, the Central Asian sands heaped up on the streets and in the courtyards. I could find no joy or distraction: neither the solicitude of my brother Shura, nor the amazing stories of what he had lived through (I never read or heard anything later as poignant as the stories he told me, not even in the masterpieces of concentration camp literature), nor Simon's letters telling of his tragicomic scurrying about between university and ministerial offices, where the functionaries could not believe their eyes or ears (An exile in Moscow! and not a fugitive? Would you believe it, a man released by Lubyanka, why even with its blessings, so that he can take the university exams!), nor my two-month-old granddaughter Katya—nothing gave me solace.

Only later did I realize how selfish I had been, how unfeeling I had been toward my brother. He had no prospect of freedom; all he could look forward to in the event of our liberation was being sent back to his former place of exile in the Far North.

At long last the dénouement came: a summons to the *komendatura,* a discharge certificate, a visit to the "militia" and the securing of a new passport. All this remains murky in my memory except for one detail: Ksil Pokhis assured me Simon would not have to come back especially to pick up his passport—Kzyl-Orda was not Moscow with its red tape and bureaucracy; people trusted each other more. Simon's passport was delivered to me. The police in Moscow would never have shown such flexibility or liberality.

We left Kzyl-Orda July 9. Lyalya and her husband were detained a few days longer, and they went straight to Kiev. David and I boarded the train. A huge crowd of people were on the platform to see us off. The thought came to me: They exiled us so as to isolate us, to keep us away from people, to suffer in solitude. But we were always surrounded by people, and people were kind to us. That may explain why we never felt afraid, did not become embittered or withdraw into ourselves, but always went toward people with trust and an open heart.

Farewell "Exile"-Orda! Many exiles joked good-naturedly, but I am sure many left a part of their hearts there.

19 / Ilya Ehrenburg

IT WAS THE BEGINNING of August 1954 when we stepped out on the wooden platform of Kazan Station. The life of dusty and pallid Moscow had not changed in the least—as if there never had been the blood, the lawlessness, the death of Stalin. . . .

We learned we would have to live with my mother in her one and only room, inasmuch as our apartment was occupied. Two of the rooms had been given over to an old retired doctor, who had once worked in one of the MGB's hospitals, and his daughter; another room was occupied by a physical education teacher and his wife, their daughter and his mother-in-law; and the fourth and final room had been let to a military procurator, who had just had it repainted. However, when he learned "through channels" about our imminent return, he decided not to move in. But we could not move in either, since there was a lot of red tape involved.

Markish had still not been rehabilitated, and we continued to be in the dark about his fate. I was informed by the office of the military procurator that "his case is under investigation." That was all. Supposedly they had no further information.

While I was in exile, my former employer, Professor Victorov, and his blind wife had died. His successor took me on as his secretary, and so I resumed my old routine.

The first opportunity I had to take a few days off from my work, I went to Leningrad to rest up a bit as well as to visit a few relatives. Soon after my arrival, I had a telephone call from Simon. "Mama," he said, "don't come back to Moscow. They've taken away our passports and are planning to send us into exile again."

He told me that, of course, "in coded language"; in the USSR you don't ever say such things openly, and certainly not over the telephone.

That same night I returned to Moscow. I learned that all the wives and children of Jewish writers had had their passports withdrawn and had been notified by the "militia" (police) that they could not reside in Moscow. Furthermore, Leningrad, the capitals of the Union Republics, the "heroic cities," and the coastal cities were also declared off-limits. This left no doubt that the stage was being set for our second exile, and this time it would be for life. Something had to be done and quickly, since we had been given only forty-eight hours to pack. If we stayed beyond that in the "capital of the socialist motherland," we would be in contempt of the law and put into jail for violating the passport regime.

I left immediately for Peredelkino, the writers' colony not far from Moscow, to see Fadeyev, the secretary of the Soviet Writers' Union. Unfortunately he was away, so I retraced my steps, but as I was trying to find my way off of Fadeyev's immense property, I stumbled into an adjoining property. There, on the open terrace of a cozy dacha, I caught sight of Vsevolod Ivanov, his wife Tamara, and their children. My first impulse was to turn back from the path into the undergrowth—Markish had not been rehabilitated, and I was not sure how the Ivanovs would react to my sudden appearance. It was too late. They had already noticed me, and Vsevolod came rushing over.

I told him the whole story.

"What can I do, how can I help you?" he wondered. "I don't have to tell you how little influence I have. I'll write a letter to Rudenko, the procurator general—

we sat alongside of each other at the Nuremberg Trials and there's a chance he remembers me."

With that, Vsevolod sat down, and wrote the letter, and gave it to me. He then suggested I stop by and see the "venerable" Leonov, his neighbor, who had lots of connections and surely could be of some help.

Tamara thought there was little point in my seeing Leonov, and I tended to agree with her. I remembered the incident at the Chistopol bazaar during the war when Leonov had bought that whole barrel of honey by offering twice the price. In the end, though, we decided it would do no harm to call on him. She left me at the entrance to the high fence surrounding his dacha, and I went in alone.

I rang the bell at the gate and the maid appeared.

"I would like to see Leonid Maximovich," I said.

"Who shall I say is calling?" she asked. "He's over there in the garden."

Leonov was bent over a rosebush. Servants were hurrying about.

"Ah, so it's you!" Leonov recognized me. "Well, what a surprise!"

"They're getting ready to exile us again," I said. "Help us!"

Leonov assumed an air of gravity. "Come by tomorrow or the day after, during visitors' hours."

"That's not possible," I said. "Listen to what I have to say!"

"During visitors' hours, visitors' hours!" Leonov repeated.

I turned around and began walking down the golden, sand-covered path.

"And where's your husband?" he shouted after me.

"There is no husband!" I choked, holding back my tears."

Leonov returned to his rosebushes.

Tamara and I walked through the streets of Peredelkino in silence. The children of writers gaily rolled by on bicycles; the roofs of writers' luxurious dachas could be seen behind the high walls that protected them.

I now decided to go to see Alexei Surkov in Vnukovo, a neighboring writers' colony. He was away in India, but his wife, Sonya, welcomed me warmly, "Alyosha will be back and will think of something. In the meantime, Fira, why don't you spend the night with us? Nobody will come looking for you here. Those forty-eight hours will soon be up, and there's no telling what will happen!"

I thanked her from the bottom of my heart, but it was out of the question. I returned to Moscow.

It was also impossible for me to spend the night at my mother's: the forty-eight hours had already expired. So my children and I went off to various friends' houses—we had to hide. The next morning I went to the office of the procurator general with Vsevolod Ivanov's letter.

While I was sitting in the waiting room, a woman called out, "Don't you recognize me? Remember, we met each other when we were bringing parcels to the prison—you to your husband, me to my daughter."

I did remember. This woman was the mother of a young girl who had been a student at Moscow University. Once, while she was on an outing with friends in the countryside near Moscow, her attention was attracted by a sickly birch tree, and she said jokingly, "Hey, look, this is a counter-revolutionary birch tree. It has withered under the sun of the Stalin Constitution!"

There was an informer among her companions, and the girl got twenty-five years in the camps for her joke. Now she had been rehabilitated, and her mother had come to the procurator's office for certain papers.

I told the woman our story.

"I'm going to give you one telephone number," she said. "Better not write it down, just try to remember it. It's the number of a bigwig in the Central Committee who deals with rehabilitations and the like. Give him a call—he may be able to help you."

After drawing up a declaration, I left for the building where the bigwig in the Central Committee had his office. I called him from the phone booth on the ground floor. After listening to me he said, "Draw up your declaration and come to see me tomorrow."

"I've got it with me."

"In that case, wait a minute; I'll send my secretary down to pick it up. Call me in a few days."

Two days later—the children and I were living "underground"—Surkov got back from abroad. I went to see him at the headquarters of the Writers' Union.

"We'll do something for you," he said, after I had explained the situation to him.

"I'm not the only one. There are lots of others, the whole family," I said.

Surkov began telephoning to someone on the *vertushka*—the official telephone—and asked me to wait outside in the reception room. From there I put in a call to my mother. She shouted excitedly over the phone, "It's all straightened out. They've called off the exile!"

At that very moment, Surkov came running out to me. "Everything's okay, Fira! I spoke to Rudenko. It turns out that he already received a letter from Vsevolod Ivanov. It was just another one of those bunglings!"

The next day, we all were given back our passports, and from then on we were left in peace.

During those difficult and perilous days, I also went to see Ilya Ehrenburg. He was old, not to say decrepit—the poet Yunna Morits has described him well as a "silvered monkey." After hearing what I had to say, Ehrenburg thought for a moment and then started ticking off names of people whom he would approach on our behalf. Then suddenly, without any transition, he began this story:

In February 1953, somebody called him from the office of *Pravda*'s editor-in-chief asking him to come over immediately. The editor read him a letter that had been sent to *Pravda,* a letter that was a virtual incitement to a pogrom. It dealt with the "doctor-assassins in white coats" and pointed up the collective responsibility of Jewry for "that crime."

The editor went on to explain that "the letter has been signed by Jewish personalities in the field of culture. You, I trust, will also give your signature."

"I'd like some time to think it over," Ehrenburg replied.

"Well, all right, we can wait a day or two. . . ."

The moment he got back home, Ehrenburg telephoned Stalin's secretary and requested an appointment with Stalin or, at least, an opportunity to talk to him over the phone. The secretary promised to look into the matter, but two days passed without any word. On the third day, Ehrenburg was again called in to *Pravda*, and the editor, once again, proposed that he sign the letter.

"Is Stalin acquainted with that letter?" Ehrenburg inquired.

The editor thereupon handed him a copy of the letter which bore certain handwritten revisions. Ehrenburg recognized the handwriting as Stalin's.

"The letter must be published tomorrow," the editor continued.

"I will not sign it," Ehrenburg declared. "I cannot."

On returning home, Ehrenburg asked his wife to get his things together, whatever he would need in the event of his arrest. The night passed uneventfully. Ehrenburg rose early the next morning, before the mail arrived, and went out to get a copy of *Pravda*. The letter had not been published.

At the time, Ehrenburg did not reveal to me the exact contents of the letter or the names of its signatories. But later evidence suggested that the letter concerned the well-known appeal, subscribed to by the poet Yevgeny Dolmatovsky—and there is reason to believe that the composer Matvei Blanter also signed it—for the application of the death penalty against the "Jewish doctor-assassins."

"I will not affirm categorically," Ehrenburg said by way of conclusion, "that my refusal to sign the letter prevented it from being published, but it may have had something to do with it."

In the summer of 1959, on the Riga seashore, the late Igor Nezhny who, before the war, was director of the Moscow Art Theater, told me the following story.

In February 1953, just about the time the "doctors' affair" was to be brought to court, Nezhny was arrested. (At one point during his questioning, his interrogator, Ryumin, took exception to the way Nezhny answered something and struck him. As a result of the blow, Nezhny became stone deaf.) He was implicated in the affair of the "Zionist Center," directed by the pianist Grigory Ginzburg. All of the people who had been arrested in connection with the "Center" came from the world of the arts. The Soviets had conceived of the following plan of action:

On March 6, 1953, the trial of the "doctor-assassins" would open in the Hall of Columns of the House of the Trade Unions. The "assassins," condemned by the entire Soviet nation, including all honest Jews, would, of course, by an overwhelming majority, be sentenced to hang publicly. This public execution would be a new, important contribution to Soviet legal theory and the penal system. But then the discovery would be made that the Zionists had not desisted from their plotting after all: they had enlisted musicians, artists and the like who were bent on poisoning Soviet culture. A new trial would therefore be scheduled for the beginning of May, once again in the Hall of Columns. And once again the evildoers would be sentenced to hang, but this time the people (not the mob, but the people!) would express their righteous indignation, snatch the condemned from the hands of their guards and lynch them on the spot.

The next step in the scenario would be a second letter addressed by Jews to *Pravda*'s editorial office, the gist of which would be that the wrath of the Soviet people was justified and uncontrollable, but insofar as the overwhelming majority of Jews were true Soviet patriots who must be protected, leading representatives of the Jewish people request the Party and the government to take measures to ensure that Soviet Jews are placed in conditions of security. (The fact is that while Stalin was still alive, the Soviets began building barracks in Magadan Province.)

This scenario was very much in accord with Stalin's sadistic practices. He almost never acted with one fell swoop, but proceeded gradually, step by step, as the way in which he liquidated all of his political rivals, beginning with Trotsky.

Ironically, history intervened in this proposed scenario. Instead of the grandiose spectacle of a ritual trial staged by Stalin and his henchmen in the Hall of Columns on March 6 to finish the job the tsarist pogromists had begun with the Beilis affair, there was an incomparably more grandiose spectacle: the funeral of the most terrifying criminal of our terrifying epoch, Josef Vissarionovich Stalin, who died March 5, 1953.

There were other occasions when I met with Ehrenburg, particularly when he was engaged in writing his memoirs, *People, Years, Life,* which contain material on Markish. During one of these meetings, Ehrenburg told me how an effort had been made to drag him into the Malakhovka trial at the end of the fifties. A Jewish synagogue was burned down in the city of Malakhovka, not far from Moscow. An agent of the KGB called on Ehrenburg and suggested he testify as an expert at the trial.

"I know nothing about it," Ehrenburg said. "I haven't seen a word about it in the newspapers."

The agent handed Ehrenburg some of the documentary material that had been gathered. Among these papers was an incendiary anti-Semitic pamphlet that bore the signature *B.Zh. C.P.*

"What's this signature?" Ehrenburg asked.

"Bei Zhidov Spasai Rossiyu [Kill the Kikes, Save Russia]," explained the agent.

"I can appear at the trial as a public prosecutor, but not as an expert," Ehrenburg said.

"Well, we'll be in touch," his visitor said as he took his leave.

That was the end of it. The trial was never held.

On several occasions Ehrenburg insisted on talking about the rumors that connected him with the loss of Markish and other members of the Jewish Antifascist Committee. He denied them, of course, and said that he knew nothing about the fate of our loved ones.

Ehrenburg was too intelligent not to understand the shameful role of *shirmach* that had been assigned to him during the period of the pogrom, 1949–1952. (The word is Russian thieves' jargon for the member of the gang who distracts the attention of passers-by by acting as the *shirmach,* or "blind," while the victim is being robbed.) At a time when anti-Semitism in the USSR was assuming Nazi-like proportions, Ehrenburg, always parading his Jewish affiliation, traveled all over the world making speeches in defense of "Stalinist peace policy," and refuting the "slanderous allegations" of an anti-Semitic campaign in the USSR by the very fact of his participation in international gatherings.

Ehrenburg did half admit that role in Book 6 of *People, Years, Life* (first published in *Novy Mir*, Number 2, 1965). He starts off by claiming that in 1949, he didn't understand a thing—Stalin was a master of camouflage. But how could a man like Ehrenburg, who had gone through fire, water and all kinds of trials, not have understood? Jewish persecution had surpassed even the levels of the 1936–1938 purges. . . . Entire peoples were accused of treason and deported. . . . Victims of the prewar purges who had survived and been set free were sent back behind barbed wire. . . .

Ehrenburg then tells about his reluctance to attend the Peace Congress in Paris because his heart was so heavy. But he went, nevertheless, and he delivered a speech about how repugnant racial and national arrogance were, about how peoples must and always will learn from each other. He had chosen this theme as a sign of protest against anti-Semitism, against the chauvinistic campaign against "cosmopolitans" (read: "Jewry") that had been raging in the Soviet press since February 2, 1949. And even Stalin, Ehrenburg noted, had missed the point of his speech: in the margin alongside the most antichauvinistic passages he had written the word *magnificent*. I just can't believe that a man as shrewd and experienced as Ehrenburg could have been bamboozled by this typical Stalinist subterfuge: at the height of the purges, for example, there was more talk than ever about democracy and the rights guaranteed by the new Constitution!

Louis Aragon and Elsa Triolet asked Ehrenburg what was going on. What was this fuss about cosmopolitans all of a sudden? What is the press up to, publicizing old pseudonyms, harping on the fact that the cosmopolitans are people with Jewish names? "They were my friends," Ehrenburg wrote. "I had known them for a quarter of a century, but I was unable to answer their questions." Who knows what might have been the fate of Markish and his comrades had Ehrenburg been "able" then to speak the truth? A little farther on, he even goes so far as to admit that all that night he dreamed of Markish!

Ehrenburg calls that the terrible price he paid for "loyalty to people, to the age, to fate." Why such high-flown phraseology, why such low-down evasiveness? I do not reproach Ehrenburg *a posteriori*. I merely wish to make it clear that his cowardice should not be taken for courage.

We were finally given authorization to occupy the room in our old apartment that the procurator had declined at the last minute. The doctor and his daughter accepted our reinstallation with good grace, but the burly physical education teacher was furious. No doubt he nurtured the hope that he would eventually take over that room.

As I mentioned earlier, the fellow lived in what was formerly our dining room together with his wife, daughter and mother-in-law, a wizened old lady. After a lifetime spent in a communal apartment where squabbles and scandals were an everyday occurrence, she was completely bored. To relieve the monotony, she would occasionally pour sunflower seed oil on the floor of the kitchen we all shared, or would sprinkle sand and soil into her own pots and pans, afterwards accusing David of such mischief. The physical education teacher and his wife naturally joined into the fray, which all but ended in blows.

Actually I felt a bit sorry for the old lady. She couldn't expect to live much longer and her life was pretty bleak. In all the time we lived together, I never heard either her daughter or her son-in-law address a single word to her. Moreover, the old woman lived in mortal fear of the brute and secretly detested him. Four times a week she retreated to the kitchen and sat there until the wee hours of the morning, her head resting on her bony fist, waiting for the indefatigable athlete to gratify his sexual appetites.

Finally, the court ordered them to leave and we got back our dining room. The doctor and his daughter, however, stayed on in our apartment, since they were not subject to eviction, and they were still living there after we left the Soviet Union. Our battle to emigrate from the USSR undoubtedly caused them a great deal of trouble. Since they were party members, the KGB must have called them in frequently to obtain information about us and our friends.

In the spring of 1955, before the rehabilitation of his father, David graduated from high school. He tried to get into the Medical Institute, but he didn't pass the competitive examinations: there was a tremendous number of candidates, and priority was given to children whose fathers were killed during the war or worked in the regions of the Far North. When he learned about David's situation, Boris Lavrenyov wrote a letter to the minister of Public Health. Unfortunately, I have not kept a copy of his letter, but the gist of it was that a boy whose adolescent years had been maimed and poisoned by exile had as much right to be accepted as the children of men who had given their lives in the fight against fascism or who had not spared their health in the struggle with the frosts and blizzards of the Far North. David was finally admitted, but he was not meant to be a doctor. After one semester, he dropped out of the Medical Institute and in the autumn of 1956 he enrolled in the first year of the Institute of Literature.

Meanwhile, Simon began working as an editor in the State Literary Publishing House, one of the most important in the Soviet Union. Lyalya graduated from the Faculty of Sculpture of the Kiev Institute of Fine Arts. The life of our family was gradually returning to normal.

Our old house on Gorky Street—a house without a father—also began to find its familiar routine amid a circle of old and new friends and acquaintances. Many writers, Jews and Russians, came to the house of Peretz Markish as to a shrine and talked about the great literature that had been destroyed by the wave of terror.

The very young also came—friends of Simon and David, aspiring poets and novelists, literary translators.

240

Our house gradually became a focal point for the literary intelligentsia. Foreigners who had either known Markish or admired him as a poet were also frequent visitors. Their visits, which were not wholly without risk, made our place even more fascinating for Soviet citizens anxious to have firsthand news about literary and political life in the West. The KGB, as might be expected, also took an interest in our house. The telephone began functioning erratically; strange chirping noises came over the line, strange voices broke in on our conversations, or else we were cut off. David received several threatening, anti-Semitic letters. He opened one envelope to find a photograph of a Nazi gas chamber that had been clipped from a magazine; it bore the caption "Soon it will be the turn of all of you!"

Once we put in our application for immigration to Israel, though, the literary influx began to ebb, and we found ourselves resorting to the primitive rules of conspiracy: whenever it was a question of our personal affairs, of confidential meetings and the like, we wrote them down instead of speaking (the walls have ears). Afterwards, we burned the notes, folding them in such a way that they did not smoke.

20 / "We Still Owe You a Little Something"

NOVEMBER 25, 1955, marked the sixtieth birthday of Peretz Markish. My children and I gathered with a few of our closest friends in our room on Gorky Street. Simon, my elder son, raised his glass of wine in a toast: "I do not know whether I am drinking to the health of my father, or to his memory. . . ."

Two days later I was summoned to the Military Collegium of the Supreme Court. I was not the only one: in the waiting room I ran into the wives (widows?) of Bergelson, Kvitko, Hofstein, Lozovsky—who was responsible for the work of the Jewish Antifascist Committee—and Shemiliovich. Lina Stern was also there; the noted biologist and physiologist—and the first woman to be admitted to the Soviet Academy of Science—was now old and stooped.

I was received by General Borisoglebsky. The walls of his office were as bare and forbidding as a dissection laboratory except for the cheaply framed portraits of Lenin and Stalin.

"You probably can guess why I've asked you to come," the general said.

"No," I answered. "I've come to hear what you have to say."

"I am in a position to tell you," he continued, "that your husband has been rehabilitated."

"Where is he?"

"Your husband was shot by enemies of the people," said the general, resorting to the stock phrase as he placed a glass of water before me.

"Let me see his dossier," I said. "I would like to examine it."

"Come now, you're not a jurist, it won't mean a thing to you."

"I want to see my husband's dossier."

"Impossible."

"When did he die?"

"Sometime in August 1952."

"I want to know the exact date."

"But what difference does it make?" the general asked, a touch of annoyance in his voice.

"My children and I have to know. Where is his grave?"

"He doesn't have a grave."

"You must tell me the exact date of his death."

The general picked up the telephone; a few moments later his adjutant came in with a thin folder under his arm.

"The twelfth of August 1952," the general announced after glancing through the folder. "Is there perhaps something I can do for you?"

"Yes, you can expedite the review of the case of my

242

brother, Lazebnikov, Alexander Yefimovich," I said. "He is not guilty of anything, and his rehabilitation is only a question of time." (Three days later, my brother was rehabilitated.)

When I came back to the waiting room, Lina Stern came over to me. "Come and see me—I have something to tell you."

Realizing it had something to do with Markish, I went to her place with the children. Lina Stern was the sole survivor of the trial of the members of the Jewish Antifascist Committee. The other women who had been incriminated—Mira Zheleznova, the secretary of Itzik Feffer; Chaika, a journalist and onetime American citizen who had worked as a translator in the committee; and one historian, whose name I can't recall, who sat on the committee's presidium—were all shot August 12.

Lina Stern had immigrated to Russia from America at the end of the Thirties. She had evidently been taken in by Communist propaganda and decided that she would make her contribution to the "triumphant proletariat." They came after her early in 1949, explaining that the minister of State Security wanted to have a "chat" with her.

No sooner had Lina Stern stepped into the office of Minister Abakumov than he started raising the roof: "We know everything! Come clean! You're a Zionist, you were bent on detaching the Crimea from Russia and establishing a Jewish state there!"

"That's the first I've heard of it," she said in a strong Jewish accent.

"Why, you old whore!" Abakumov roared.

"So that's the way a minister speaks to an academician." Lina Stern shook her head in dismay.

Until May 1952, the only person whom Lina Stern saw of the group arrested with Markish was Itzik Feffer. She had a personal meeting with him. He looked sick, pitiful, demoralized. "Well, Lina Solomonovna," Feffer began, "no use trying to deny it. You know only too well that you were involved in an underground Zionist organization. . . ."

"What *are* you talking about?" she exclaimed. "What organization?"

243

"Admit it, admit it!" Feffer repeated, as he caught the eye of the interrogator.

That same month a closed trial began or, to be more precise, a parody of a trial. The defendants were led to the building of the Supreme Court, where the Military Tribunal was in session. Of course, they had no defense counsel.

Lina Stern saw with her own eyes the bloodied Shemiliovich, Zuskin, half-crazed, and Bergelson, who had grown old and feeble. And she saw Markish, too.

None of the defendants pleaded guilty except Feffer. In his final statement, Lozovsky, former deputy minister of foreign affairs, charged Feffer with being a "witness for the prosecution."

Lina Stern told us Markish had delivered an eloquent and devastating speech at the trial. No one interrupted him—after all, there was nobody in the courtroom except the judges and the defendants, and the judges were dead sure nobody would ever learn what Markish had said. In his final summation, Markish lashed out against his tormentors and their mentors with all the power of his creative genius. While Lina Stern could not recollect his exact words, she remembered that he spoke not as a defendant but as a prosecutor.

Shortly after our meeting, Lina Stern died, and as far as I know we were the only ones with whom she shared her recollections of the trial. However, I subsequently met a number of people who told me about Peretz Markish's scorching indictment, although none of them was able to explain to me exactly how they had learned about it.

I do not know who condemned Markish and his comrades.

I do not know who else was sitting in the courtroom across from the "prisoners' dock."

I do not know where people obtained information about Markish's final statement.

The prosecutor demanded prison terms of twenty-five years for all of the defendants. Someone at the top, however, most probably Stalin, felt that the sentence was too lenient, and the decision was referred to the Military Collegium of the Supreme Court for review. On June 18, the defendants in the trial of the Jewish Antifascist Committee were condemned to death by firing squad. Only Lina Stern was spared; she was sentenced to five years' exile.

To this day, many of those responsible for that crime are at liberty.

After the posthumous rehabilitation of a writer, it was standard practice that a commission be set up to deal with his literary legacy. There were already a number of such commissions at work (or, at least, constituted) under the aegis of the Writers' Union. I had no doubt that a Markish commission would be formed, and I was also sure that, as his widow, I would be named secretary. This meant, moreover, that if I was interested in seeing new editions of Markish's work published, I would have to devote myself full-time to this undertaking to have any chance of pushing these editions through the cordons of the publishing houses. I therefore quit my job at the Society of Microbiologists and, prior even to any decision by the Board of the Writers' Union to establish a commission, I began working on the archives, textual variants, and the plans for future editions. I would often bring together friends of Markish who had survived to seek their advice and help.

We were in the middle of such a meeting one day when the telephone rang. A voice on the other end of the line said, "This is the finance department of the KGB calling. We still owe you a little something."

"What are you referring to? You know as well as I do that you reimbursed me for all the money I sent to my husband." (As mentioned earlier, during the years of his incarceration, Markish did not receive a single kopek of the money I had passed on to the administration of the Lefortovo and Lubyanka prisons.)

"No, you still have something coming to you for the teeth."

"What teeth are you talking about?"

"The gold crowns."

I screamed in a voice that was not my own. My friends came rushing out into the hallway and caught me; I had fainted. The receiver dangled and swayed on the cord while the voice of death's tallyman continued its angry gurgle. Someone grabbed the telephone and shouted, "Damn your soul! Leave her in peace!"

The next day I went to see Surkov. When I told him about the incident, he went white with rage. The only thing I asked him was to make sure that my older companions in misfortune were spared such indecencies. A woman like Tsilya Bergelson, for example, who was now over sixty, might very well suffer a heart attack if she were importuned by a story of crowns torn out of the mouth of her murdered husband by the accomplices of the executioner.

Whenever I subsequently heard or read something to the effect that it would be better not to stir up the evils of a bygone day, reopen old wounds, that it would be better to bury and forget them, I always said to myself, "The teeth!"

As I had anticipated, a commission was finally set up under the chairmanship of Pyotr Ivanovich Chagin, former director of the State Literary Publishing House and a friend of the great lyric poet Sergei Yesenin. In the name of the commission, I wrote to a number of prominent poets asking them to collaborate on the translation of Markish's poems into Russian. Anna Akhmatova responded with gratitude to my letter. The young Yevtushenko told me frankly that Markish was too overpowering for him to do justice to a translation. Boris Pasternak sent a courageous and awesome reply to my appeal:

December 31, 1955

Deeply esteemed Esther Yefimovna:

I bow my head before the immensity of your sorrow. Besides his significance as an artist, Markish was an uncommon phenomenon of life itself; he was its smile, its radiance, which, touched by beauty, left its heart-warming mark wherever it shone.

I vividly remember his visit to me, our conversation and the substance of the interlinear translation of his verses in memory of Mikhoels.

246

But contrary to the opinion of your co-editor Ye. Permak, who wrote me that my memory is more faithful than any photograph, I not only have no recollection of my translation [of those verses], but I don't even recall ever having translated them. I think what really happened was that I promised to translate them and intended to do so, and the misunderstanding arose from this.

No one—neither you nor anyone else—can possibly imagine how disorganized my life as a writer is—no books, no correspondence, no traces of what I have written, no personal archives, my letters and manuscripts destroyed, and only the most essential conserved in my heart and soul.

The verses have to be translated anew (or perhaps for the first time). This ought to be done by somebody else like Petrovykh or Martynov; we have no lack of splendid translators, some of whom are no worse than I am, and others who are even better.

I am pressed on all sides by requests for translations. In some instances, they are as noble, as worthy and as awesome as yours. But if people were kind and considerate to me, they would do well to inhibit and discourage me from doing translations, and not ask me to undertake them. The time has come for me to think about myself.

Your son, a charming boy, has spoken to me about translations, about Shelley and Edgar Poe, among others. I told him everything. I leave it to him to say a good word to you in my behalf.

That the years of our life have been filled with monstrous and terrible and countless examples of martyrdom, that is something I suspected long ago, and my incapacity to reconcile myself to such a state of affairs, as far back as forty years, was the decisive factor in my life and tied my hands.

Don't be angry with me.

Yours,

B. Pasternak

"To Mikhoels—Eternal Light" was translated into Russian by Arkady Shteinberg, a fine poet and translator. The poem provoked the hostility of Nikolai Lyusechevsky, director of *Sovietsky Pisatel,* the publishing house that was preparing the first posthumous edition of Markish's poetry. When he examined the dummy of Markish's *Verses and Poems,* he said to me, "What do you mean trying to slip in a photograph of a dead man! And you've deliberately chosen a blood-red cover. No, you won't get away with it. . . . Furthermore, 'To Mikhoels—Eternal Light' is a nationalistic piece of verse. Who ever told you that he was murdered? Everybody knows that he was run over by a truck!"

It took the intervention of Alexei Surkov to put the fascist Lyusechevsky in his place. The book was published as we had originally conceived it. The thaw, however, did not last too long, and in all subsequent editions of Markish the censor cut the ode to Mikhoels. And Lyusechevsky spared no effort to prevent Markish's works from being published. For a number of years he delayed the appearance of Markish's novel *The March of Generations,* accusing the author of bourgeois nationalism and Zionism. He had no trouble finding supporters, among them Tevekelyan, author of detective stories, a former collaborator of the MGB, and a keen Party sleuth. They both swore they would turn in their Party cards if Markish's novel was published. "The hero of the novel is an out-and-out Zionist," they trumpeted. "He dies wrapped in a tallith! That is religious-nationalistic propaganda!" Had it not been for the special authorization of the Board of the Writers' Union, the novel would never have seen the light of day.

People like these two, with their sterilized consciences, are representative of a large part of the Moscow literary scene today. These mediocrities are given every encouragement by the Party mandarins who direct the destiny of literature from the headquarters of the Central Committee of the CPSU. All of them continue to be in direct or indirect contact with the KGB, and many are former KGB agents. The benediction of the KGB is regarded by the vast majority of Soviet writers as the supreme recompense. Since they are incapable of making a career in literature, they climb on the Party bandwagon and are made Party organizers of the Writers' Union and its numerous subdivisions. This gives them the power to make or break the career and personal life of their colleagues, who fear them—and with good reason—like the plague, and grovel before them even as they beat their breasts for their own spinelessness.

One day I went to Peredelkino to see Afanasy Salynsky on matters connected with Markish's literary affairs. The dacha of Salynsky, the most honest of all the Writers' Union secretaries, was located on the same large plot as Tevekelyan's. One fine day, Salynsky told me, he discovered that a fence had been put up dividing the lot in two. It seems that his neighbor suspected that Salynsky's children were helping themselves to raspberries from his bushes. The fence, of course, had been built at the expense of the Literary Fund, in which Tevekelyan occupied a high post as a reward for toeing the Party line.

"That man," Salynsky said derisively, "is the hero of our time. Everybody thinks highly of him. A rogue, a nobody! Impossible to shake his hand—what I mean is, you can't bring yourself to it."

A quarter of an hour later, I got into the car with Salynsky so he could drive me to the railroad station. Suddenly, "the hero of our time" appeared on the road. Salynsky got out of the car and, casting a sad and, I thought, somewhat guilty glance in my direction, strode over to greet the "mighty ignoramus." Cordially, he shook his hand.

Boris Lavrenyov, the eminent Russian writer and a true friend, wrote the preface to the first posthumous edition of Markish's poetry. That was in 1956, when it was possible to write—and have published—lines like the following:

> Markish's enormous talent was in full bloom and he undoubtedly would have produced even more magnificent works had he not been cut down in the prime of his life. Unjustly calumniated, he

fell victim to his enemies. Enemies of the Fatherland snuffed out the life of a remarkable poet,
but they were powerless to silence his muse.

A few years later, when the thaw was over, the
censors deleted even the slightest allusion to the tragic
way in which Peretz Markish's life had come to an end.
In 1969, I saw something that the ordinary Soviet
citizen is never permitted to see: the censor's correc-
tions on the galley proofs of the last book of Markish
to be published in the USSR. The censor had red-
penciled the word *Jew* wherever it appeared—as it
did frequently—in the volume, and he suggested that
the editor replace this "unacceptable" term by words
such as *man, citizen,* or *passer-by.* The word *Jew*
was taboo. The censor, moreover, threw several poems
out of the collection: "Jerusalem," "Galilee," a few
chapters of "The War"—all of which were seen as
infused with Jewish nationalism—and, it goes without
saying, "To Mikhoels—Eternal Light."
As a matter of fact, what concerned me most was
the poem "The Forty-Year-Old," which David had
translated into Russian. He too was apprehensive about
it. The only thing we could count on was the abysmal
ignorance and stupidity of the censors, and they
did not disappoint our hopes. They couldn't make
head nor tail of this difficult poem, and they gave their
okay. Similarly, they let a poem like "The Red Monks"
slip by:

No churches are in view, and no psalms do they
    sing—
But hordes of monks mill around in the valley.

Their every step exudes a stink of decay.
The wick of the law smolders in their censers.

They emerge from the darkness—
Their eyes asquint, their mouths askew.

For every question, for a smile, for a scowl—
A chapter of the law they recite from memory.

Their shoulders are bent, their faces white as
   chalk.
Commanded they are by their statutes to do
   evil. . . .

But my mouth is on fire. Through the storm,
   through the gloom
I shall rise up to you and speak to you thus:

Though night has retreated from the white gates—
The red darkness shall rise, shall spread.

A star is in its sleeve, but night is in its bosom—
And the monks whisper, for speak they must.

They vow they will destroy the darkness—
And with that they fall off to sleep in a cold
   sweat.

With a blind love loving their faith
They castrate themselves in ecstasy.

They are omnipresent. With relish they take
   vengeance
On men for their laughter, on a flea for its bite.

But the day is triumphant, the future bright—
And the sun will reduce the monks to ashes.

A good deal could be said about the troubles connected with the publication of the six books that
appeared after Markish was rehabilitated. But the
human atmosphere that surrounded their publication
is of considerably more interest than the negotiations
with the publishing houses. For it reflected the duality
so characteristic of Soviet intelligentsia today. In private meetings, generally speaking, a spade was called
a spade: anti-Semitism was anti-Semitism. But in official meetings involving Markish's literary legacy, even
the most outspoken intellectual shied away from this
word.
   When I quit my job to devote myself entirely to
Markish's literary affairs, I forsook the extremely mod-

est income that had allowed me to scrape by. If I were to resume my former occupation of translator and earn my living from it, I would have to have the support of "highly placed individuals." No matter how reluctant I was to pull strings, I had no choice but to turn to the Writers' Union once again. This time I went to see Boris Polevoi, who headed the Committee on Foreign Books. I told him about my difficulties and apologized for the bother I was putting him to.

"For heaven's sake," Polevoi exclaimed, "if any apologies are to be made, they should come from us."

He thereupon wrote a letter to the director of the State Literary Publishing House, A. K. Kotov. As a result of Polevoi's intercession, I received my first translation assignment since Markish's arrest—a part of the diaries of Romain Rolland that were published in one of the last volumes of his *Collected Works*. From then on, practically right up to the time I left the Soviet Union, I was engaged in literary translation. (Naturally, once I applied for permission to emigrate from the USSR, I put an X on my career as a translator and all doors to the publishing houses were closed to me.)

I had another meeting with Polevoi soon after our first, this time at his request. The American journalist Shoshkis had come to Moscow and was anxious to meet members of the Jewish community—that is, what remained of it—and Polevoi wanted to talk to me about it.

"The past is the past," he said. "No matter how sad and terrible it is, you can't resuscitate the dead. Now it is the task of all of us to prevent our common misfortune from becoming a weapon in the hands of our common enemies. Many people will be interested in you and will want to see you. I think it advisable you should not tell all you know to visitors from abroad. If they ask you about the fate of Markish, I suggest you say he died of a heart attack."

"No," I said, without a moment's hesitation, "that's not possible. People coming from abroad, you know, can be persistent, or curious, or genuinely concerned with Markish and his family, and they'll want to visit the grave of a person who died of a heart attack.

Where am I supposed to take them? To the photograph on the wall above the shelf where I always keep a vase with flowers?"

Polevoi said no more, and let it go at that.

21 / My First Contacts with Israelis

LATE ONE EVENING in 1955 the telephone rang in our apartment. It was a call from the Central Committee of the CPSU.

"Get ready to receive the general secretary of the Communist Party of Israel, Mikunis," a voice said. "He is on his way over right now."

To tell the truth, I was frightened. A foreigner, that was bad enough, but . . . an Israeli! For all I knew, I could find myself back in Kazakhstan tomorrow.

Mikunis showed up around midnight and stayed until five o'clock in the morning. It turned out that he came from the same small town as Markish, Polonnoye, and remembered Peretz very well as a young man. A frequent visitor to Moscow, Mikunis had tried to locate us as early as 1952, but he was told we had dropped out of sight.

We talked rather freely, but not with complete candor. Much as I would have liked to, I simply couldn't ask the Communist Mikunis, an intelligent and very likable man, how we might get out of the USSR. About Israel, its kibbutzim and its cities, he spoke with love and enthusiasm, but when it came to politics, it sounded as if he was parroting editorials from *Pravda*.

Subsequently, whenever Mikunis came to Moscow, he always spent some time with us. With each successive visit, he became more and more outspoken and,

253

I would say, increasingly disheartened. He was on the point of breaking with the Communists in the Kremlin, but I don't think that was what really troubled him; it was, rather, that he had begun to discover the truth when it was already too late.

This was the time when, primarily under the pressure of Western liberals, an attempt was made in the USSR to resuscitate the lifeless body of Jewish culture. Jewish singers began to perform again, artists gave public readings of Jewish writings, a Yiddish-language journal, *Sovyetish heymland,* edited by Aron Vergelis, got started, and so on. But it took more than these initiatives and the performances of even such wonderful singers as Nekhama Lifshits and Venyamin Khayatauskas to give Jewish cultural life a new start. To the consternation of the Communist authorities, however, they did make a distinctive contribution in quite another sense—they reawakened a feeling of national pride among Russia's downtrodden Jewry. The fact that people flocked to Jewish concerts was in itself a repudiation of the assimilationists. The Jews wanted to remain Jews in the Communist empire, which had stopped at nothing to bring about the fusion of nations with different cultures into a single, faceless, docile monolith. Moreover, the appearance of members of the Israeli embassy at Jewish concerts added to the ferment: Jews saw with their own eyes other Jews who not only wanted to be free but who had won their freedom.

Our first encounter with "real" Israelis occurred some years before the Jewish concerts got started, in 1959. In the fall of that year, a gala evening in honor of Shalom Aleichem was held in the Moscow Literary Museum. It was a very special occasion, indeed, for it had been many years since an evening devoted to the works of a Jewish writer had been organized. We had been invited, and David had been asked to read poems about Shalom Aleichem.

An hour before the performance was to begin, a dense crowd of gate-crashers had gathered in front of the museum. It was made up of both young Jews and those of the older generation. The museum auditorium was too small to accommodate all of them.

Five or six Israelis were seated in the first row, the insignia of the State of Israel displayed prominently on their lapels. Immediately the hall crackled with rumors that the Israeli ambassador was in the audience.

I was anxious about David and about his performance. Ilya Ehrenburg, the chairman of the evening, had just introduced him, and now David began to recite.

His poems exuded the fragrance of the Middle East, with its palm trees and deserted seacoast, so dear to the readers of Shalom Aleichem. I saw the Israelis exchanging glances with one another as they broke into applause. The entire audience applauded when David said that now that the Jews had become strong, they need no longer laugh through their tears.

After the performance, the Israelis went backstage to congratulate the artists, and they asked David to give them his poems. He was only too happy to do so. But no sooner had he returned to the auditorium than he was approached by an "admirer in civilian dress," an agent of the KGB.

"I liked your poems tremendously," he said. "Could I have them as a souvenir?"

"Sorry, I don't have them," David replied.

"How's that? Why, you just finished reading them a moment ago."

"I've lost them," David said. "You know how it is, the crowds and all."

"Do you mean to tell me the organizers don't have a copy? I'm sure they must have looked over your poems before you gave your reading."

"No," said David to the zealous informer, "they did not. I had the original, I've lost it, and I don't remember the poems by heart."

Even at the height of the thaw, the ideological section of the KGB had its ear close to the ground and kept a tight watch on "Jewish undertakings"—particularly when Israeli diplomats were involved. The KGB didn't trust "its" Jews, and rightly so.

On November 25, 1960, an evening held in commemoration of the sixty-fifth anniversary of the birth

255

of Peretz Markish proved particularly troublesome to the Soviet "custodians of political morality." The celebration was held in the main auditorium of the Writers' Club, and it drew a large audience. Outside, a huge swarm of people spread through Herzen Street, stopping all traffic. The police were called in "to keep order." Gate-crashers poured into the club. The auditorium was filled to overflowing; people pressed together two to a seat, while others stood in the aisles. At first, club officials refused to admit representatives of the Israeli Embassy, citing some obscure regulations. It was only with the greatest difficulty that I succeeded in getting the Israelis through and finding seats for them.

A major exhibit illustrating the life and works of Markish was set up in the foyer. Speakers at the meeting included Anna Akhmatova, Pavel Antokolsky, Semyon Kirsanov, Wilhelm Levik as well as other poets and interpreters. Particularly heartening was the fact that the audience was composed largely of young people.

The high point of the evening was undoubtedly the message sent by Ilya Ehrenburg, whose attendance was prevented by illness:

I deeply regret that I cannot be with my friends tonight who have gathered to honor the unknown grave of the well-known poet, Peretz Markish. I would like to remember him as the young and uncompromising man he was in Kiev, where sadness and hope hung like a cloud over his handsome face and narrowed the pupils of his dreamy eyes. I would also like to call to mind our meetings in Paris where he spoke inspiringly of the revolution and poetry, of Guillaume Apollinaire and Mayakovsky, of the ancient Chasidic legends, and of the dawn of a new age. I would like, too, to tell about our last meeting, our last brief talk, the last time we shook hands—also in the corridors of the building on Vorovsky Street, where many of us cast a final parting glance at each other. I would like to say something about a wonderful poet. But all this will have to wait until another time, and I hope I'll be able to write about it some day.

I feel sure that at an evening honoring the memory of Peretz Markish, a great deal will be said about his stirring poetry. I would like to say what drew me so close to the murdered poet—besides a devotion to art and the pleasant times we spent together many years ago. What I feel is perhaps best expressed by the Polish poet Julian Tuvim, whose poetry Peretz Markish loved. In 1942, Tuvim explained why he was proud to call himself a Polish Jew: "It's a matter of blood. Racism, you will say? No, not in the least. Quite the contrary. Blood sometimes possesses a dual quality: there is the blood that flows in the veins and then there is the blood that flows out of the veins. The first is body fluid and is of interest to the physiologist. . . . The second is the blood that the ringleader of international fascism drains out of humanity in order to prove the superiority of his blood over mine, over the blood of millions of persecuted peoples. . . . The blood of Jews (not 'Jewish blood') flows in deep, broad streams; the blood-blackened streams converge into a swirling, foaming river, and in this new Jordan I receive my spiritual purification and enter into the bloody, fervent brotherhood of martyrdom with the Jews." Peretz Markish knew these words. Like many others, he spent hours of grief and pride over them. Then, Peretz Markish was no more. . . . Can there be anything more senseless than such a death in spite of its profound and tragic sense? His poems remain with their vibrant ring. The image of a pure, courageous and good man remains. It uplifts multitudes, it radiates warmth in moments of solitude, it rejuvenates those in the twilight of life. Yes, it was worth writing like that, and a life like that was worth living.

Five years later, in 1965, another evening was held in Markish's honor, this time in his birthplace, Polonnoye, a small town in the Ukraine. The arrangements for that celebration in the name of a "distinguished local citizen" were accompanied by a number of difficulties.

About a year before the event took place, I went to Polonnoye to have a look at the place where Markish had grown up. The local residents—as a result of the war there were few Jews among them now—regarded Markish as one of their "honored sons." When I mentioned to the Town Soviet the idea of some kind of commemorative ceremony, however, the municipal authorities were scared out of their wits.

To perpetuate in any way whatever the memory of a Jewish poet would have been an inexcusable stupidity on the part of the local leaders. At the moment, to be sure, the situation of the Jews was reasonably satisfactory; no longer were they being branded rootless cosmopolitans, no longer were they the victims of organized persecution, and a Jew, Dymshits, had even been named Kosygin's deputy. Yet, had not Stalin also had his Jew, Kaganovich? And look how things turned out. Kaganovich outlived his patron, but still the Jews had been broken on the rack. Tomorrow, the clock could always be turned back, and if it was, Maisterchuk, the chairman of Polonnoye's Town Soviet, would receive no praise for anything he had done to perpetuate the memory of Peretz Markish. In Stalin's day, a lack of political flair under similar circumstances could have gotten you twenty-five years in jail—that is, if you weren't shot just for having associated with a Zionist element.

Maisterchuk was willing to do something for Markish —set aside a corner in the local museum for an exhibition, for instance—but only if he received an unequivocal green light from the authorities in Kiev. So I decided to make a trip to Kiev. The authorities there proved to be much more "understanding" than the unsophisticated Maisterchuk. The Kievans agreed, in principle, to help organize a gala evening commemorating the seventieth anniversary of Markish's birth. They notified the province Party officials in the city of Khmelnitsky of their decision, and the latter, in turn, notified Maisterchuk. Now that he had been relieved of any personal responsibility, Maisterchuk felt free to act.

Toward the end of November 1965, my children and I arrived in Polonnoye. Maisterchuk, leading a delegation of the Town Soviet, rolled out the red carpet for us at the railroad station. We were escorted to the hotel, and from there to a dinner at the local café. As we were led through the café to the private dining room where our table had been laid, the customers stared openmouthed at us, since that room was reserved for the province and republic bigwigs and rarely used. We insisted, however, on being served in the regular dining room, and they acceded to our wishes, if reluctantly.

The new, freshly printed menu listed "golden consommé," "roasted chicken gizzards," "gefilte fish." David's eyes popped out. He knew the country well, and in an ordinary café in a town like Polonnoye, such a selection of food was unheard of.

"How much is the consommé?" David asked the waiter.

"Fifteen kopeks," the waiter answered, without batting an eye.

"And the roast gizzards?"

"Twenty."

Why, this was fantastic! You'd have to be out of your mind not to go and settle in Polonnoye for the rest of your life. Where else could you find prices like that?

The next day it all came out. We were told confidentially that the special menu and the special prices were in force for the three days we would be staying in Polonnoye. As soon as we left, the party would be over for the local citizens, and they'd be back to their old diet of red cabbage and pasty macaroni.

We made another discovery, too: how the Town Soviet had raised the money for such a pleasant improvement in the life of the local populace. It seems that a few days prior to the Markish Evening, Maisterchuk brought together a dozen "citizens of Jewish nationality" who were playing a prominent role in the organization of the forthcoming festivities. He took each one of them aside and said something like this:

Maisterchuk: Are you interested in seeing the Markish Evening is a big success?
A Jew: Why naturally.
Maisterchuk: Can you contribute any money to it?
A Jew: I don't have any.
Maisterchuk: Then put this statement in writing: "I hereby request a nonrepayable loan in the amount of five hundred rubles." Now, hand it over to me. I'll approve it.

The money so received was immediately turned back by the Jews to the town treasury and was expended on "cultural activities" and the special menu with special prices.

As a climax to the festivities, it was announced that one of the streets in Polonnoye would be given the name of Peretz Markish. Naturally, we were anxious to see the street that had been selected, but it took some doing before they agreed to show it to us. The "street" turned out to be a vacant lot earmarked for development. You can imagine how disappointed we were; Maisterchuk's mellifluous phrases about the future architectural beauty of the site were scant consolation.

Seeing our distress, the writers who had come from Kiev for the celebration immediately got on the telephone and made a series of calls to Kiev and Khmelnitsky. Following protracted long-distance discussions, the decision of the Polonnoye Town Soviet was overruled: the name of Peretz Markish was given to a quay along the river. (I would be very much surprised to learn that it still bears his name now that we have left the Soviet Union.)

Also in connection with Markish's anniversary celebration, I made a visit to Alexander Chakovsky, editor-in-chief of the *Literary Gazette* and a Jewish anti-Semite who sold his national birthright and civic conscience for a mess of dripping Party porridge.

"I would like to offer you for publication a chapter from Markish's novel *The March of Generations*," I said.

"Why exactly in the *Literary Gazette*," Chakovsky asked, visibly annoyed, "when there is a special organ for writers of national minorities, like *Friendship of Peoples?"* (This magazine, *Druzhba narodov,* was at one time edited by Vasily Smirnov, a notorious and pathological Russian anti-Semite, who claimed that if Solzhenitsyn was such a "mediocre writer," it was because he was a Jew and his real name was "Solzhenitser.")

"How come *Literary Gazette* publishes ethnic writers like Rasul Gamzatov, Chingis Aitmatov, and so many others?" I asked.

"I'll be quite frank with you," he said. "The fact is I don't like Jews."

"And I'll be just as frank and tell you that the Jews don't like you either," I countered.

With this, I took my leave of the "prominent Russian writer and public figure" Alexander Chakovsky, who, you will remember, traveled in the baggage rack of our compartment on the Tashkent-bound evacuation train. . . .

The evening organized in Markish's honor in the Central House of Writers in Moscow in December 1965 turned out to be much more than just another milestone in our family's personal history. What distinguished that evening was not the fact that, as five years before, the hall was packed full, nor that hundreds of people were left standing outside the doors of the Writers' Club surrounded by a cordon of police. No, the extraordinary thing about the evening was that every speech reverberated with the cry, "They murdered him! They murdered him!" And this outcry against yielding to the temptation of forgetfulness and, by extension, to uniting "in the struggle against the common enemy," came as a terrifying blow to the literary authorities seated on the platform, while it touched a responsive chord among those in the auditorium.

Our whole family was together that evening: Simon, who had given up his editorial position at the State Literary Publishing House and had been admitted into the Writers' Union (he did translations of classical and modern literature and also wrote about the literature of antiquity and the Renaissance); David, who, following in his father's footsteps, was trying his hand at poetry, prose and journalism; Lyalya and her husband Nikolai (whose magnificent portrait of Peretz hung above the stage), who had both achieved a solid reputation among Ukrainian artists, Lyalya in the field of plastic arts, as a porcelain designer and ceramist, and Nikolai as a sculptor; my brother Shura, who had resumed his journalistic career after an eighteen-year interruption; my mother, and my two grandchildren, who were already twelve years old.

Next to me I recognized the florid bloated face of Nikolai Tikhonov, a onetime poet who had become a pillar of the regime and a militant defender of the purity of Russian culture in the struggle against the "cosmopolitans." (It was he who, as I mentioned earlier, wrote the anti-Semitic article attacking Nusinov in the first issue of *Soviet Culture,* a magazine that got its start during the postwar *Zhdanovshchina.*) If the choice had been mine, I would never have sat down at the same table with him. As I listened to the words of pain and resentment, of intransigence and implacability spoken that night, I felt that they were aimed directly at Tikhonov.

The atmosphere of that evening is no better conveyed than by the words spoken by my son, Simon:

We are gathered here tonight not only to commemorate an anniversary, but to honor the memory of a poet. I would like to say something about memory.

To paraphrase Mandelstam, we can say that memory is both our torment and our treasure. It is in the nature of man to want to forget—to hide from his memories like a coward, to put on blinders, to block his ears, to pretend to the outside world and to himself that the past did not exist. But it is still more terrible and tormenting when memories recede and grow dim, when you no longer hear the voice that was the sweetest in the world to you, no longer apprehend the pungent odor of thinning curls on the top of a head, no longer see the hands with the large, ribbed fingernails, and you feel like a traitor and a criminal. You have to summon all your strength, all your courage, to resuscitate the past, no matter what the cost, like Ulysses, who restored to the shades of the netherworld a voice and a semblance of life by infusing them with the blood of a ewe. But not with the blood of a black sheep do we revive our memories, but with our own blood and sorrow.

During the last few years, memory has reasserted itself with increasing authority and vanquished the perfidy of forgetfulness and the dishonesty of half-remembering, which is as vile as half-truths. This is happening everywhere, in every country, in every corner of life and art. May this evening of ours be one more contribution to, one more milestone in our noble cause.

For those who disappeared without a trace—perishing in fires or drowning in the waters or vanishing in the deserts—the Greeks raised cenotaphs, empty tombs. Peretz Markish has no grave, no tombstone. But he needs no cenotaph, for he has not disappeared without trace, as those who murdered him hoped and desired. His monument is not his books, old or new, but solely and uniquely our memory, whole and impartial. The memory of his beauty, his talent, his stormy and colorful life, his visions and delusions, and his tragic end.

Returning home one evening, I was met by my neighbor: "While you were out, you had a visitor, a foreigner, she left you a note."

A Soviet always recognizes a foreigner, even if he or she speaks impeccable Russian. Merely talking to a foreigner is risky business and is enough to get you into hot water. But the visitor of a foreigner to your house is something extraordinary! A decade of espionageitis has left its mark on the Soviet citizen, who is inclined to see a spy or a saboteur in every foreigner. Even those who are more intelligent and sophisticated, who know that not every American carries a pistol in a holster, not every Italian a dagger and a spy camera in his bag, even they avoid meetings with foreigners simply to keep out of trouble. Our neighbor belonged to this second category. She was convinced that my association with foreigners would land me, sooner or later, in considerable trouble.

My unexpected visitor, as I learned from the note she had left, was Maria Varshavskaya, the wife of the Jewish writer Oizer Varshavsky, a friend of Peretz's from his younger days. Maria had come to Moscow with a group of tourists from Paris and would be leaving that very evening. I telephoned to say that I would be right over. I didn't want to go empty-handed, so I grabbed a small souvenir of Moscow and also took along a few photos showing Markish and Varshavsky together. A half-hour later, I was knocking on the door of her hotel room.

Maria opened the door. She was holding some photographs in her hand—the very same ones that I had brought along.

Maria turned out to be a wonderful person and a real friend. For a number of years we kept in contact with one another. She was a constant source of support during a particularly difficult period in my life—after we had begun our fight to leave the Soviet Union.

The first time we met, Maria told me about the tragic fate of her own husband: Oizer had been taken by the Germans and had perished at Auschwitz.

I was now increasingly in touch with institutions and publishers in the West who were interested in Markish's writings. I received Jewish newspapers regularly, "left-wing" papers, of course; the others, mostly from the U.S.A., but also from France and Poland, were confiscated by the postal censors. Markish's works were published in the United States, Argentina, Israel, and France.

I developed an extremely interesting correspondence with Nakhman Maizel, head of the *Yidisher Kultur Farband,* a leading authority on Yiddish literature in the West. Up until his death, we exchanged about a hundred letters concerned with various aspects of Markish's writing. A major event in our lives was the visit from Israel of Gitl Maizel, Nakhman's sister, who was also a writer and a critic. With Gitl we could speak with complete candor and share our hopes and plans. She provided us with valuable information about the state of Yiddish culture in Israel.

Thanks to our contacts with Israelis and with others from the West, our plans for the future took on more concrete shape. The question was never *whether* we should go to Israel, but *how* . . . With every month that passed, this question took on greater urgency.

Then, the Six-Day War broke out.

22 / The Voice of Israel

PSYCHOLOGICALLY, the Six-Day War in the Middle East was a tonic for Russian Jewry. By the end of those six days, during which the Israelis defeated the Arab armies in the Sinai, on the Golan Heights, and on the West bank of the Jordan, everything had taken on a new perspective.

Beginning June 6, 1967, we sat by the radio night and day, listening to the "Voice of Israel." (Few people took seriously the Soviet newspapers' clamorings about the "victorious offensive" of the Arab armies.) The first hint there was of any realignment in the position of the contending forces was a report that the Arabs were fleeing. Soviet Jews rejoiced, congratulated each other: *"Our* people are on the offensive!" With the life of Israel imperiled, a great many Russian Jews made a choice: "Israel is our family; Russia is, at best, a relative, if not a total stranger." Not only the Jews who had decided to somehow get to Israel felt that way; even those who asserted the contrary in public glued themselves to the radio at home—turned very low so that their neighbors could hear nothing. Later, this anecdote made the rounds of Russia: Dymshits,

Kosygin's deputy and the most powerful Jew in the USSR, is holding one of the periodical press conferences of "trained Jews" to castigate the Israeli aggressors. Suddenly, glancing at his watch, Dymshits becomes visibly nervous and terribly impatient. He quickly winds up the press conference, exits hurriedly, rushes to his car, and orders his driver to step on the gas and take him home. The moment he arrives, he dashes to his bedroom, locks himself in, closes the shutters, slips into the covers, head and all, and . . . switches on the transistor already tuned to the "Voice of Israel."

But it was still too early to talk about demonstrations in front of the headquarters of the Central Committee of the CPSU, about skirmishes with the police, about hunger strikes at the Moscow Central Telegraph office. All that came later, after people had taken the first, most daring step: trying to obtain an official invitation from Israel, where they had distant relatives who had escaped from fascist or Communist persecution. Photographs of aunts, uncles, or third cousins who were living in Israel had long been stashed away in bottom drawers, and no mention was ever made of their existence in conversations or on questionnaires —having relatives abroad could mean nothing but trouble. To succeed in life, a Soviet citizen must be as sterile as a surgical dressing. How can there be any claim to "sterility" if you have relatives in a foreign country, especially in Israel?

The idea of going to Israel was something we had been dreaming about ever since our return from exile. But we realized that, having done away with Markish, the Soviets would do everything in their power to prevent us from leaving the country. Dead men tell no tales.

Then we began to make contact with Israelis, following the restoration of diplomatic relations with Israel, which had been broken in 1956 during the Sinai War. We went to Jewish concerts and Israeli embassy receptions. Our ties with Israel, our homeland, slowly became a tangible reality, and this gave us strength.

David, who as early as 1958 had made an unsuccessful attempt to reach Israel via Poland (the KGB gave him a rather bad time after that), established clandestine contacts with Israelis. He never removed the chain with the Star of David from his neck, and in those days it took plenty of courage to wear one. He came back from every meeting with Israelis bursting with new vitality. Mostly, I knew nothing about these meetings: David didn't want to upset me, knowing such contacts might lead to dire consequences both for himself and us as well. In 1960, David began publishing Zionist poems in Israel under the pen name of D. Magen. For a long time, I knew nothing about that either.

The 1967 war broke open the carapace of fifty years of fear. Now we knew Israel would stand behind us, would not abandon its Jews in distress. The only thing we had to do was obtain an official invitation from Israel—and follow through. We did not have to grope in the darkness; the way had been lighted by people like the poet Joseph Kerler and the singer Nekhama Lifshits. It had been a difficult road, and they had been among the first to tread it.

We had relatives in Israel: first cousins of Markish's and some of my own family from my mother's side. (According to family legend, a first or second cousin of my mother's had married the brother of Chaim Weizmann, Israel's first president, making the famous General Ezer Weizmann a distant cousin of mine. We didn't take the idea we might be related to him very seriously, any more than the story that one of Markish's ancestors was the Portuguese admiral Lourengo Marques, whose name had been given to the capital of Mozambique.) We had no information about Markish's cousins, except that they had gone to settle in Israel before the October Revolution. But it was enough for a start.

One fine day we found a thick, oblong envelope in our mailbox. It contained an invitation from one of Markish's cousins. The die was cast—and we knew from the encircled "7" stamped on the envelope that the KGB censors had acquainted themselves with its contents. We also knew this was not our first invitation from Israel; the previous ones had simply never reached us.

The official document bearing the state seal of Israel with red silk ribbon was locked away in a drawer of my desk like a precious treasure. The invitation covered not only myself, but my son Simon and my mother. The next step was to submit the invitation to appropriate agencies. There were two possibilities: they would permit us to leave immediately, preferring to avoid any complications with the Markish family, or else draw us into a long battle, the issue of which would be uncertain. Our resolve was strengthened by the fact that in submitting our documents to OVIR (Visa and Registration Department of the Ministry of Foreign Affairs) we would be encouraging others to do the same thing.

It would take us quite some time to wind up our personal affairs. In the first place, we didn't have enough money to process our documents and visa application. In the event our visas were delivered, we would have to pay more than one thousand rubles per person for an exit permit, not to mention the cost of transporting our baggage. Second, my mother, who was in her eighties, was seriously ill. Finally, Simon was planning to marry a Hungarian citizen, and if we put in for our visas immediately, this would complicate his marriage plans tremendously (in the USSR, marriage to a foreigner is no easy matter).

The first problem presented no particular difficulty. After many years of perseverance, a collection of Markish's verses and poems appeared in Leningrad, and there was a considerable sum of money coming to us. My translation of Armand Lanoux's *Maupassant*, my fee for which would also help, was at the printers. Then, too, David had written the scenario for a film, which was in production, and a book of his short stories had been accepted by Sovetsky Pisatel, the Moscow publishing house.

On April 21, 1970, Simon was married. We had a few close friends and relatives in to celebrate the occasion. My mother had, of course, come for her beloved grandson's wedding; she didn't look too well, but she was in good spirits and joined in the general merriment. But the following day she took to her bed, and she never got up again: on May 2, she died of lung cancer.

Simon's wife had just completed her work in Russia and had to return to Hungary any day now. The whole family got together and we all agreed to wait a bit longer before submitting our papers to OVIR so as to allow Simon time to apply for permission to leave for Hungary and take up permanent residence there with his wife. (If we put in our applications at the same time as Simon, he would surely have been turned down.) So he went ahead with his application, and we did nothing pending the outcome.

In early September, the answer came from OVIR: Simon's application was approved. He decided to leave at the beginning of October. When the time came for us to say good-bye, we were not sure whether we would ever see each other again.

At this time the Jews of Russia were following closely the proceedings of the First Anti-Jewish Leningrad Trial. The defendants had been accused of attempting to hijack a plane to Sweden, with the intention of making their way to Israel. It was clear to all of us that the regime was using this trial to intimidate Jews and discourage them from seeking greener pastures. Nobody knew better than our own family what Soviet show trials were, how they were fabricated, and how they ended up. If the defendants managed to escape the firing squad, it was evidence that the Soviets felt compelled to consider public opinion in the West. And if, God willing, things turned out that way, there would be rejoicing on our street and we would be successful in our efforts to get out of the Soviet Union.

The condemnation to death of Kuznetsov and Dymshits, the two principal defendants in the Leningrad Trial, enraged the Jews in Russia. Hatred welled up in their hearts against the monstrous, perverse regime that disposed of their destinies, that inflicted its black will on people who had been born free. Their hatred grew and with it, their determination. I do not know of a single person who, as a result of the barbarous sentences meted out at the Leningrad Trial, changed his mind about leaving Russia for Israel. On the contrary, hundreds of Jews laid siege to the offices of OVIR throughout the country to put in applications to leave the Soviet Union. Far from intimidating the Jews, the Leningrad Trial emboldened them.

But of course the prostituted Soviet press trumpeted about the "success" of the trial, using phrases like "just vengeance," and "devious scheming of international Zionism." And many Jews—some coerced, others freely—wrote boot-licking letters to the newspapers in which they heaped opprobrium on their own people and Israel. It left an ugly taste in our mouths to find among the authors of these letters people of recent acquaintance. . . .

By the time the money from the publishing houses and the film studio finally came, we had assembled the considerable number of documents required. In early February 1971, David and I went to Kolpachny Lane, where OVIR was located. The Department of Visas and Registration occupied a small, two-story house. ("Where does the homeland begin?" the Jews used to joke. "With OVIR!") The first time, they refused to accept our documents because some information was lacking. We obtained the information and went back a second time, but again we met with a refusal: certain other information was required. Finally, on the twenty-third of February, a wet, snowy, windy day, our documents were accepted. As we left OVIR, David and I threw our arms around each other. We felt almost free now, for we had dared to tell the regime: "We are Jews and we want to go home."

We spent almost the entire day at OVIR. The place was teeming with people, mostly Jews. The formalities connected with the submission of documents are time-consuming, and Jews arrive at OVIR early in the morning to take their place in line. Two policemen— where they came from and why they were there was a mystery—spelled each other, alternating days. They spent their time scrutinizing with hostile eyes the forty or fifty Jews packed into the reception room. One was particularly rude; his chest was decorated with row upon row of medals. Now and then, the stentorious voice of a guard keeping order was heard: "No smoking! No milling around! Sit down! Anyone who hasn't got a seat can clear out!"

After an hour of waiting. we knew the faces of the guards, of the deputy head Zolotukhin, nicknamed the "Gold Behind," and of the two women inspectors Kosheleva and Izrailova. The latter was, by all appearances, a Tatar, and her name, posted on the board, caused her lots of trouble. Could anything be more ludicrous than a Soviet police lieutenant with the name Izrailova processing the applications of Jews trying to get to Israel? Lieutenant Kosheleva was a young, attractive woman with a known weakness for tall men and a distaste for short men. The shorter Jews, therefore, tried to fall into the hands of Izrailova, but Yura Aronovich, an orchestra conductor, absentmindedly let Kosheleva take care of him, although he couldn't have been more than five feet two inches, a head shorter than her. She measured him with a disdainful glance.

"Look here," she said, pointing to his application form, "you say your father was buried in a Jewish cemetery. How come?"

"Allow me, citizen lieutenant, to ask you a question," the sharp-witted Yura countered.

"Well!"

"I have no desire to be indiscreet, but could you tell me what your nationality is?"

"What do you mean?" she said, not at all pleased by the question. "Why, Russian, of course!"

"And your mother, she's also Russian?"

"Certainly!"

"Well, now, when she dies," Yura was coming to the point, "she'll be buried in a Russian cemetery, won't she? You'd never think of having her buried in a Jewish cemetery, would you?"

Kosheleva was furious, but there was nothing she could say.

Then there was Senior Inspector Akulova, who occasionally came down from her office on the second floor. Her name, which means "shark," suited her to a tee. The Jews told the story of how, one March 8— Woman's Day in the Soviet Union—a disappointed applicant had sent her a gift by mail . . . a dog muz-

271

zle. Akulova treated the Jews with contempt and arrogance, as if they were a species of a lower order. It made no difference if she were dealing with a worker or a professor; the only thing that mattered was that he was a Jew.

Major Fadeyev, the deputy head of the OVIR section dealing with foreign nationals, was in fact an agent of the KGB, notwithstanding his policeman's uniform. Who is better qualified to handle foreigners than a KGB agent! Fadeyev was a boor with the face of a hangman. Since "Gold Behind" couldn't cope alone with the surging tide of Jewish applicants, Fadeyev was often called down from the second floor to lend a hand.

The number-one man in OVIR, Smirnov, was completely disconcerted by the influx of Jews continually asking for something and making his life generally miserable. Only a year before, OVIR was as quiet as a hospital; the number of people applying for visas could be counted on the fingers of one hand. But now, hordes of unruly Jews were storming the doors of OVIR from morning on! Smirnov had issued strict orders forbidding any Jews to enter his second-floor office, and he had his telephone number changed every month—but all to no avail. The good old days when there was nothing to disturb his tranquillity were gone forever, and nothing but trouble lay ahead. . . . Ah, those Jews, whoever would have expected they would play such dirty tricks?

One entry on the questionnaire read, "Is there anything particular you wish to say about the motives for your action?" Both David and I wrote, "We consider Israel our ancestral home." Which was an act of open defiance, but we committed it with a light heart.

The days dragged interminably as we waited for a decision. In early March, a policeman suddenly appeared at the apartment. At first, he pretended he was just dropping in to see how we were getting along. Then, out of the blue, he asked, "You're not by any chance expecting visitors from abroad, are you?"

"No, we're not."

"Are you, perhaps, planning to go away yourself?"

"We have filed an application to leave for Israel."

"I see," the policeman muttered, as if this was news to him. "And your furniture, are you going to take it with you? You have lovely furniture."

After jotting something down in his notebook, the policeman left. We interpreted his visit as a favorable sign that perhaps some positive decision had been taken in our case.

The next thing that marked our period of waiting was the decision taken by Sovetsky Pisatel to "kill" David's book.

There was no beating around the bush: "Is it true that you—how shall I put it—are planning . . . ?"

"Yes, it's true all right," David broke in. "I'm planning to go to Israel."

"Well, in that case you can easily realize nothing can come of your book."

"But it's already been announced in the program of forthcoming publications."

"It's none of our doing; we're just carrying out orders. The best thing for you is to take back your manuscript."

As was to be expected, many of our old acquaintances became invisible, but we found new friends among petitioners, who, like ourselves, lived under the sign of the three "V"s—*Vyzov* ("invitation"), *Viza,* and *Vyyezd* ("departure")—and spent hours talking about Israel, listening to the Voice of Israel and discussing the broadcasts, and making conjectures about the future. And we continued preparing for our departure. We sold our furniture and anything else that was not essential, and we started packing our books. David got rid of his hunting rifle and collection of daggers, sensing that the authorities might take advantage of the opportunity and slap him into jail for illegal possession of arms. He may very well have been right. Had a pretext not been found for trumped-up criminal charges against the film director Mikhail Kalik, who had also applied for immigration to Israel? The charges had been dropped within a few months, but the whole thing left Kalik a nervous wreck.

David and I grew closer than ever to Mikhail Zand, a very old friend of my two sons. Thanks to his knowledge of Judaism and Hebrew, and a number of other qualities, this brilliant and sensitive man had become a leading figure among the "Israelis of Moscow." Everybody turned to him for advice and help. His reputation was further enhanced by his breaking up at the Moscow synagogue a meeting of "trained Jews" that had been organized for the benefit of some visitors from abroad. Rabbi Levin had been engaged for the occasion to paint a glowing picture of the life of the Jews in the Soviet Union and debunk the stories that Jewish culture was being throttled. He claimed that, except for a handful of renegades, Soviet Jews had no desire to go to Israel!

Once Zand had succeeded, with considerable effort, in breaking through the police cordon guarding the entrance to the synagogue, he confronted Levin and accused him point blank of betraying the Jews. The assembled foreign guests and journalists were wide-eyed with astonishment. Zand was arrested on the spot but since he did not resist, there were no grounds for jailing him. The KGB, however, settled its score with him some time later: they gave him fifteen days for "disturbing the peace." Throughout the entire fifteen days of his detention, Zand refused food and water. On the twelfth day of his hunger strike, a "medical" team was dispatched to the jail to feed him by force.

"Are you going to resist being fed?" a man in a white shirt asked Zand.

"With all the strength I have," Zand calmly answered.

"I warn you," the "doctor" said, "you may die if you do, and then we'll simply enter your name in the profit and loss column."

Though tied down on a bench with prison guards sitting on top of him, Zand still resisted. They decided to call the whole thing off, and Zand continued his hunger strike until his release on the fifteenth day.

Such examples of courage forced even the most irresolute and downtrodden Jews to face up to their oppressors and look them squarely in the eye. There were Russians, too, who could not but esteem this show of courage.

The first period of our wait came to an end in mid-May. A postcard arrived in the evening mail with the message, "Contact Inspector Akulova at OVIR." There was a telephone number, and that was all.

Such postcards from OVIR always come in the evening mail, and usually on Friday, the eve of the weekend, so as to prolong the anxiety of the recipient. It would seem that nothing would be simpler than to write on the card "Request granted" or "Request rejected." But no, that would be too great a luxury. Let the Jew have a few sleepless nights, pacing back and forth in his room wondering for the millionth time if his request has been granted.

Early the next morning, we telephoned OVIR.

"Your application has been rejected," Senior Inspector Akulova informed me.

"On what grounds?"

"I tell you your application has been turned down," she repeated. "As to the reasons why, that you can find out from the appropriate agencies."

My hope that they would think twice about harassing the Markish family collapsed like a house of cards. But the loss of this fragile hope was compensated for by the firm conviction that in the end we would prevail. Our staunch friends, the "Israelis of Moscow," comforted us: the first refusal is only "the baptism by fire." Yes, there are a few lucky ones who make it the first time, but not everyone is lucky. That evening, Volodya and Masha Slepak, Vitya Polsky, and the Kaliks came by to see us. They had fared no better than I; we were all in the same boat. We ate around a cheerless table, remembering those who had made it to Israel: Nekhama Lifshits, Iosif Kerler, and a few young people. There was some consolation in the fact that exit permits were being granted; it was no longer a supernatural phenomenon. Our minds went back to the "March Events"—the first sitdown strike by Jews in the hall of the USSR Supreme Soviet, in the very heart of Moscow. As a result, nearly thirty people had been allowed to leave. The strike had come as a hard blow to the authorities, who never suspected that the Jews were capable of such a desperate act, or anybody else in Russia, for that matter. But the next time the strike weapon was used, it led not to departures but to arrest. New forms of protest now had to be discovered.

Immediately after our application was turned down, we registered a demand that our case be reexamined. While we were waiting at the entrance to OVIR, we happened to see two people to whom it was absolutely impossible to gain access: Shutov, the commissar of the "militia" (chief of police), and Georgy Minin, a "civilian" KGB official (rumor had it that he held the rank of general and was head of the Jewish section of Lubyanka). The crowds of Jews on the sidewalk in front of OVIR swarmed around this unsavory pair. One little girl shouted "Uncle general, let me go to Israel!" I shouldered my way through to Minin and stopped him. David was by my side.

"We are the Markishes," I said. "Perhaps that name means something to you."

"Why, yes," he answered with a sardonic smile.

"We have received a refusal, and we would like to make an appointment to see you."

"Fine," he said. "I'll telephone you."

"It might be better if we called you," David chimed in.

"I'll find your number in the directory," the general joked as he went toward his car.

We waited in vain for Minin's phone call, but did succeed in locating his phone number (not in the telephone book, since the numbers of KGB officials in the Soviet Union are unlisted) and calling him. Minin agreed to receive us at OVIR. (He did not publicize his affiliation with the notorious KGB. According to the official Soviet version, the KGB has nothing to do with the problem of Jewish emigration from the USSR; in reality, they enjoy complete jurisdiction in this domain, and their authority extends down even to individual cases.)

David and I went over to OVIR in the morning. We expected a great deal from this meeting with a general of the KGB, because we would make it clear to him that our detention in the USSR would inevitably attract the attention of international public opinion, with undesirable consequences for Moscow. We had never met a KGB general face to face before, and we were anything but relaxed. Maybe, I thought, just for old time's sake, they'd clamp us into prison.

Flashing his stainless steel dentures, Minin received us with the cordiality of an actor playing a role.

"My advice to you is to take no further action until the fall," he said. "Meanwhile, why don't you get away for a rest? We have such a marvelous seaside—in the Crimea, in the Caucasus."

"We also have a lovely sea," David countered. "The Mediterranean, the Red Sea—that's where we'd like to go for a rest, to our own country."

The general smirked. "Come now, what do you know about Israel? Do you know how many theaters they have there? One! Here, if you want, you can go to a different theater every day. Also, theater tickets are very expensive there. And medical care! Here, for nothing at all, you just pick up the phone and a doctor comes over immediately. But there, just try to get a doctor to come to see you, and if by some miracle he does, it won't be for nothing."

"We haven't come here to discuss the situation in Israel with you," I said. "Tell me, why have we been refused?"

"It's a complex problem," he said, tossing up his hands. "The official explanation is that a sufficient degree of kinship does not exist." The general eyed us scornfully. "To sum up, I advise you not to pursue the matter any further until the fall." The audience was over.

But I couldn't deprive myself of the pleasure of quipping, "Are you suggesting by the time fall comes around, our distant relatives will have turned into close relatives?"

"We'll have an opportunity of seeing each other again." The general smiled graciously as he got up from his desk.

When people around us received permission to leave, we went to see them off at Sheremetyevo Airport, our eyes staying on them until they disappeared behind closed doors. Just a few hours away there was freedom, human dignity, a homeland, eternity. . . . The more people we saw leave, the more our hearts were filled with pride and optimism: the Jews were on their way, and our turn would come, too. The only question was . . . when? Would we live to see that day? Would we be able to stick it out? Of one thing we were all certain, however. Were it not for the support we had in the West, we would long since have been rotting in the ground.

23 / The Last Battle

OUR SECOND REFUSAL came that summer. We took it in stride and filed a protest that same day. But on August 12, the date of the nineteenth anniversary of Markish's death, David and I decided to organize a demonstration. After giving the matter considerable thought, we decided the best place would be the Hall of the Supreme Soviet, not inside the building itself, but just opposite the main entrance that adjoins Red Square, in the heart of Moscow. We also decided to demonstrate wearing a yellow Star of David pinned to our chests, as was mandatory for Jews under Hitler. It was a risky enterprise: the Communists loathe being reminded of the fascistic nature of their regime. But if we were arrested precisely on the twelfth day of August, it would have a dramatic impact on world public opinion and the Soviets would be forced to release us. Nineteen years after his own disappearance, Markish would be instrumental in our liberation.

We planned the operation with painstaking care. We would enter the Hall of the Supreme Soviet as soon as the doors opened in the morning and give a letter to the attendant. The letter would serve notice that we were going to stage a demonstration to protest our detention in the Soviet Union; that the six-pointed yellow stars were a reminder of the immense sacrifices the Jewish people had suffered as victims of Nazism and anti-Semitism; and that we had chosen this place and this date for a demonstration because Markish had perished nineteen years ago to the day and there was no grave at which we could gather.

On the eve of our demonstration, we notified members of the foreign press corps and asked a group of young Jewish activists—the Krimgold brothers, Victor Yakhot, and a few others—to take up positions at various points near the site of the demonstration; in the event of our arrest, they would immediately scatter and spread the news.

The next morning at ten o'clock sharp, we handed our letter to the attendant in the hall.

"This letter, is it a collective letter?" he inquired. From the look on his face, I could see that he took David, who had handed him the letter, for a Jew.

"No," David affirmed. He was anxious to avoid the letter's being opened and read on the spot, since this could have resulted in our being detained on the premises. Soviet functionaries are extremely reluctant to accept collective letters: either they refuse to accept them altogether, or else they raid them at once and then refuse to accept them.

As soon as we left the hall, we pinned on the yellow stars. To have done so before delivering the letter would surely have meant being detained. As far as I know, this was the first time that yellow Stars of David had ever been worn in a demonstration in the USSR.

Meanwhile, the word was going around among the "Israelis of Moscow" that we had begun our demonstration. David and I stood on the curb of the narrow sidewalk. As the unending stream of pedestrians passed by, we continually noticed familiar faces: friends or acquaintances who had come by to verify the rumors of our demonstration.

The moment we had left the Hall of the Supreme Soviet, the foreign correspondents were on our heels —representatives of Western newspapers and wire services. We gave them copies of the letter addressed to Podgorny and spoke to them. Our mission was completed. There was nothing more for us to do but to wait around quietly until we were arrested.

The KGB arrived in force in the wake of the journalists. They had been loitering nearby, ridiculously wearing dark glasses and carrying newspapers under their arms. I spotted a few familiar faces—agents who "worked" with the Jews and covered Sheremetyevo Airport, OVIR and the Central Synagogue. They sent the policeman posted at the doorway to the Hall of the Supreme Soviet over to us.

"Why have you been hanging around here since early morning?" he asked menacingly. "Get a move on!"

"What's wrong?" David asked. "Is there any law against standing here?"

The guardian of the public order was at a loss for words, for we were not in violation of any law.

"We're going to stand here until six o'clock this evening," David continued. "The letter we've left with the hall attendant explains why."

"Your papers!" he commanded.

We handed him our passports and he checked them.

"Move on!" he repeated. "If you don't, I'll call the patrol, and they'll send you packing."

"Well, go ahead and call them," I said as calmly as I could.

While all this was going on, our cohorts, led by Slepak, sent three telegrams: to Podgorny, to Brezhnev, to Kosygin. The message concluded with the words "Pharaoh, let my people go!"

After two in the afternoon, there were fewer KGB agents around; apparently they had gone off for lunch. We began to feel the effects of the hot sun beating down on us. Passers-by glanced with frightened astonishment at our yellow six-pointed stars—which Soviet propaganda has transformed into a symbol of fascism—but we detected no sign of hostility, only curiosity or sympathy. The Jews had a particularly sharp reaction: they either quickened their steps or stopped dead in their tracks, as if struck by a bolt of lightning.

Five o'clock came and the Hall of the Supreme Soviet closed its doors. When we didn't budge, the KGB intensified their activity: they couldn't guess what we were up to and this alarmed them. Again they dispatched a policeman to intimidate and abuse us. When his efforts failed, he spent his wrath on our young Jewish friends who were there as observers and sent them flying.

At six o'clock sharp, after our eight-hour stand without food or water (my feet were swollen and I was feeling faint), David stepped into the street to hail a cab.

"What do you mean jaywalking!" the policeman bellowed, rushing over to him. "I'll haul you in for a traffic violation!"

We paid him no heed but got into a taxi and drove home, where our friends were waiting for us.

Not surprisingly, our demonstration did not bring immediate results. We weren't discouraged, though, and began devising other methods of resistance. Election time was nearing and the residents of our district were called upon to vote for Kosygin, who was up for the post of chairman of the Council of Ministers. By that time, we had already been notified of our third refusal, and Kosygin was one of the key people to whom we had sent letters of complaint that were never acknowledged.

Two weeks before election day, Kosygin received another letter from us, in which we asked "our candidate" to do something about our problem. If he replied to our letter, we wrote, he would receive our votes.

It is worth noting that attempts to shirk voting are not all that infrequent in the USSR. Every citizen is well aware of the fact that whether he participates in the voting or not, it has no effect whatever on the political fate of the government-endorsed candidate, and that the elections themselves as well as the ballot count are a complete fraud. Nevertheless, no efforts are spared to get out the vote. Those who repeatedly refuse to appear at the polling places find themselves under the surveillance of the KGB and the district psychiatrist.

We did not, of course, receive any reply from Kosygin. On election day we stayed at home and waited for further developments. At noon, aides of the election committee, student "volunteers," came by to see us.

"You haven't voted yet?"

"No, and we're not planning to."

"What do you mean, you're not planning to?"

"Just that," we said. "We have our reasons. You can tell the chairman of the election committee that our position has been set forth in a letter we sent to our candidate, Kosygin."

"Please try to put yourself in our shoes," the students pleaded. "If you don't come with us, we'll be in hot water. Come on now, you know it's no problem at all, if that's what's stopping you. The polls are just around the corner."

We felt sorry for the student "volunteers," but we refused to budge.

A few hours later, the chairman of the election committee himself appeared.

"If one of you is sick," he said, "that's no problem. We'll bring you the voting box, and you can vote at home."

"But we have no intention of voting, and that's that."

"But why?"

We thereupon produced a copy of our letter to Kosygin. As he read it, his face fell.

"It's people like you who spoil the voting record of the district," he complained.

There was nothing we could do but express our sympathy to him.

At subsequent elections—for the district soviet, for the peoples' judges, and other posts—we were no longer bothered. They had, apparently, given up on us.

So as to lose no time and to prepare ourselves properly for life in Israel, we decided to begin studying Hebrew. At the time, there were ten or fifteen illegal study circles functioning in Moscow. The regime was powerless to do anything about them: people simply got together in somebody's apartment, as if attending a social gathering, opened their notebooks and studied the language. It was difficult for the authorities to break up these "evenings" without proceeding to arrest all the students along with their teacher. The KGB was reluctant to apply such an extreme measure.

Owing to an oversight on the part of the authorities, there had once been two legal Hebrew study circles in Moscow. The teachers of the two schools had called on the tax division of the Ministry of Finances and declared that they were "teaching a foreign language and would like to pay the required tax."

They were then told to fill in some cards, which they did on the spot.

"And could you tell us what Hebrew is?" the clerks inquired as they filed away the cards.

"Oh, just another foreign language" was the casual answer.

"You don't say!" one of the clerks exclaimed, utterly amazed. "My, the number of foreign languages in this world! Why, Hebrew isn't even listed among the languages we have on file. . . ."

The authorities soon put two and two together, however, and demanded Hebrew-teaching diplomas of the two teachers. There was no such thing, of course, since Soviet schools had no Hebrew-language departments. The teachers declared that they fully met the requirements of their students, but to no avail. The schools were discontinued.

Our teacher was a young man by the name of Yasha Charny, who had learned Hebrew on his own. He had been dismissed from his engineering post after applying for permission to go to Israel, and he now had a job as a loader in the same bakery where David worked, also as a loader.

After he had given us ten lessons, Yasha's permission to emigrate came through, and he left. Volodya Zaretsky, an unsuccessful applicant for emigration, took over. He had given us only one lesson when suddenly he, too, was given permission to leave. These coincidences gave rise to a joke among the "Israelis of Moscow"—"if you want to go to Israel, all you have to do is give Hebrew lessons to the Markishes."

On October 22, a policeman visited the parents of David's wife, Irina, and ordered her to appear at OVIR at once. It was in the evening, and Irina happened to be at her parents' quite by chance. She took a taxi to OVIR, where she was informed that she was

283

free to leave for Israel and had one week to quit the territory of the USSR.

"And what about my husband?" Irina asked.

"He'll have to make his own inquiries," they told her.

The next morning, David put in a call to Pristansky, deputy director of the Administrative Agencies of the Central Committee of the CPSU, who was responsible for supervising the work of OVIR. He knew our family and our case very well, for we had talked to him several times. David explained the situation to him.

"You'll have an answer in a few days," Pristansky said. "You'll find it satisfactory, I think, and you'll be leaving."

"May I take your words as a formal declaration?" David asked.

"You know very well whom you're talking to," Pristansky replied.

A few days passed, however, and there was nothing new. David decided Irina should leave by herself, maintaining that any Jew who received permission to leave ought to at the first opportunity, since it was by no means uncommon for a visa to be canceled out of hand. And besides, Irina's was due to expire shortly anyway.

So, for the umpteenth time, we drove out to Sheremetyevo for the Moscow-Vienna flight. But this time we were seeing off a member of our own family. I tried to persuade myself we were saying good-bye for only a short time—a few days, perhaps, or a week at most—and that Irina would do well to wait for us in Schönau, but common sense dictated otherwise. What are the promises of the Soviet authorities worth, whether they come from the Central Committee, the KGB, or the MVD?

Two and a half weeks later, we received our fourth official refusal. This time the reason given was "considerations of State." Pristansky, whom David immediately telephoned, declared: "You evidently misunderstood me, Citizen Markish."

After still another refusal—the fifth, I think—David and I decided to repudiate our Soviet citizenship. By this time, we had already acquired Israeli citizenship and were in possession of the numbers of the relevant decrees of the Israeli Ministry of Internal Affairs. The documents themselves had been mailed to us from Israel and had, of course, been confiscated by the KGB. We were completely cut off from contact with the outside world: the KGB had our home phone disconnected. David came home less and less frequently—he was being hounded by the police and the military authorities, who had decided to conscript him into the army. Conscription would have meant that all doors out of the Soviet Union would be shut to him for at least three years. After weighing the pros and cons, David decided to go into hiding. He proceeded to knock around the country, staying in no one place for any length of time.

David's last travels in the Soviet Union would have been fascinating had they not been fraught with danger. At the beginning, we hid out together, at the dacha of David's in-laws. It was a flimsy wooden structure without heat or electricity about twenty-five miles from Moscow. We had come to the dacha just before a sharp drop in the temperature and so had nothing but light summer clothes with us. Thus we could not make our way to the railroad station without attracting considerable attention, the weather being what it was. We had no choice but to stay in our wooden refuge wrapped up in blankets and tablecloths. Fortunately, a few days later, one of David's friends showed up with overcoats and boots. When darkness fell, we made it safely to the train station.

Without even stopping by the apartment, David went directly to Leningrad. But there was no question of his stopping there either. He could have stayed with an aunt of mine, except that she lived in a communal apartment, and there was always the possibility that one of her neighbors had been listening to a foreign radio and had heard something about our affairs. The Voice of Israel, the BBC and other stations had carried the news that a group of Jewish activists, David among them, were hiding from the military authorities. So David continued on to Karelia, where he took a room in a remote village and went about finishing his novel.

285

Now and then, he would cast a forlorn glance at the Finnish tourist buses carrying travelers toward Vyborg and points north, beyond the frontier.

David's next stop was Riga. From the Latvian capital he telephoned his wife, who was then in Paris, and the KGB stumbled on his trail (at the telephone office they asked to see his passport before putting through the call to his wife). He managed to shake his pursuers and board the train for Moscow, where he also succeeded in eluding the KGB control—in those days, Jews were forbidden to enter Moscow and were taken off the trains and planes.

It was then that we decided to renounce Soviet citizenship. It was, more than anything else, an act of protest and a risky one: in the event that the authorities did accede to our request, we could be expelled to a region about sixty miles from Moscow, I would lose my rights to a pension, and, if worse came to worse, we could be placed in preventive detention in a labor camp. To be sure, we already had Israeli citizenship, and the Soviets knew it. And the fact that we did inspired us with confidence in the successful outcome of our enterprise.

A declaration of renunciation of citizenship is not receivable unless it is submitted on the detailed, official forms especially for that purpose. They are exceedingly difficult to come by. Only the Moscow OVIR is authorized to deliver them, but categorically refuses to do so until you have introduced a formal request that the requisite forms be issued to you. Your request can be studied for three months, or six months, or a year, for that matter, since there is no specified time limit. Fortunately, we managed to obtain in a roundabout way one copy of the form and made three copies of the original. In addition there is a fee of five hundred rubles, which meant that David and I had to cough up one thousand rubles to the Treasury out of the money we had put aside for our departure from the Soviet Union. To transfer such a large sum of money through our savings account—and there was no alternative—is no simple matter: the bank may suspect something fishy, contact the appropriate agencies, and simply refuse to allow the transaction.

And unless your declaration is accompanied by a receipt confirming that the money has been deposited to the treasury, it has no validity.

We managed, though, merely telling the bank that the transaction was a pure formality connected with the issuance of our passports for foreign travel. Hypnotized by the size of the sum involved, the bank clerk stamped the receipt and in the column marked "purpose," David entered the words "repudiation of Soviet citizenship." We sealed the forms, the receipt and declarations in a large envelope and sent it by registered mail, with receipt to be acknowledged by the addressee (this is very important since you retain a receipt and a record of the materials sent). The envelope was addressed to the Supreme Soviet, the attention of Podgorny. Once again, there was nothing for us to do but sit back and wait.

Six months later, in response to a telephone call, we were told (verbally, of course—nothing is ever put in writing in cases like this) that a decision was still pending and that our dossier had been referred to the KGB for "verification." It turned out that the "voluntary" bonds between the citizen and the State were extremely difficult to break.

Several weeks were spent tracking down our file in the KGB Klychkov, who would have nothing to do with us except by phone, declared, "So you want to leave for Israel. Well, as soon as you receive permission to do so, we will strike you off the list of Soviet citizens."

"We see no connection between our repudiating Soviet citizenship and our departure for Israel," I explained. "We simply no longer wish to be Soviet citizens. That is our right, after all."

"How can you be so thick-headed!" the colonel exploded over the telephone. "I'm telling you in plain Russian: as soon as you leave, you'll lose your citizenship!"

"I take it, then, that our request to renounce citizenship is rejected."

"That's right, rejected."

"And that's your own decision?"

"Whose else?" the colonel exclaimed, not suspect-

287

ing that it was a loaded question. "Of course, it's our decision!"

"But you know that the decision on matters of citizenship lies with the Supreme Soviet!"

The colonel didn't know what to say, but one thing was clear: they wouldn't allow us to give up our citizenship. Naturally, we didn't let the matter go at that, and we wrote the following letter to the Supreme Soviet:

> Within the time limit set by law—half a year —we have received no answer to our declaration of repudiation of Soviet citizenship. We hereby inform you that should we not receive the requested reply in the next two weeks, we will consider ourselves divested of Soviet citizenship.

The bureaucratic style of the declaration was repulsive, but we had already learned to speak to Soviet officialdom in their native language.

There was no reply to our letter, so when the two weeks had elapsed we began calling ourselves foreign nationals. Moreover, in the event that we did receive an official, documented rejection, we had a ready plan of action. We would bring suit, demanding the restitution of our thousand rubles. The district court would unquestionably dismiss our action against the Presidium of the Supreme Soviet. In that event, we would file a complaint against the district court with the municipal court. The latter would have to hear our complaint in open court before interposing a demurrer. We would see to it that Western correspondents were present at the hearing, which would then be publicized in the press. A precedent would be established, and if there is one thing the Communist bureaucracy doesn't like, it is a precedent.

Our battle to renounce Soviet citizenship continued right up to the day we left the USSR: the regime would not permit a precedent to be established that could have paved the way for a mass repudiation of Soviet citizenship—and not by Jews alone.

Those final few months were, I daresay, the most

oppressive and bleakest period of our long, interminable wait. We had no desire to see anyone or go anywhere. There was only one place in all of Moscow that kept its charms for us, and that was the home of our dear friends Lucia and Jean Cathala.

Jean Cathala was a French journalist, writer, and a long-time resident in the Soviet Union. His cozy apartment on Sivtsev Vrazhek Street was a gathering place for the French, English and American members of Moscow's foreign colony, free men from the free world. An evening spent at the Cathalas' was like escaping from prison for a few hours. Jean Cathala, a man of great charm and intelligence, and Lucia, his lovely and sympathetic wife, may never have suspected what a bracing effect their company and that of their guests had on me.

One evening David and I were the only guests in their hospitable home.

We talked high-level and low-level politics, we spoke about the future. . . . At one point in the conversation, David said, "We can't wait forever. We've already done practically everything in our power. The time has come to set a deadline, say two or three months, and call it a day. In the long run, our suicide may be of some use to others."

Cathala turned green.

"What are you talking about? You mean you're more concerned with others than with yourself?" Cathala ventured.

"No, I'm thinking first and foremost of myself."

"In that case, why don't you take a pistol and at least knock off one of your persecutors."

I think David got the point.

Right after the murder of our athletes by Arab terrorists during the Olympic Games in Munich, we decided to stage a protest demonstration. We had to act rapidly and decisively; all previous attempts by Jews to demonstrate officially had been disrupted by the authorities. We immediately set about drafting a letter to the chairman of the Mossoviet (Moscow Soviet) that clearly stated the firm intention of the authors to stage a demonstration in front of the Lebanese embassy. At the same time, we decided to give a letter of protest to the Lebanese ambassador. The letter to the chairman of the Mossoviet was signed by Professor Alexander Lerner, Professor Vladimir Mash, and my son David. The three of them left for the Mossoviet to deliver the letter.

They were received by a deputy chairman, who declared, "All of us regret what has happened and share your grief, citizens of Jewish nationality. But as far as the demonstration is concerned, you'll have to contact the Committee on Sports. Why exactly do you want to demonstrate before the Lebanese embassy?"

"Precisely because the headquarters of the terrorists are located on Lebanese soil," they answered.

Apparently the authorities were reluctant to outlaw the demonstration, but they would do everything possible to interfere with it.

From the Mossoviet, Lerner, Mash and David went over to the Committee on Sports. The officials there became alarmed.

"We have not come to ask your permission," our delegation declared. "You can, if you like, join in our demonstration."

"Give us time to think it over and make a few phone calls," the committee officials said, "and let's meet tomorrow."

Whom they were planning to call was no mystery.

"We're holding the demonstration today," our spokesman affirmed. "You can postpone a holiday, but not a funeral."

It was agreed they would telephone the committee at the end of the working day.

The telephone call might just as well have not been made.

"We will not take part in the demonstration," the committee officials informed them, "and we advise you not to.'"

Around six o'clock that evening, more than one hundred Jews, individually and in small groups, started marching on the Lebanese embassy, which was already ringed by cordons of police and military detachments. As we drew near the building, we exchanged discreet signals with a French newspaper correspondent who had been alerted to our plans. We proceeded to push through the regular, rush-hour crowds until we had broken through the first, rather loose police cordon. Alongside the walls of the embassy, a second cordon of police was in position, supported by a contingent of soldiers stationed near their military trucks.

"Scatter!" a police colonel barked, as he lunged forward.

On the steps leading up to the embassy entrance, a KGB agent in civilian dress was shouting orders to the police colonel below. The colonel waved his hand, and buses pulled up to the curb. The police cordon closed ranks and started channeling us toward the buses. There was a flurry of resistance. A throng of people on the other side of the street observed the scene in silence. Soviet citizens, regardless of nationality, enjoy the spectacle of resistance to authority.

Upraised arms and fists churned the air. A few people had already been shoved into the buses; others were being dragged. They had Boris Moishezon in tow, a doctor of physicomathematical sciences; he was searching on the ground for something: they had knocked a book out of his hands.

A humorous incident occurred on the bus David and I had been herded into. A young man, whose face was not familiar to us, was yelling at the top of his voice and putting up desperate resistance. He was causing such a commotion an enraged policeman jumped into the bus after him and continued to clobber him. Finally, the hapless victim somehow managed to extract from his pocket a little red booklet— his KGB identity card—and waved it under the nose of the startled policeman. In the tumult, the police had taken the KGB man for a Jew and dragged him on the bus.

When our bus was packed to bursting, the police colonel signaled the driver to pull out. We drove through the center of town in the direction of the Leningrad Highway. Those of us who had already participated in earlier demonstrations figured that we were on our way to the Voikovsky Disintoxication Center: for some outlandish reason, the KGB has chosen this place for Jewish demonstrators.

That evening, the center did not take in any drunks; otherwise, there would not have been enough room to accommodate the Jews. They had hardly had time to sort us all out and assign us to various cells when the last demonstrator to be seized in front of the Lebanese Embassy was brought in. It turned out to be academician Andrei Sakharov, who had joined with the Jews to demonstrate against the Munich assassins.

Our long martyrdom came to an end on the morning of November 3, 1972. The evening before (naturally) we were summoned to OVIR—one more sleepless night added to the countless others we had spent during the past twenty-one months.

They informed us at OVIR that our request had been granted, that we had seventy-two hours to leave the territory of the USSR. I was on the point of protesting—how could we ever pack up in such a short time?—but David stepped on my foot.

"We won the war in six days," he reminded me after we had left the office. "You can't tell me we won't be able to manage in three!"

The three days whizzed by; I can't even recall who came to say good-bye to us. We had to pick up our visas and have them validated, we had to return our apartment to the State (a procedure that normally takes a full week), we had to buy tickets, pack up some belongings and ship out the rest.

The only thing I do remember is going to the cemetery and lingering at the grave of my parents.

At dawn on the fifth day of November, we drove for the last time to Sheremetyevo. More than a hundred friends had come to see us off, but we were not allowed to say good-bye to them. Many are with us now, here, in our homeland. Many, but not all of them.

Two and a half hours later, our plane landed on the tarmac of Vienna Airport. We fell into the arms of new friends who had come to meet us.

The flight from Vienna to Tel Aviv on *our* El Al plane, our family reunion at Ben Gurion Airport, our first footsteps on *our* soil. . . . But already three years have gone by since we arrived in Israel, and I have enough material for a whole new book.

I came here knowing scarcely more about Israel than about another planet: the information I had in the USSR about the land of Israel was either erroneous or deliberately misleading. My knowledge has naturally undergone a transformation by this time, but one feeling I carried away with me from Russia has not changed: the feeling of love I have for my people. Today, many people talk or write about the difficulties of assimilating Jews from the Soviet Union in Israel, about the "psychological incompatibility" between former Soviet citizens and Israelis. There are, undeniably, difficulties in integrating adults and especially the elderly into a new fabric of life—particularly those who did not bring with them (or lost it somewhere along the way) a love for their land and for their brothers and sisters engaged in the building of a Jewish state. "Without love, even a tree will not grow," according to an old Russian proverb, and proverbs know no national boundaries.

The happiness of being a Jew in the land of Israel is not an easy happiness. It is not given those who put a premium on the glitter of material riches. It is given to people who are strong in spirit and staunch in their moral convictions. Those who do not possess these qualities are impoverished; they will never be happy anywhere. There are some among the former "Israelis of Moscow" who prefer rich and powerful America to war-beleaguered Israel. But there is no army in the world without its deserters, and it is not the deserters who determine the bearing of an army.

INDEX

Diplomatic Department for Assistance to Foreign Nationals, Soviet Union, 99

Dnepropetrovsk. *See* Yekaterinoslav, Soviet Union

Dobrovolsky, Victor, 170

Dodrushin, Ezekiel, 74, 75-76

Dolgorukova, Princess, Gymnasium of, 15

Dolgy Most, Soviet Union, 204, 215

Dolidze, Dr. Teimweaz, 201, 208

Dolmatovsky, Evgeni, 113

Donbass mining region, Soviet Union, 56, 57

"Do Not Grieve" (Markish), 45-46, 48, 53

Druzhba narodov, 261

Dymshits (Kosygin's deputy), 258, 265-66, 269

Dzhaparidze, Alexei, 14

Dzhigan (comedian with Jewish Miniature Theater), 102, 103

Dzhusaly station, Soviet Union, 201, 202

Ehrenburg, Ilya, 81-83, 225, 234-39, 255, 256-57

Ehrenburg, Lyuba, 81-82

Eikhenbaum, Boris, 66

Epstein, Shakhno, 142

Eye for an Eye, An (Markish), 96

Fadeyev, Aleksandr, 80, 98, 136, 142, 231

Farklepte tsiferblatn (Markish), 34

Feffer, Itzik, xi, 97, 140-41, 142-43, 144, 150, 243, 244; arrested, 151, 153, 171-72; murdered, 172

Fifth Horizon, The (Markish), 56

Finn, Konstantin, 70-71, 170

First Anti-Jewish Leningrad Trial, 269-70

Fischer, Kurt, 24

Fonvizin, Ivan, 139

"Forty-Year-Old, The" (Markish), 38, 101-102, 151-52, 154, 250

Friendship of Peoples (magazine), 261

Gabrichevsky, Professor (microbiologist), 166-68 '

Gabrilovich, Yevgeni, 65

Galliulin (chief of ROMGB, or District Branch of the Ministry of State Security), 192-93, 194, 195, 201

Gamzatov, Rasul, 261

Gavrikov, Lieutenant (head of the special *komendatura*), 224, 227

Gavrila (yardkeeper), 7

Germany and the Germans, 143, 218, 219, 264; Russia and, during World War II, 70, 98, 99, 100, 102, 103, 110, 112, 114-15, 119-20, 121, 130

Gide, Charles, 19

Gilkina, Tsilya, 196, 200

Ginzburg, Grigory, 236

Glevneft' (Chief Oil Administration), 21

Gobulov (theater critic), 144, 145

Golodny, Mikhail, 154

Golodnyi, Misha, 31, 84

Gontar (poet), 140

Gori, Soviet Union, 83

Gorky, Maxim, 23, 74, 120

Grade, Chaim, 102

Granovsky (GULag Deputy Chief), 104, 105, 108

"Great Purge," 80-81, 238

Grechko (minister of Defense), 88

Gribachov, Nikolai, 193

Gudzy, Nikolai, 139-40

GULag, 104

Gusatinsky (Jewish prisoner), 63-64

299

We know you don't read just one kind of book. | That's why we've got all kinds of bestsellers.

Available at your bookstore or use this coupon.

___**THE SEVEN PER-CENT SOLUTION, Nicholas Meyer**   24550 1.95
Sherlock Holmes meets Sigmund Freud in this, his most incredible case. At stake are Holmes's mental health and the political future of the Balkans. This #1 Bestseller is "a pure delight!"—CHICAGO NEWS

___**SOMETHING HAPPENED, Joseph Heller**   27538 2.50
The number-one bestseller by the author of "Catch-22" is about greed, ambition, love, lust, hate and fear, marriage and adultery. It is about the life we all lead today — and you will never be able to look at that life in the same way again. "Brilliant."—SATURDAY REVIEW/WORLD

___**HOW TO BE YOUR OWN BEST FRIEND,
Mildred Newman and Bernard Berkowitz with Jean Owen** 27462 1.75
This highly-praised book by practicing psychoanalysts tells you how to make yourself a little bit happier ... just enough to make a difference.

___**THE SENTINEL, Jeffrey Konvitz**   25641 1.95
A novel that takes you to the very boundaries of belief — and one shattering step beyond.

___**THE WIND CHILL FACTOR, Thomas Gifford**   27575 2.25
Icy tension and hard-hitting action uncover a sinister network of key men in high places plotting the birth of a Fourth Reich — and only one man can stop it.

___**PRAISE THE HUMAN SEASON, Don Robertson**   24526 1.95
An old-fashioned panoramic story of two people who shared a lifetime overflowing with warmth and wisdom, people and events. It will make you believe in love again. "Magnificent."—SAN FRANCISCO CHRONICLE

___**THE SAVE YOUR LIFE DIET, David Reuben, M.D.**   25350 1.95
The doctor who told you everything you always wanted to know about sex now reveals the most important diet discovery of our times — high fiber protection from six of the most serious diseases of American life.

BB **Ballantine Mail Sales
Dept. LE, 201 E. 50th Street
New York, New York 10022**

Please send me the books I have checked above. I am enclosing $........................ (please add 50¢ to cover postage and handling). Send check or money order—no cash or C.O.D.'s please.

Name_____

Address_____

City_____ State_____ Zip_____

Please allow 4 weeks for delivery.

L-7